MW00781902

# ARGUMENT & SONG

# ARGUMENT & SONG
## Sources & Silences in Poetry

STANLEY PLUMLY

HANDSEL BOOKS

an imprint of
Other Press • New York

Copyright © 2003 Stanley Plumly

Production Editor: Robert D. Hack

Text design: Kaoru Tamura

This book was set in 10.5 pt. Caslon 540 BT by Alpha Graphics of Pittsfield, NH.

10 9 8 7 6 5 4 3 2 1

All rights reserved. No part of this publication may be reproduced or transmitted in any form or by any means, electronic or mechanical, including photocopying, recording, or by any information storage and retrieval system, without written permission from Other Press LLC, except in the case of brief quotations in reviews for inclusion in a magazine, newspaper, or broadcast. Printed in the United States of America on acid-free paper. For information write to Other Press LLC, 307 Seventh Avenue, Suite 1807, New York, NY 10001. Or visit our website: www.otherpress.com.

### Library of Congress Cataloging-in-Publication Data

Plumly, Stanley.
   Argument & song : sources & silences in poetry / by Stanley Plumly.
      p. cm.
   Includes index.
   ISBN 1-59051-076-3 (acid-free paper)
   1. English poetry—History and criticism.   I. Title: Argument and song.
II. Title.
   PR503.P58 2003
   821.009—dc21

                        2003004366
                           Rev.

*for Stephen Berg, David Bonanno,*
*and Arthur Vogelsang*

# CONTENTS

Acknowledgments ix

The Abrupt Edge    1986    1

Words on Birdsong    1992    21

Wistman's Wood    1993    41

Whistler's Nocturnes    1985    51

Season of Mists    1997    61

Reading Autumn    2002    73

Dirty Silence    1981    95

Sentimental Forms    1978    115

What Ceremony of Words    1985    125

Lyric Yoga    2001    141

Autobiography and Archetype    2001    151

Chapter and Verse    (1983)    163

   I.   Rhetoric and Emotion    1977    165

   II.   Image and Emblem    1978    210

   III.   Narrative Values, Lyric Imperatives    2003    263

Author Index    319

# ACKNOWLEDGMENTS

These essays first appeared in the following publications:

Journals
*The American Poetry Review*: "Chapter and Verse," "Narrative Values, Lyric Imperatives," "Words on Birdsong"; *Antaeus*: "Dirty Silence," "Sentimental Forms," "Whistler's Nocturnes"; *The Greenfield Review*: "Season of Mists"; *The Ohio Review*: "The Abrupt Edge," "Wistman's Wood"

Books
*After Confession* (eds. Kate Sontag, David Graham): "Autobiography and Archetype"; *Ariel Ascending* (ed. Paul Alexander): "What Ceremony of Words"; *How We Live Our Yoga* (ed. Valerie Jeremijenko): "Lyric Yoga"; *The Planet on the Table* (eds. Sharon Bryan, William Olsen): "Reading Autumn"

Special thanks to Megan Riley in the preparation of this book.

THE ABRUPT EDGE

*In robes of green, in garments of adieu.*

A Brontë postcard—

At the top of the High Street, Haworth parsonage, of a cold brownstone, stained by two centuries of weather, and behind it, and above—the sky half thick with cloud, half blue—Haworth Moor, in outline, in too-brilliant a summer green, the high grass caught permanently, it seems, in a wind directly from the sea, while in front of the house, and flanking it, gravestones and pines and stunted fir and perhaps some beech trees and a few rooks for heavy punctuation and moor-grass running to the church just below, then starting to the right, out of the picture, the cobblestones that still lead into the village and the Black Bull. . . .

Like most visual clichés, this one is not hard to imagine, though it changes with memory. What I remember being struck by at my first visit to the village of Haworth was the completeness of its world, the circumscription but completeness of the idea of village life, the sense of self-containment and limit that nomadic Americans in particular have trouble relating to. You could live the provincial life here in Haworth or in any number of a thousand little towns like it and not miss much: a concept of the microcosm that George Eliot, Thomas Hardy, and even Agatha Christie share. You could stand on top of the house and count the world and know the numbers, though small, were perfect. You could see the boundaries, mark where the basic needs of flesh and spirit would be met—the butcher, the baker, the candlestick maker, and God. In a place like Haworth, confinement could mean concentration, focus, perspective; you might be forced, in fact, to come to terms with yourself, to know and accept and thrive in limitation.

I remember drifting in this fantasy awhile. Then I walked around, measuring the town's circumference, and had lunch at the Black Bull Pub. To come to Haworth, which sits high in the wind above Worth Valley, West Yorkshire, you have to pass through some of the ugliest Lawrencian industrial scabpockets in England, of dead-black mill and ironworks and smokestack holy purity. You also pass through some of the most beautiful countryside on earth, great sweeps of the near-moorland climbing away from the road right up the sky, divided into pasture by stone—green pastures made to lie down in. Haworth is in recess from both extremes, tucked and diminutive, but for the Brontës it was large enough to be divisible by four: the moor, the parsonage, the graveyard, and the pub. It was their whole world because of the juxtaposition of its parts—the great moor looming against the back of the house, the house pressed (and doubtless oppressed) by the churchyard below, and lower still, the twilit, carnal, interior space of the Black Bull. Charlotte and Anne, in the best of their fiction, either longed to leave or rejected Haworth, both its Gothic isolation and its proximity to industrial violence and drabness; their brother Branwell—a real-life inspiration for Heathcliff—finally wanted only to disappear and painted himself out of the sibling portrait and drank himself to death at the Bull. Emily came to terms with the contradictions of Haworth by embracing the wildness and dark-ness of the landscape surrounding the isolated, repressed, and dull safety of the nest. Having survived them all, wife and children, the Brontë preacher-father, in later life, would often show visitors, especially Ameri-cans, the room his daughters worked in, now still almost undisturbed, the furniture intact, their books and memorabilia everywhere. He was oddly proud of his daughters, but was still preaching—from Job, remembered one visitor—with his eye on the graveyard: "There the wicked cease from trou-bling; and the weary be at rest."

I remember standing, not on a house, but on a flat gravestone in order to better see the whole of the place and how the parts of Haworth fit. From high on the horizon, the silver and green of the deep moor-grass seemed to pour, like a wind, down on the parsonage right on through to the church and churchyard, and though it fell in stages and in different lengths, inter-rupted by fence and path or clump of trees, the grass should have made the transition between territories more natural; instead it heightened the dif-ference. And where the grass ended, the cobblestone picked up the rhythm and carried it on into the town. I began to understand that what ought to provide continuity was in fact underlining the difference between the wild and open moor and the tiny island of church and citizen. Standing there, try-ing to get perspective, the moor at the top of the land and the milltown of Keighley at the very bottom, in the valley, I began to see that a landscape is

4

many scapes, many entities, many walls, invisible sometimes, sometimes visible but permeable. It is no secret that Emily Brontë came to see the open, ocean wilderness of the moor as freedom from the strictures of space and consciousness in her father's house, as liberation from the vacuum of small rooms viewing graves. Yet when she contracted consumption—the poet's disease—she chose to withdraw from her loved long moorland walks and die at the window. Her brother chose the closed space of his own stupor. He could not, apparently, imagine a life beyond the circle of Haworth or at least did not have the talent to cross and embrace the wild outside. He simply sank deeper into the well of himself. He died against his father, in the town's one pub. He got stuck at the edge.

Standing in a graveyard that seems more attached to the house than to the church is unsettling. Matthew Arnold, not exactly a cup of cheer himself, in an 1855 elegy for Charlotte Brontë entitled "Haworth Churchyard," makes the spatial arrangement clear: "the church/Stands on the Crest of the hill,/Lonely and bleak;—at the side/The parsonage-house and the graves." The graves, as I recall, were rough, with that handmade, hand-dug roughness of the animal, the ground over the bodies still heaped a little, the stones handset, off-center, weathered and natural-looking, the names driven in with a hammer. Many of the names and dates named and dated children or people who, like the Brontë children, did not make it much into or out of their thirties. The cold and the damp and the Yorkshire grim and the black north wind would have made short work of most of us—the weather had the feel of the congenital. Yet the green ground against the black and deeper green of the towering graveyard trees, with the stones lit gray like fieldstones, and the rooks calling what sounded like the names of the dead from above, all had a kind of beauty, a sense of ceremony. The humanity of the place felt at one with the nature of the place—loss was piled on loss, yet the spirit felt fed. What the earth pulled down, the branching of the trees and the greening of the grass returned to light. The rooks could be witnesses or angels, depending. The richness went to the root. Death lived here, in rest and in peace, next door, one of the choices.

In ornithology there occurs the phrase *the abrupt edge*, which, according to the bird books, is "the edge between two types of vegetation . . . where the advantages of both are most convenient." In the less precipitous sense such edges are gradual, over a distance, sometimes up to miles, where a woodland thins out to shrub and grassland or a hedgerow drifts into ellipsis and disuse and finally pasture. In the more abrupt forest-at-the-edge-of-the-field sense, however, trees will stand isolated in a grove, in open country, or clumped in a thicket by a good river, like islands; closer to home, the protective hedge and shrub corners of a garden will act as a border, while the line of young maples or the understory of pyracantha and azalea will mark the boundary between safety and vulnerability. The advantage of the edge is that it allows the bird to live in two worlds at once, and the more abrupt the more intense the advantage. From a position of height, of secrecy, the bird can spy for danger or prey; it can come and go quickly, like a thief. Where the vegetation is more varied, the shade and cover thicker, the insect life rising, the tanager can sweep down from its treetop, the thrush can fly out from the gloom, and the redwing can sit on the fencepost all day in the summer sun. The edge is the concept of the doorway, shadow and light, inside and outside, room and warlde's room, where the density and variety of the plants that love the sun and the open air yield to the darker, greener, cooler interior world, at the margin. It is no surprise, then, that the greatest number of species as well as individuals live at the edge and fly the pathways and corridors and trails at the joining of the juxtaposition. That is where the richness is, the thick, deep vegetable life—a wall of life, where the trees turn to meadows, the meadows to columnar, watchtower trees.

A man of sense, coming to a clearing, a great open space, will always wait among the trees, in the doorway, until the coast is clear.

You cannot walk the moors forever. You cannot live in the daylight at the Black Bull. The list of abrupt edges is endless, but for the American Crow and English Rook through to the Wren and Yellow Warbler the general list is Waterside Vegetation, Isolated Prominence, Mixed Brush and Grass, Margin on Open Country, Broken Openings, Deep Mixed, Deep Conifers, Deep Deciduous. And to negotiate the edge there is the long glide-and-search, the ground hunt, and dash-and-hide. But always there is the return to coloration and safety and the nest. In order for the habitat to be whole it must be divided—inside and outside, tower and open field, island and ocean. Like most principles and techniques of survival, the edge is ultimately a rather domestic arrangement. For birds it is the way the race thrives, the way the day is made, the way work and the rest from work are defined. I have to remember that Emily Brontë wrote her work in her father's house, as I must remember that without the moors there might have been no work to do. If we are fed or inspired in the open, the spirit and the hand must labor in the cloister. Without work to do the edge is meaningless. That is why the Brontë brother had to paint himself out of the picture—he had no work to do; only the night world of further and further withdrawal.

Far from the Yorkshire moors, south, about the year Emily Brontë was born, at the edge of the village of Hampstead, John Keats used to sit out in the summer evenings, claret in hand, and let the day go dark in long, blue, infinite graduations all around him. He was usually with friends, from what would later be known as the Keats circle; based on his own reports and those of others, the conversation was exciting and diverting, both at the level of gossip and philosophy. The company was changeable, but Leigh Hunt was often there—or they would all be at Hunt's, in the Vale of Health—and the painter Robert Haydon, and the poet Percy Shelley, and perhaps Joseph Severn, and of course Charles Brown, and occasionally Charles Dilke, and later William Hazlitt and Richard Woodhouse, and so on. Hampstead is still famous for its heath, a great wild park now part of London. But then, in the early nineteenth century, it was forest and hill and understory almost exclusively, thick and green and burly, with country paths. The Charles Brown/Charles Dilke house, where Keats was staying, was right at the border of the heath and Hampstead proper, a good place for people to gather. Keats was about to enter his greatest period as a poet, between the awful autumn, 1818, of his brother Tom's illness and death and his own contract with tuberculosis, a year and a half later. Keats, a Londoner, was habitually restless and whenever and wherever he was living in London he had three haunts: the busy commercial area around Fleet Street, the intimacy of tiny Hampstead, and the enclosure and canopy of the heath itself. He seemed, primarily, to prefer the place in between, the place now known as the Keats House, Keats Grove, Hampstead.

I have thought a lot about John Keats over the past few years. For all of his restlessness and planning, he was not the great long-distance walker many of his Romantic contemporaries were, including the unromantic Charles Brown. Keats nearly died an even earlier death from a Brown-instigated weeks-long walking tour of the Lake District and Scottish Highlands, all

7

cold rain and haggis. He once grew so unhappy on the Isle of Wight that he fled, after great expectations, because its isolation turned out to be too much solitude, space, and vista. And he would have been uncomfortable, without question, on the open, empty Yorkshire moors just to be walking. He preferred the walks between near-places—the populated few miles from the Thames to Hampstead or the much shorter path of "beechen green" between Brown's house (Wentworth Place) and Leigh Hunt's cottage in the Vale. When he lived in Winchester, during the period of "To Autumn," he took the water–meadows walk along the River Itchen every day—from the cathedral to the St. Cross Abbey and back again, about forty-five minutes one way. He would go out, in other words, only so far, to reveal only so much. He loved intimate, small space, the closed distance. That is why he seemed to love the evenings so much, with friends, at the darkening and blurring edge of worlds, the arcadian sublime of the near-house with the secure green of its grounds opposed to the rich, green space and chaos of the forest and underlife starting across East Heath Road, a chaos he would find compelling.

We cannot read Emily Brontë without an awareness of the impressive graveyard just beyond the Brontë windows. The correlative of the moors is obvious in her work, but the graveyard is the darkness. The weight and gloom and pull of its presence have everything to do with the tone and undertow of *Wuthering Heights*, and, at the last, with the novel's farewell.

> I sought, and soon discovered, the three head-stones on the slope next to the moor—the middle one grey, and half buried in the heath—Edgar Linton's only harmonised by the turf, and moss creeping up its foot—Heathcliff's still bare.
>
> I lingered round them, under that benign sky; watched the moths fluttering among the heath and hare-bells; listened to the soft wind breathing through the grass; and wondered how any one could ever imagine unquiet slumbers for the sleepers in that quiet earth.

While the moors may have been Emily's freedom, Haworth Churchyard is the place, in the short distance, of simplest riches. The graves are her final emotional resource, the resonance under the work. The graves bring the outside inside, right into the parsonage, into the writing room, through the eye to the mind—they make intimate the space between life and death and give that edge its complexity and richness, and its powerful attraction. We cannot read "Ode to a Nightingale" without accounting for the weeks, in the fall of 1818, that Keats spent with Tom in their little rooms above the Bentleys in Well Walk. Keats was ill himself with a very bad sore throat, having just returned from his bone-soaking northern tour with Brown. Tom, though, was dying, and until the end in December Keats would be his nurse. In the gray, tubercular air of the sick-room, Keats would himself slowly become marked with the mark of youth that "grows pale, and spectre-thin." It is not hard to imagine Keats, the physician, bending over the sad and wasting body of his brother, knowing somewhere in himself what he was doing and risking.

Severn, Keats's last great friend, was fond of reporting how the poet would suddenly disengage himself from the group, when they were gathered after supper for the evening, at Hunt's or Brown's, and wander off onto the heath, lost, apparently, in a long thought. Severn would claim of later finding Keats lying on a hillside, scribbling, listening to a thrush. Severn was convinced, against Brown's better-distributed opinion, that it was during these absences, in the early spring of 1819, in the first rush of warm and healthy Hampstead air and green, that Keats started thinking and speculating about the poem that became the nightingale ode. It is a nice story. Brown's version that Keats wrote the poem in a single extended sitting, on a May morning no less, right in front of the house, better fits our vanities of emotion quickly recollected in tranquility. Yet what appeals to me in the Severn story is what appeals to me in the poem itself: the sense of secret, intimate space within or abutting the larger, enclosing, impending mystery of trees and the interlacing vegetal and floral network at their trunk and root—a wall of green. It takes no scholar of Keats's poetry to notice how much he is impelled and empowered by that mystery, and how sensual he finds its attraction though it overwhelm him with its palpable, physical, total information. At the edge of the small room, the small found space out of time, is the immensity and threat and gravity of the other world, all that is not the condition of art. When we bend over the face of the dead, or the dying, as Keats did, everything opens; suddenly everything seems possible, in a moment. The mind begins to collapse into the imagination, into dimensions of another size and density. Keats's nightingale is a miracle for what it promises: at the crucial, heart-filling moment, at the edge, at the green wall, it sings from the other side. It makes no demands, calls no questions, shows no apparent interest. It simply sings of mortal summer from the depth of the mystery with full-throated ease.

To write a poem like the "Nightingale" you have to be in the right place at the right time, and to know it, and to know the difference between whistling and the "plaintive anthem." Keats cannot follow his nightingale, and yet he does—"past the near meadows, over the still stream,/Up the hillside . . . into the next valley-glades." At one level, his "imaginative leap" is a flight from weariness and fever and fret; at another, it is an understanding, an insighting of his long suffering with Tom. His intimacy with this moment, at this edge of spaces, is to know absolutely, and at last, the distinction and ultimate disinterest between life and art, that edge where nature, beyond the human, the egotistical sublime, does its richest business. My impression of the nightingale ode has always been that the so-called green chaos and the "embalmed darkness" become synonymous at the point at which Keats cannot see the flowers underfoot nor identify the soft incense on the boughs, so he guesses—which is a form of acceptance—

> Wherewith the seasonable month endows
> The grass, the thicket, and the fruit-tree wild;
> White hawthorn, and the pastoral eglantine;
> Fast fading violets cover'd up in leaves;
> And mid-May's eldest child,
> The coming musk-rose, full of dewy wine,
> The murmurous haunt of flies on summer eves.

Through the motion and medium of the falling evening dark, the abrupt green edge has been blurred and moved to include Keats; rather passively, in his waking dream, he has, in imagination, passed over, passed through the wall, to the place where he can say, meaningfully, that he too has been half in love with easeful death and that now more than ever seems it rich to die. Because he has been so prepared and so patient, the wall has come to him, though his complaint is the familiar complaint of the listener who would hear more, whose fantasy of immortality is the closure of the past: of hungry generations, of emperor and clown, of Ruth among the alien corn. To close off his poem is to leave him back at the edge, in silence in a question, but also in the clearing.

Life, of course, for Keats, will imitate art. He will perfect his vision only to see it end. I have often wondered how such a mimesis happens: how our lives can seem so emphatically plotted and predicated by the poem or story. The obvious answer is that our lives themselves have done the plotting, the materials were there from the start, and that the imagination lets us see, forces us to see who we are and what will become of us. The imaginative leap is a leap from memory, from the edges of experience. The other world, the other side of the green wall, the graveyard, the intimate understory of the heath, may or may not be the future; they are certainly the simultaneous present—a parallel, disinterested order of a different order, a wholly terrible and powerful otherness enacted at the speed of light. Imagination is the body alchemized, through fire, into spirit. When I lived in Devon I thought of Plath—"The hills step off into whiteness." Thus when I lived in Seattle I thought of Roethke—"The edge is what I have." Both poets confronted the wall in their lives; both were committed to the imagination at the peril of their lives.

In Devon—as on the Yorkshire moors or on Hampstead Heath—the happiest necessity is walking. The weather is dramatic, the landscape is dramatic. The clouds come in off the ocean in armadas, stacked with rain to the top-sail, tinged with sunlight. The weather is six things a day. The landscape is in rhythm with the sky: it rolls, it opens, it closes, it runs right up to the edge of the open water, then drops straight down, hundreds of feet. Devon blue is a color; so is Devon green, a luminescent, bristling, gorgeous green of infinitive version. As the sky and ocean beat against it, the landscape holds its own only more or less domesticated—fisherman and farmer, laborer and shepherd. The land and off-land work. The excitement of the place comes mostly from the melodramatic wind, which is constant and omnipresent and vocal, a third scape between sky and land, sky and sea. A wind that is filled with birds and the sounds of birds and the skim from the saltwater. Perhaps the strongest visual link in the Devon countryside is the hedgerow, a history of the common life of the vegetable, animal, and human kingdoms. It runs head-high or higher in seams all over the shire. The trope of knitting, of weaving, is appropriate. If you walked the road between the rows in the evening, the sun would light candles on top of the hedge, while in the hayloft underneath, in the bramble and thicket, the sounds, except for the thrush, would be settling into sleep.

In her poem "Wuthering Heights," Sylvia Plath complains that "there is no life higher than the grasstops/Or the heart of sheep, and the wind/ Pours by like destiny. . . ." A short time later, when she takes her own Devon walk, in her poem "Blackberrying," the dimensions of pastoral life will substantially increase, though the same claustrophobic fear of closure becoming enclosure will obtain. It is the richness, the fecundity, the almost grotesque fullness of the bramble hedge hugging both sides of the road that disturbs her—"a blackberry alley"—and, at the same time, the pull of the antithetical open ocean at the end of the lane that compels her to go on. She has no place of safety. Having already filled, by the end of the first stanza, her blackberry quota, she must either retreat or go on, though either way in its own way is closed. She goes on, to the open end of the lane. Unlike Brontë or Keats, Plath seems to be seeking the edge, an extreme edge, an edge that would, given the opportunity, shut down imagination. Even overhead, as if to blind and mute the sky, "the choughs in black, cacophonous flocks" congregate, like the berries. Theirs is the only voice, protesting, protesting. "Blackberrying," written in 1960, has more and more struck me as a poem certain of suicide, a suicide of that moment when the heart-deep imagination overloads or precipitously empties and will not work anymore, cannot lift. It can only, simply, metaphorize the moment. Which is exactly what Plath does once she reaches the place where "the only thing to come now is the sea." The imagination, or something, seems to shut down and the brilliant, painful inventing machine takes over. The cliff face, she says, at the edge of the Atlantic, looks out on nothing, "nothing but a great space/ Of white and pewter lights, and a din like silversmiths/Beating and beating at an intractable metal." The world of the hedgerow, the great green world, is overwhelming, and now the great shining space of the open water and the shout of the sea-wind overload, seal off the senses—this time a white wall rather than a green. And though she tries and tries, and ends her career writing nearly anorectic forms, the richness and promise of the edge, closed or open, green as well as white, drive her back into her own perfection and fears, so that instead of finding a way through the wall, whatever its texture, she retreats to the child-sized dimensions of the grasstops and dies in a tiny kitchen, with her head in a tiny oven.

The open, light-refracting undifferentiated surface of the ocean may be too alien, too non-human a wall, in spite of the human figure of the silversmiths. Yet the ripe looming hedge is also too thick for Plath, too threatening. Theodore Roethke, in "The Far Field," declares to have learned, half-way through the journey of his poem, "not to fear infinity/The far field, the windy cliffs of forever." Brave words, from a brave man. As we know, by the finish of this wonderful poem, Roethke will have joined, imaginatively, all the air and water; at the edge of his far field he will have begun to be absorbed into the natural cycle in order to wind, like a Yeatsian spirit, around the waters of the world. Bainbridge Island, where Roethke lived in the American Northwest, is just west of Seattle and next to the Olympic Peninsula. In Roethke's time it was much less populated than it is today, which means there were even more trees—big pines and spruce and fir and Pacific yew, a wall of evergreen, standing and mixing with a variable but almost continual wall of mist and fog and rain. An interaction of the green and white, on a landscape of forest just above sea-level. Plath might have suffocated in such closeness—at least the white noise of the Devon coast feels separate at the edge.

One of the essential differences between "Blackberrying" and "The Far Field" is that Roethke begins his poem where Plath chooses to end hers. The extreme edge, the apparent dead-end where the imagination is in trouble, is, in "The Far Field," the condition to be overcome. Roethke starts off by saying that he dreams of journeys repeatedly, yet offers examples of the cul-de-sac—first with the bat flying into the narrowing tunnel, expressed as a simile, then, extensively, with the speaker driving alone, without luggage, out a long peninsula, in the cold of the year, alternate snow and sleet, no oncoming traffic, and no lights behind . . .

> The road changing from glazed tarface to a rubble of stone,
> Ending at last in a hopeless sand-rut,
> Where the car stalls,
> Churning in a snowdrift
> Until the headlights darken.

Roethke then sets himself the task of solving this suicidal position—by, in effect, stepping out of his car and addressing the edge of the natural,

13

mortal world, which is not quite yet the abyss. "I suffered for birds," he says, "my grief was not excessive." He makes no secret of the fact that the richness he is about to embrace is ordered in his mind with the thought of his own death, "The dry scent of a dying garden in September,/The wind fanning the ash of a low fire." This end-of-summer poignancy continues outside him, with the wrens bickering and singing in the half-green hedgerows, the flicker drumming from his dead tree in the chicken yard, and himself lying naked, like a body projected, in the shallows of a coastal river, fingering a shell. Then the river turns on itself, becomes two rivers, and returns toward the sea.

At one point, in the middle of his poem, Roethke apposes his sweeping line about the windy cliffs with "the dying of time in the white light of tomorrow." This image seems to me to be more than simply another effective generalization in his sequence—it has particular emotional content, an especial quality of surrender, as distinguished from Plath's brilliant but combative pewter and silversmith strategy at the close of "Blackberrying." Roethke is yielding to the rest of his journey; Plath has no further to go. I am reminded of another of Plath's telling Devon poems, "Sheep in Fog," that concludes:

> My bones hold a stillness, the far
> Fields melt my heart.
>
> They threaten
> To let me through to a heaven
> Starless and fatherless, a dark water.

Here the extremity of the edge threatens by its promise of a starlessness and fatherlessness, with no chance of renewal or return. The far fields become a dark, deadly water of dissolution. It is too simple to say that Plath killed herself and that Roethke died a longer death. The difference is that both poets are animated by similar edges with different results. Roethke reads renewal, Plath reads the perfection of the closed rose "when the garden/Stiffens and odours bleed/From the sweet, deep throats of the night flower." Is Plath's a spiritual suicide as well? I have said that the edge is where the richness is, the clearing, the open space, the water of the green wall. The bird flies back and forth between worlds because the risk is exactly where the richness is.

Plath's is the art of divestment, Roethke's the art of acquisition. Plath wishes to forget, Roethke to remember. Plath wants more than to disappear into her emblem; she wants to be perfected by it—dissolve into it completely, traceless, like the arrow and dew, as she says in "Ariel," at one with the drive into the cauldron of morning. She wants to melt into the wall. She wants the air emptied behind her. At the point of richness and energy and intensity and the potential of return, she wants only absence, absolutely. She wants to be transformed without the further burden of transcendence. Emily Dickinson speaks of "just the Door ajar/That oceans are . . . /And that White Sustenance—/Despair—." Plath's genius and beauty, in those poems at the utter edge, is that she is willing to admit when the imagination is terminal and the body carnal and the spirit slow dissolve. She is willing to yield to the impermeability of the wall itself, willing to melt into it. Yet once at the edge we cannot stay there; we must go into the openness or density of the other, the natural, the green world and we must find our way back again. The sustenance of white is the death of the spirit, a flight into oblivion and the absolute, and Plath's greatness lies in her willingness to risk it.

Roethke, though, is dressed "in robes of green,/in garments of adieu." He knows he will join, must join, the "silence of water above a sunken tree:/ The pure serene of memory in one man." He will give himself up to the world in detail, to the immensity, he says, of change. Roethke's spiritual analogue could never be found, like his Yeatsian mentor's, in a golden bird on a golden bough, in the announcement of an artifice. Instead, Roethke's soul is in the analogue of the tree, roots in one world, branches in the other, with that oldest symbol of the soul, the wren, the warbler, the brown thrush, hidden in the leaves. Sitting here also, in parallel, like unconscious life itself, as one in the *wylder ness*, is the green man, who cannot be killed, though we strike him dead. At the edge of his secret position, from the gloom and intimacy and complexity of the root and branching, he beckons that we put off this flesh and be one with the flowering of the tree—magical in the natural, green and evergreen—even the florid shade tree at the grave. His seduction is effectively sexual.

Near the end of his exhaustive elegy for Lincoln and the Civil War, Whitman does the most curious thing ever done in an elegy—certainly as antithetically arcadian as a Lycidian elegy could be. He has arrived at part 14 of his 16-part poem. And he is at the edge of the lilaced dooryard, at the close of day, at the edge of the swamp, at the edge of a vision.

> Now while I sat in the day and look'd forth,
> In the close of the day with its light and the fields of spring,
> 	and the farmers preparing their crops,
> In the large unconscious scenery of my land with its lakes
> 	and forests,
> In the heavenly aerial beauty, (after the perturbed winds
> 	and the storms),
> Under the arching heavens of the afternoon swift passing,
> 	and the voices of children and women,
> The many-moving sea-tides, and I saw the ships how they
> 	sail'd,
> And the summer approaching with richness, and the fields
> 	all busy with labor,
> And the infinite separate houses, how they all went on,
> 	each with its meals and minutia of daily usages. . . .

He continues in this rhythm, and rhapsody, for several more lines ("Be with me, Whitman, maker of catalogues," says Roethke), setting the scene, taking the long perspective, confusing even the grammar of the sequence, in order, apparently, to create a context for the wild elegiac assumption he is about to make: that by befriending the enemy he can win a victory; that by befriending death he can know it, and its thought, and its sacred knowledge; that by walking—"as walking" he actually says—with the knowledge of death on one side and the thought of death close-walking on the other, as with companions, "as holding the hands of companions," he can understand the night and the green wall of the swamp and the solemn shadowy cedars and the ghostly pines so still. He continues in this rhythm in order to show that "then and there/Falling upon them and among them all, enveloping me with the rest/Appear'd the cloud, appear'd the long black trail"—in order to show that life-in-death is whole, and in order to prepare for the song outside the cycle, from the other side, the song of the gray-brown thrush, from the swamp. It is the song that will tally with the voice of his own spirit into a hymn of acceptance, a carol of joy—"Come lovely

and soothing death/Undulate round the world, serenely arriving, arriving"—
and it is this song of the soul's tally that will permit Whitman passage to
his further and transcendent vision, "long panoramas of vision," far beyond
the original object of his concern. His word for his new understanding will
be "askant": or sideways, angular, slant, sublime.

> And I saw askant the armies,
> I saw as in noiseless dreams hundreds of battle-flags,
> Borne through the smoke of the battles and pierc'd with
>     missiles I saw them,
> And carried hither and yon through the smoke, and torn
>     and bloody,
> And at last but a few shreds left on the staffs, (and all in
>     silence),
> And the staffs all splinter'd and broken.
>
> I saw battle-corpses, myriads of them,
> And the white skeletons of young men, I saw them,
> I saw the debris and debris of all the slain soldiers of the war,
> But I saw they were not as was thought,
> They themselves were fully at rest, they suffer'd not,
> The living remain'd and suffer'd, the mother suffer'd,
> And the wife and the child and the musing comrade suffer'd
> And the armies that remain'd suffer'd.

These lines, so rich in repetition and detail, so generous, so empathic,
so embracing, are remarkable for what they posit: an afterlife here on earth
in the long reflective moment and realism after death. The corpses are as
they were, *the corpses are as they were*: what a simple and profound act of imagination. Sitting in his dooryard, in the spring, at the edge of the whole green
world and ghostly swamp, Whitman has seen beyond the green man, beyond the garments of adieu, beyond grieving, beyond the renewal in the
cycle of the leaf. He has heard and understood the song of the bird, who is
also in the tree, who wants nothing from us—a song of the joy of the spirit
that tallies with our own, that tells us not to be afraid, not to turn away,
that this richness too is ours, if we accept it, as we might accept the richness of the dream at the end of the night, and the daydream in the evening,

out on the lawn. Whitman has imagined the unimaginable because he has prepared for and listened to the spirit in the wood, the hermit thrush—solitary and secret except at the articulate edge. The lilac as well, Whitman says, with its mastering odor, holds him, and the great western star. But they are merely marvelous. The loud human song, as he calls it, "with the voice of uttermost woe," that is the sound at the edge of our hearing, that is the sound and symbol, in the crisis of imagination, we become.

One early October morning I was being driven by a friend from Billings, Montana, to Sheridan, Wyoming. My first visit. We had the time, so she asked if I would like to stop off at the Little Bighorn, which was on the way. I said sure, why not, with no idea. The weather had turned sour, with an intermittent ice-cold drizzle and a black sky. The rain, in fact, had been falling all night and had given the land more weight, as if it needed it. The tourist season was long over, but the drive into the main area of the Custer Battlefield National Monument was still open. It was on a rise, though not too high. Through the cloud and ceiling of the sky there was little, it seemed, to see, as the open landscape diminished into lush endless moorland and undulant sameness and a gray wall of weather. It was a landscape to get lost in, even on a good day. You could see that much. Yet standing there awhile, within the isolation of the cold rain, staring out at the long undulant ground, I was moved, more moved than I have ever been by a landscape, except the grounds at Gettysburg, which are also mapped and discovered and toured until one day you pass by accident and see, perhaps, askant. Men had died here, bravely, and had been buried, in pieces, where they lay. Even in the obscurity of the weather you could feel the presence of the power of the dead in battle. You could feel it in the roll and secrecy and totality of the land, which was a series of blind-sides and which was nothing else but this one history. It was human and it was alive. And though the dead could not humble the land, they were now an intimate part of it. Its richness.

So we say life and death, as if that were the edge of ultimate concern to the imagination, when the real edge is between life and more life, memory and wish. The powerful imagination does not work, as every good poem reminds us, unless it comes to an edge, makes its pass, and, one way or another, returns. It surely, in a lifetime, gets harder and harder to get back. And a lifetime can be barely thirty years, as it was for Plath and Emily Brontë and almost for Keats. They were nourished by the very thing that would bring them down. That was their intensity. Plath, at the end, was cold with intensity: so little of the spirit seems to make it back to the woman, the person inside the poet. Roethke lasted longer; still, his *Far Field* is a post-humous book. Whitman writes and rewrites until he is subsumed, body, beard, and great soul, into the organicism of his poems. In the late pictures, he looks like a natural object, like part of an oak or a shock of wheat, the green man grown old. It can look like freedom—the open, the far field or the forest-building protective coloration of the trees of the sublime vision of the afterlife. It can look like ecstasy. But the imagination leads only a half-life, a fantasy-life, if it does not come back from the other side, no matter how compelling or consuming. If it does not return, renewed by its risk-taking. But it will have no life at all if it does not fly, as Keats says, with new phoenix wings at its desire.

1986

WORDS ON BIRDSONG

Not long ago I heard a young poet, in a public lecture, talking about the source of one of his poems—a poem, perhaps because it was new, that he thought one of his best—and how he had had to change the primary story of the experience in order to accommodate what became the secondary story of his poem. I understood his point to be that since actual, linear experience is relative to its language anyway, language somehow preempts experience—the experience of the language, that is, supersedes the language of the experience. On the face of it his point seemed familiar enough and abstract enough to be philosophical rather than polemical. It seemed no more, really, than another paraphrase of Marianne Moore's concern about the ways in which poetry's "raw material in all its rawness" becomes transformed arbitrarily into language, its language. His discussion sounded like the small talk in an interesting workshop. Simple enough, until he got to his example, the original, initiating experience.

Apparently a friend of his, who suffers from a terrific but intermittent psychosomatic disorder, was driving across country when he had an attack. So he stopped, midday, at a motel to rest and cool down by lying on the tiles of the motel's bathroom floor and then immersing himself in a tepid bath. This was a summer journey. The young poet, for no doubt a mixture of empathetic and voyeuristic motives, appropriated this difficult moment, this story—potentially a road story—as his possible subject. Which is how he put the matter. There was something about his friend's problem, as well as his feeling for his friend, that appealed to him—a classic combination of experiences, of perceiver and perceived, of compassion and curiosity, of a journey interrupted, of a possible Chekhovian moment in the midst of the larger day; all that, perhaps, and the cool black-and-white-checked tile floor on a warm summer afternoon. His subject had possibilities, though its center of gravity remained the friend's painful passage.

Having written a draft of his poem, however, the poet found that his language had turned too elevated for the illness, was too hyperbolic—the poet's word—for his senses of the subject, whatever the subject would ultimately be. But rather than "lower the level" of his language, the poet decided to "meet the construct" by raising the stakes of his material. So he kills off the friend, has him die of a kind of involuntary suicide right there on the black-and-white tiles, messy but final, details to follow. Thus, instead of writing what might be called the representative poem, the one of the difficult, actual, mitigated moment, the poet decides, for the convenience of the language he has written himself into, to invent an elegy, which means that he must also invent an emotion and the occasion for that emotion, a "real" grief. His point to us in the audience was that the literal experience—the raw material in its rawness—was expendable for a higher claim, a more suasive calling, the siren song of the language. At the end you felt this was all meant to be a tough-minded lesson in the school of poetry-writing realism—the realism of priorities.

I am reminded of Chekhov's criticism of *Hedda Gabler*, which is that the real tragedy lies in Hedda's not killing herself. In playing with death our poet was playing with fire. I wonder if he had not tipped us off if we would have felt any oddness when he read his elegy, any hollow ring, any self-consciousness. Or, if it is all language-invested anyway, if poetry is only language, if we would have felt his use of language was alone the test. Except that he was making a case, why, in the first place, would he bother to tell us? At the end of his life, in exasperation with the didact H. G. Wells, Henry James writes in a letter: "It is art that *makes* life, makes interest, makes importance . . . and I know of no substitute whatever for the force and beauty of its process." The question is, Can art make death, can it invent a death, then mourn it? Had the poem let us in on the poet's fantasy, had the exaggeration of the consequences of his friend's pain been treated as part of the ironic text, we would have known where we stood in relation to the poem's presiding elegiac emotion. The poet could have written an elegy-just-in-case. But in allowing the language itself to be the source and not the servant, the poet seemed to have compromised his sympathetic contract with his reader.

Changing fundamental emotional experience is entirely different from rewriting or revisioning a poem in order to find the power of the original experience; is entirely different from colluding fact or collapsing time, from using a persona or standing in the wings of the third-person personal pronoun; is different from changing or insisting on the literal names and dates. Revision is different from supposition. Whatever his subtractions and conflations, Wordsworth is the great poet of memory because we can believe him. Dickinson draws half her power from her discretion, even her secrecy, but we never doubt the cry of the occasion. The fact that he is our great Symbolist poet does not in any way obviate the intimate autobiographical content of Yeats. Lowell's best work may be no more psychological journalism than it is confession, but it is nevertheless rooted in graphic, accurate detail—"why not say what happened." Fundamental emotional experience, regardless, is as irrefutable as death.

The issue of sources is not simply an issue of where a poem comes from but how it comes into being: the integrity of the muse experience directly connects to the quality of the means. When our poet lies about death he voids the substance of his elegy. He, in effect, lies about memory, calls into question its very resonance. He acts as a Narcissus rather than an Orpheus; is captured by the mirror, the self-image in the water. The object, which is his subject, on the other side of the window, disappears, and takes with it its history, its vital context. Even more, in denying the potential associations of the absolutes of memory, the liar denies the suggestions of a structure, a form for the reality of his content. He robs himself of the opportunity of discovery, with its natural and inherent limits, the limits that define, shape, embody what is possible. If all a poet had to do was make things up, Plato would be literal in saying the poets lie too much. Contrivance is endless, a kind of lottery of the imagination. Poets cannot make things up. Poets make things *from*—from memory; from matter that cannot be changed, only transformed; from the rock of fact that may disappear, eventually, from erosion but that cannot be willed, out of hand, to evaporate.

"We keep coming back and coming back/To the real," says Stevens, "to the hotel instead of the hymns/That fall upon it out of the wind." Perhaps the incident our poet abuses has too recently occurred, does not yet have the weight of memory, the distance needed for the transfixing eye. What if he had allowed the report of the experience to live in time, allowed it to develop its particular absences and presences, its own resonance of initiation? What if he had allowed the experience to develop its own language instead of employing the will to do the work of the imagination? What if he had thought twice about his friend's reaction to "a report of his death being greatly exaggerated"? Wordsworth's point about recollecting in tranquility is that it is not just the deep past but emotional perspective that is being called to and called for, since the muse, in order to take power, requires a seduction ritual. In trying to convert experience too quickly into significance, our poet was forced to impose a language, a hype, and a lie, since he was trying to sell us something.

The trouble with language unburdened from time, from the awkwardness of truth, from the gravity of memory, is that it tends to free-float, untethered. It becomes responsible only to itself. Of the many sources of poetry, experience tied to time is fundamental, and, finally, archetypal. It is almost as if the language good poetry is formed into were itself part of the past, part of the discovery of the experience, were part of the memory and now the archetype. And of course it is. Our poet sacrificed the potential power of the fetal image of his friend lying on the bathroom floor for the sentimentality of a convenient death, *deus ex machina*. He could not or would not rewrite himself out of the moment, into the silence of patience. He could not or would not wait out his subject. Yet even if he had been able to wait it out, even if he had got it right, language can be so difficult, it might not be the best right. There is right, and there is better.

In "Among School Children," Yeats cannot lie about Maud Gonne's aging face—it is too well known for one thing. We are all too well known. If Yeats cannot lie, however, he can at least change his mind: hence, the original "mass of shadows for its meat"—as published in the 1928 American book edition—becomes "mess of shadows for its meat." Her face is

> Hollow of cheek as though it drank the wind
> And took a mess of shadows for its meat . . .

Mass into mess is not lying, it is transforming one terrifying grace into a greater one; it is discovering language within language, memory within memory, based on the truth of factual, physical evidence. The changing of this one vital noun is the difference between the inferior 1928 version of the poem and subsequent, more powerful publication. When the painter Degas one day said to his friend Mallarmé, "But I have all these great ideas, why can't I write a decent poem?," Mallarmé responded by pointing out that poetry is not made of ideas, it is made of words. It is the words at their source that we are talking about: "mess," in Yeats's great poem, becomes truer to the facial, emotional, and autobiographical fact than "mass." It also thereby constructs the more graphic, meaningful metaphor. Yeats, the kindly old scary scarecrow, has no need to falsify his memory of the present image of Maud Gonne's face; he needs only to articulate its sculpture, create it out of the scatter of raw materials. The rush of his impression of her at this moment in the poem is at the heart of his interior argument with himself, the argument with reality, as we all know, that generates the imagination. The argument with mortality really.

Without the truth-telling knowledge of its source, poetry's language is a siren song, a call from a cave of winds. But such knowledge is not isolated or limited to the individual talent. There is also the tradition. Anyone who writes a poem marries, for better or worse, the experience behind the poem as well as the experience it engenders, while at the same time acting as a connecter of the art to the poetry of the past, to specific, relevant poems, and becoming, in turn, a transmitter of poetry into the future . . . to, again, specific, relevant poems. The archetypes of our common and communal experience find their forms in our poems; the integrity of their expression depends on the individual truth of the archetype, on how responsible the poet is to individual, archetypal experience. Just as our poetic forms are reinvested generation after generation, so is our community of experience. If we can lie about the death of a friend for the happy convenience of our small moment with the art, clams will play accordions, and fancy replace the imagination. Lying about death, about this fundamental shared experience, we call into question, by implication, the values of all the elegies that have preceded us—we call into question the very name of the experience. Lying about death makes death itself a lie. And turns it into the anonymity of an abstraction, a linguistic construction.

For the sake of argument, if I were to choose against the hollow siren song of the language, of experience by convenience, I would choose an archetype that is classically employed as both a personification of and an alien to the voice of our grief emotions, a song both representative and removed: I would choose the archetype of birdsong, the mating song against the loneliness in the mirror of words. Birdsong, as a lyric connecter and transmitter, is one of our most perfect signatures in poetry, from Shakespeare's virtual aviary of voices to Shelley's "unpremeditated" skylark, from Poe's crusty raven to Frost's noisy oven bird and Stevens's whistling blackbird, from Roethke's lists of warblers to Plath's mute rook in rainy weather— birdsong and approximations of birdsong, such as Coleridge's Eolian harp and Dickinson's buzzing fly. Birdsong, in fact, in all its actualizations and silences, forms and suggestions, is like an aural and spiritual backdrop for all poems, a natural correlative for projections of the human voice, though, as in Frost's poem "Never Again Would Birds' Song Be the Same," the tolerance can be turned around: here it is the birds that do the learning, "having heard the daylong voice of Eve."

Of all the birdsongs, the nightingale's, of course, is the purest and most popular with a poets. The nightingale's song itself, which is male in spite of the lamentable mythological conversion of Pandion's daughter, Philomela, is famous for the quality, variety, and duration of its notemaking, beginning with a hard-to-liquid succession of repeated notes, *chooc, chooc, chooc*, mounting, over time, to a fluting, almost pleading *pioo, pioo, pioo*. The clarity of the music is unmistakable, nearly electric on a still early spring evening, especially in times before the white noise of modernism. The hermit thrush, the American version of the nightingale, and the bird Whitman celebrates in his elegy for Lincoln, makes a song similar to the English songbird but with a bit more melody and tremolo, with more notes per phrase. It may even be more shy than its English cousin. Nightingales everywhere spiral their songs as if composing while singing, which in a sense they are. One serious birdwatcher reports from 1929, on Hampstead Heath:

> I have never seen a bird so brimful of emotion as a male nightingale that I watched at close quarters for a week. On the day the young were hatched the male only brought food. Each time he visited his brooding mate he sang such a song as I have never heard before. His beak was full of juicy grubs for the family but this did not hinder him from pouring out a stream of liquid bubbling notes so soft and sweet they were inaudible at the least distance.

For poets the nightingale is as much a sign as it is a songbird, hence the sometime gender conversion, since the Philomela myth arbitrarily excuses the human connection/projection by permitting the writer to identify, within the limits of the rules of the correlative, feeling with hearing. The bird becomes one sex, one song. The sensitivity of the song suggests an artifice beyond nature. But whether the bird is male or female, nature or myth or sublimation or combination of these, the resonance of the song itself is remarkably consistent, genderless, beyond convention, the natural object being the adequate symbol. Nightingale etymology emphasizes not only the sweetness of the song—"She sings as sweetly as any nightingale"

(*Taming of the Shrew*)—but its poignancy as well, its ability to pierce—"It was the nightingale, and not the lark/That pierc'd the fearful hollow of thine ear" (*Romeo and Juliet*). It emphasizes, to quote Izaak Walton, "The clar airs, the sweet descants, the natural rising and falling, the doubling and redoubling," but also, to quote Lucrece, "The well-tun'd warble of her nightly sorrow."

This association of the piercing poignancy of the high notes of the nightingale's singing with human emotional wounds is ancient and likely comes from an innocent belief that the music's haunting quality is caused by the hidden bird's leaning against a protective thorn. Sir Thomas Browne asks "whether it be anymore than that she placeth some prickles on the outside of her nest, or roosteth in thorny, prickly places, where serpents may least approach her," that accounts for the thorn-song connection. And true, like many ground birds, the nightingale may use the thorn, willy-nilly, as part of its nest-building armor or may build its nest within a hedgework of thorns. The natural object, again, creates the symbol. The piercing notes are further emphasized in the song's bell clarity, made clearer by the fact that nightingales outlast the competition by staying up later in the day, and by singing through the entirety of a song. To quote Milton's "Il Penseroso": "Sweet Bird that shunn'st the noise of folly,/Most musical, most melancholy:/Thee Chantress oft the woods among,/I woo, to hear thy Even–Song."

The original Ovidian Philomela myth, in which the King of Athens' daughter is ravished by Tereus and has her tongue cut out to keep her from speaking his name, is not only a touching rendering of the thorn-wounding theme but a reinforcement of the notion that the grief of the song—Philomela's silent tongue has been transformed into birdsong—has real motive, a cause in experience. Philip Sidney's "The Nightingale" is the most direct and sexist retelling of the rape myth, since by his own claim—

> But I, who daily craving,
> Cannot have to content me,
> Have more cause to lament me,
> Since wanting is more woe than too much having.

—his lament of longing must needs be more painful than a complaint, as he deftly puts it, of too much having. The usefulness of Sidney's poem has little to do with the level of its considerable wit and everything to do with the terms of its closing perception—"my thorn my heart invadeth"—alluding at once to the thorn-in-the-breast idea while suggesting that the longing is not just sexual but spiritual: that the mating song is a lament in isolation, an ontological complaint.

Sidney's poem dates at 1581. Coleridge's conversation poem of the same title dates from the publication of *Lyrical Ballads*, 1798. In its wandering, modern, broody 110 lines it follows Coleridge's common evening theme of saying farewell to friends, as if for the last time, assessing, here at the end of the day, both natural and human values. Like an evensong it suggests a lament, the sweet-sadness of separating. Coleridge uses the nightingale to underwrite the happy isolation of his humanism: if the nightingale's melancholy is a strictly human projection, a reading-into nature, so is the nightingale's song of joy, its "murmurs musical and swift jug jug,/And one low piping sound more sweet than all." The poet's justification for substituting nightingale joy for grief involves, as always in Coleridge's poems of this period, his concern for his first-born child, whom he hopes will be able, in his growing up, to hear and understand that these night songs, these notes of farewell, are as filled with joy as the hush of "undropped tears."

The tone, however, of Coleridge's ostensibly outgoing conversation poem is sunset, "sunken day," crepuscular, shading into dark, a moment when "some night-wandering man whose heart was pierced/With remembrance of a grievous wrong . . ./ First named these notes a melancholy strain." Perhaps the night-wanderer, a listener, is Charles Lamb, whose sister has recently murdered their mother; perhaps it is Wordsworth, who is beginning to have questions about the value of his work, though in two months he will write "Tintern Abbey"; or perhaps it is Coleridge himself, writing against his own fears and mistakes, apprehensive for his son, as well he should be. Perhaps it is simply a mariner-wanderer, out of the poetic past. The point is not to be too literal while recognizing the gravity, the grounding, under the reference. Whatever the particulars, Coleridge's poem is an autobiography of mixed emotion, a meditation on the possibility of joy, weighted with implication. It is no accident, even if it is an allusion, that nightingale grief is expressed through the image of the thorn ("heart was pierced"). By the spring of 1819, when he writes the most famous of the nightingale songs, Keats will have behind him the backup music of not simply the mixture of joy and grief found in Coleridge and Sidney but the whole history of a metaphor on wounding—on wounded birdsong. This essential motif will then be passed on to Hardy, at the apocalyptic turning of the century, in "The Darkling Thrush," then on to Whitman, at the tragic end of the Civil War and the death of Lincoln, in "When Lilacs Last in the Dooryard Bloom'd," then on to Yeats, in 1927, at a moment of crisis of personal and artistic mortality, in "Sailing to Byzantium"—over and over, the song passed on, from century to century, the selfsame song that found a path from ancient days of emperor and clown through the sad heart of Ruth.

As the central poem in the nightingale continuum, and therefore in the continuity of all lyric poetry, Keats's ode both reflects a clear ancestry and transmits a tradition, while all the while engaging personal, archetypal raw material. "Ode to a Nightingale" is thus a fund of historical, influential, and individual transfigurations at once, and at different levels—mythic, idiosyncratic, autobiographic. At that saturated, soft incense moment when the nightingale speaker cannot, in embalmed darkness, see what flowers are at his feet, we can remember Milton, in "Lycidas," listing against their absence—"Their bells and flowerets of a thousand hues"—all those mortal English flowers that are the flowers of grief, and we can look forward to Whitman, in the dooryard, describing "the lilac-bush tall-growing with heart-shaped leaves of rich green,/With many a pointed blossom rising delicate, with the perfume strong I love." And we realize how much the bower-setting itself, as a place of birdsong, determines the tone, the feeling of the piece, and how that feeling, that elegiac emotion, is passed along among poems of similar passion and proposition. "Lycidas" is a pastoral elegy; "When Lilacs Last in the Dooryard Bloom'd" is a pastoral elegy: as a transitional lyric force between these two great poems, Keats's ode—his nightingale's song—shares their terms and concerns, so much so that the very nature of his odal intention is inherently transformed by the elegiac nature of his material—the thorn at the breast of the nightingale, the wound in the heart.

Heartache, stated nakedly as the opening finesse of his poem, is Keats's focus of the wound-grief juxtaposed to and associated with the nightingale's song. As the variation-on-a-theme from Ovid through Lucretius to Shakespeare to Sidney and Coleridge, it reenacts while enlarging the incorporation

31

of the wounded heart to include the whole of the brain and body—"My heart aches, and a drowsy numbness pains/My sense"—as if melancholy really were a complete anatomical condition. This ontological heartache, though rich with literary precedent, is nevertheless no contrivance—it is as personally thread-connected as the poetic history of the birdsong laced against it. Indeed, the combinations of grief and joy in the relevant poems by all the nightingale poets may want their larger philosophic forms, their inclusive forms, but their emotional bias is generically elegiac and conventionally personal, even when, as in the example of Sidney, the subject is romantic. Behind the poem there is always the lover or the lost one, as well as the wound, being grieved. For Keats the connections are well established in the biographies from his father's death, when he was eight, to his mother's death, when he was fourteen, to his brother Tom's death, when he was twenty-three. In the latter two deaths, Keats acted as a kind of nurse and companion: in the mother's case he is the defender, the boy with a sword at death's gate; in the brother's case, he is the physician-poet with only his words as a weapon. He fails in both instances. No wonder, in between these losses, he committed himself to medicine.

Keats's heartache, then, may have some local residence in his fairly hopeless if intense relationship with Fanny Brawne—a relationship, here in the spring of 1819 barely just begun—but it is his lost family, and emphatically the consumptive loss of Tom, that underwrites the emotional full cup of his "Nightingale." It is the absolute integrity of death as the experience of origin and the wound-healing cycle of mourning and longing that follows it that gives this middle ode in the brilliant spring sequence its special length, its resonant intensity, its narrative human claim. Tom dies just weeks after his nineteenth birthday, on December 1, 1819—Tom, who, according to elder brother George, "understood Keats better than any other human being." Keats had sat at Tom's bedside almost constantly since the end of the summer and the difficult, clumsy Scottish walking tour with Charles Brown, nursing him through the violent fevers and coughing, talking him through depression, reading him into sleep. And off and on, often late at night or in the lulls of Tom's exhaustion, Keats would work and rework his breakthrough try at the epic *Hyperion*, only to sink into a white exhaustion himself. Finally, after intermittent periods of suspension that seemed like recovery and periods that were in fact relapses, Tom had died and Keats had left the closed-in room at Well Walk to move in with his friend, Brown, at Wentworth Place, blocks away.

Purists, in acknowledging the autobiographical reference to Tom in stanza 3—"Where youth grows pale, and specter-thin, and dies"—also accuse it of its fallacy. Allen Tate, in the most famous example, an *American Scholar* piece from the 1940s, complains that at this moment in the nightingale poem "Keats has no language of his own for this realm of experience," implying that Keats has somehow not transformed the literalness of his source, its "rawness"; implying that he has merely disguised it, as if he were reporting on the general mortal human condition of things. It is certainly true that the rather stark qualifying diction of stanza 3 stands in relief against the mythic, sensual, yet ironic richness of the stanza before, but that is part of the gravitational movement in the logic of the poem, while the referential terms, the "playing-field," as it were, is no less, in both stanzas, inclusive or generalized, in just the way nightingale-song history is collective in stanza 7. I bring this point up now only to reaffirm the strength of Tom's representative presence as a *source* throughout the text—stated or sublimated—and to remember the lineage of mortality—young and old, beautiful and dull—from Keats's own life experience. Contrary to indictments of impurity, much of the energy and reach of the "Nightingale" lies precisely in its ability to bring inside the green enclosure of the evening bower "the weariness, the fever and the fret" of the palsied gray-blanched world just outside—the world of Guy's Hospital, for instance, as well as the sick room of Well Walk.

A few weeks before the writing of the nightingale ode, Keats had at last gone back to the Well Walk address to gather the remainder of Tom's personals. Among the papers, Keats found a packet of overwrought love letters from a young woman by the name of Amena, a French correspondent who turned out to be a complete fabrication. It seems a so-called friend of Tom's, Charles Wells, had dictated the letters as an elaborate hoax, sending a very adolescent Tom, in the early stages of his illness, on a wild-goose chase to France in search of this highly sexed attractive creature. Perhaps in normal circumstances the whole matter, on reflection, would have been considered a bad joke and a chance to travel. Keats, however, under severe circumstances, thought that it helped to hasten Tom's eventual death and flew into a rage, since he, like most of his contemporaries, believed that anxiety (like a hectic in the blood) was a contributor to consumption. He even threatened, in a letter to George, to kill Wells. Instead, in the calm following the storm, Keats wrote the therapeutic "La Belle Dame sans Merci," a hymn of a piece that immediately precedes "Ode to Psyche," the first of the spring odes. "La Belle . . ." will prove to be a kind of ethereal warm-up to the poet's emerging sense of lyric concentration within ambitious lyric form. Scholars have no trouble, in the content of "La Belle," with accepting Tom's pivotal place as a transformed muse-figure, especially as the allegorical terms of the poem are so distilled, intense, dreamlike, distant, and exquisite. As yet another precedent for a prelude to the heartache of the "Nightingale," written as if by another hand, this strange poem is noteworthy for its insistence on a landscape in the picture's negative ("The sedge has withered from the Lake . . . And the harvest's done.") and for its refrain of a cold hillside where no birds sing. The snow lily and the fading rose, the starved lips and the silent spring—these emblems are like ghost forms of imminent outlines of spectral figures, to be filled in and fleshed out "Through verdurous glooms and winding mossy ways." And if the "lily on the brow" becomes easily the face of youth grown "pale, and specter-thin," such an image only further enhances the complementing contrast with the fecundity and luxury of the individual nightingale moment in the mythology and history of losses and returns celebrated in the ode.

Tom's death, linked as it must be to the parental losses and to the disintegration of the family—George now somewhere in the wilds of America, Fanny now a virtual prisoner of the Keats's family guardian, Richard Abbey—and the lack of money, let alone lack of a home to go to, left Keats at the low point of his life in the winter of 1818–1819. "La Belle" is one of the signatures of the existential, emotional deprivation of these months, written at the cusp of a change of fortune—it is both a rendering and a renewal. So all the more dramatic that an early break of spring, along with a generally improving domestic life—including the resolution of where he would be spending the summer (Wentworth Palace) and who his next door neighbor would be (Fanny Brawne)—began to pull Keats out of his withdrawal, which had been manifested largely in black moods and, for Keats, more serious drinking. One good sign of Keats's emotional recovery was a new routine of walking on the heath. On a windy April Sunday—one of those coastal winds that sweeps far inland—and almost to the day that he completed his knight-at-arms ballad and just days before he wrote the first finished draft of "Ode to Psyche," Keats met, for the first and last time, another ritual walker on the heath, that "archangel a little damaged," Samuel Taylor Coleridge.

The now familiar circumstances of the encounter are nearly as interesting as their afterglow. Coleridge, by this time, though still only in his forties, was thought to be the supreme intellectual senior citizen of England, the man Hazlitt had referred to as "the only person I ever knew who answered to the idea of a man of genius," and whose mind he described as "being clothed with wings" and whose voice "rings in my ears with never dying sounds." This Coleridge was by this time, to use Keats's word for him, "a great ruin," though still gifted with the jewel of his Mariner's eye, which, like his mind, caught all the light. Keats at first did not recognize Coleridge and when he did, out of shyness, kept on walking. It was Joseph Green, Coleridge's amanuensis and a former anatomical dresser at Guy's Hospital when Keats was a student there, who said to Coleridge, "Is that not the poet Keats?," whereupon he caught up with Keats and made the introductions. What Coleridge remembered most from the meeting was Keats's disheveled dress and the fact that—as Coleridge recorded years later—there was death in the young writer's handshake.

> A loose, slack, not well-dressed youth met Mr. [Green] and myself in a lane near Highgate. [Green] knew him, and spoke. It was Keats. He was introduced to me, and stayed a minute or so. After he had left us a little way, he came back and said: "Let me carry away the memory, Coleridge, of having pressed your hand!"—"There is death in that hand," I said to [Green] when Keats was gone; yet this was, I believe, before the consumption showed itself distinctly.

He also recalled that he, Coleridge, complained about the nightingales keeping him up all night and that their meeting lasted, to his regret, too briefly.

Keats, in a paragraph in one of his journal-letters, tells a slightly different story:

> I joined them, after enquiring by a look whether it would be agreeable—
> I walked with him at his alderman-after-dinner pace for near two miles I

suppose. In those two miles he broached a thousand things—let me see if I can give you a list—Nightingales, Poetry—on Poetical sensation—Metaphysics—Different genera and species of Dreams—Nightmare—a dream accompanied by a sense of touch—single and double touch—A dream related—First and second consciousness—Monsters, the Kraken—Mermaids—Southey believes in them—Southey's belief too much diluted—A Ghost story—Good morning—I heard his voice as he came toward me—I heard it as he moved away—I had heard it all the interval—if it may be called so. He was civil enough to ask me to call on him at Highgate.

The walk, apparently, went on for an hour. The nightingales, as well as the genera and species of dreams, were close on Coleridge's mind, since in both Highgate, north of the heath, and Hampstead, just south, nightingales had been nesting early and staying up late, though they likely represented correlatives of other noises in the great man's sleepless head. Nevertheless, Coleridge kept his humor—"As to Nightingales—they are almost as numberous with us, as incessant in songs, as Frogs with you," he had written to a friend in the fen country. Nightingales must have been on Keats's mind, too, since, as reported by Joseph Severn, Keats had spent many evenings, after a sociable spring dinner at the Hunts's or at Brown's, wandering onto the moorland of the heath to listen to the songs, even taking a few notes—this in the teeth of Brown's testimony that the nightingale poem was written in a single inspired morning at Wentworth Palace under a plum tree, "the nightingale having built her nest near my house." It is not hard to imagine Keats tying all the birdsong he heard that spring together, gathering his notes, and drafting a first full version in a morning's silence, in morning sunlight, passing the song along from its many distances, once his sources had fallen in place.

Whatever the mysteries or multiples of the sources of a lyric poem—and all lyric poems, regardless of their achievement, begin with the same ambition—however distant the inspiration, however finally transformed the original experience is, the fact remains that fact itself—physical, existential fact—exerts an equivalent pull of gravity while at the same time authenticating the future. Like every other art, the making of a lyric poem exists on a time-line—the poem's future is made out of its past, its success out of its sources. "All these were spectacles and sounds to which/I often would repair, and thence would drink/As at a fountain," says Wordsworth. The imagination, an event into futurity, depends on its empiricism, on its evidentiary gravity, on events of personal history, not in order to play with the toys of personal knowledge but in order to release our powerful and catalytic experiences into archetypes. Tom, therefore, becomes the presiding fraternal figure in "Ode to a Nightingale," Coleridge one of its paternal figures: both, as presiding presences among the many other, less personal, presences, move between, like ghosts, the waking and the sleeping of the ode. Put another way, Tom is a muse, Coleridge a catalyst. Almost like a part of the palimpsest of the notes for Keats's poem, Tom's death is first traced in "La Belle Dame sans Merci," whose form itself is likely most immediately borrowed from Coleridge's own ballad, "Love."

> She leant against the arméd man,
> The statue of the arméd knight;
> She stood and listened to my lay,
>     Amid the lingering light . . .

> And that she nursed him in a cave;
> And how his madness went away,
> When on the yellow forest-leaves
>     A dying man he lay . . .

If Tom had lived a while longer, say, into the spring, if Keats had not met Coleridge and Green on the heath that April Sunday, "Ode to a Nightingale," if written, would have been a very different poem—shorter, tighter, more focused on the object, the way "Ode to Melancholy" and "Ode on a Grecian Urn" are, less interested in the narrative values that invite and report transmissions from the real and local world. It would have addressed the bird within a more completely insulated, isolated bower. This is an opinion, of course. Yet all the other odes, including the least pure, "Indolence," and the most pure, "To Autumn," are object-goddess-haunted, enclosed within their mythological paradigms, written like dramatic arguments, inside the house of art. The dramatic circumstance of "Nightingale" is contrived not only to be outside, in an announced and single setting, but to follow a single emotional moment through time, from evening dark to

37

darker. Keats's fiction is to enact his limited story with himself as a persona limited within it. His narrative sources have led him to his narrative needs, a real bird in a real garden, with a real and acknowledged past pushing the poem into its narrative future, crowding the scene. The fancy cannot cheat so well.

Physical evidence has a power of its own. You have to imagine Keats sitting all those hours with Tom in the confinement of the sick room—the coughing, the odors, the all-night vigils—as Keats himself would be sat with by Severn in just two years. You have to imagine Keats leaning over his brother, Keats the physician, who had watched the anatomical lectures and studied the diseases, who had collected as part of his apprenticeship some of the freshly buried corpses. You have to imagine the poet working and reworking *Hyperion* in a chair at the bedside. And you have to see Keats on the heath, running into Coleridge, in the company of a man Keats knew well from those medical days, when Joseph Green was a demonstrator at Guy's—you have to imagine the actual physical encounter of the young poet ("'Heaven!' said I, 'when I shook him by the hand there was death!'") and the great elder ("I heard his voice as he came toward me—I heard it as he moved away—I had heard it all the interval") and remember Coleridge as the facilitator of much of Wordsworth's finest writing, the writing coming out of the talking, just as the meeting with Keats was talking. You have to imagine Coleridge with all those insomniac nightingales in his head, and the thousand things, from metaphysics to mermaids, and see Coleridge as Keats, and so many other admirers, saw him, as a kind of Ur-voice of inspiration, a fountain, an ongoing creative process. You have to imagine Coleridge, in his way, giving Keats permission.

The writing itself is also physical evidence. In the Fitzwilliam Museum at Cambridge, you can look at the surviving draft of the nightingale ode. Under glass it seems to float in a separate space, the sepia-brown of the ink somehow still fluid above the browning texture of the paper, paper itself watermarked Ruse & Turners, 1817. At two years of age, the paper had already begun to acquire a mortality by the time Keats used it; and had his words truly been written in water, both paper and ink would have long since passed to dust. But the words make the 174-year-old paper almost immortal—almost, since the words are really written on the air. Small changes in the manuscript—crossings-out, substitutions, rewrites—take on a plastic, artist's-drawing life: the way *My*, the very first word in the poem, is at first cancelled, then left; the way *painful* in the first line is changed to *drowsy* so that *pains* can become the verb instead of *falls*; the way *spectre* is added to *youth grows pale and thin*; the way *grief*, at the end of line 27, becomes *sorrow*; the way the *voice* of the nightingale that was heard by emperor and clown becomes *birdsong* again in the sad heart of Ruth. Such changes have the effect of line and contour and shading, a quality of chiaroscuro, entities in themselves that are part of the larger drawing of "Ode to a Nightingale." This visual impression lends itself to a greater aural sensation, as if the poem were vocal on the page, physically active.

You are, of course, hearing it in your head as you read the raw material of the manuscript, and you are seeing it as an object in itself. The profundity of these words, like all words in all good poems, is what they represent, what they figure in front of us on the page, the tremendous amount and complexity of experience they focus in their signing abstract auditory character—even, as in this literal instance, their implied tactile power. The profundity of the words is also how they rescue and redeem our ordinary daily use of them, how they emerge original again in poems.

> I cannot see what flowers are at my feet,
>     Nor what soft incense hangs upon the boughs,
> But in embalméd darkness guess each sweet
>     Wherewith the seasonable month endows
> The grass, the thicket, and the fruit-tree wild;
>     White hawthorn, and the pastoral eglantine;
>         Fast fading violets cover'd up in leaves;
>             And mid-May's eldest child,
>     The coming musk-rose, full of dewy wine,
>         The murmurous haunt of flies on summer eves.

To see this stanza written out in the flawed living hand of its author is to understand at once the perishability of its utterance and the permanence of its achievement, since even this beauty will not survive without its truth, the truth of the text it advances.

Language, as such, is not the source of poetry. At best, language can become a kind of self-fulfilling prophecy, like the wave that starts so far from shore it seems self-generated. The spirit in the wind, the heartache, the longing—these are what start poems. And these things are not nothing. They themselves come from the substance of experience, palpable, fundamental experience, with the force of gravity fixing them in our common lives, our common memory, to be passed along, rewritten, and passed along again. The selfsame song, says Keats, is both a voice and a music, a plaintive anthem, a night bird on the wing, yet it is also only words. The sources of the words, the words, for instance, of Keats's pale manuscript, can never be known except as they are manifest in the work, in the words. But the reader must feel the force of where the words are calling from if the words themselves are to have force—force of conviction, force of fact. How many facts are there? Not many—the rest is detail.

1992

WISTMAN'S WOOD

# 1

Even at a distance it looks old, older than old—an extended island of three consecutive copses of sway-backed English oak the color of stone. Closer up, at walking speed, the enclosures, like ancient, pillaged castle walls, begin to flow into one another, with the undergrowth and giant clitter forming the transitions between larger structures. Then when you are almost close enough to touch it the whole thing looms and unifies, suddenly undifferentiated, simultaneous.

That is when the singular plural of the noun really kicks in: when you are at the broken wall of the wood and can begin to appreciate, even absorb, its opacity, its confusion, and can, once your eyes focus on distinctions, begin to separate one tree from another. Wistman's Wood is both one tree and multiples of that one, whose trunk and lateral branching is layered with centuries of secondary life—vines and vegetation—and whose root system, like an afterthought of itself, is rooted in stone, which is also gray-green with erosion and encrustation. One fundamental tree, one fundamental stone, with mirrors.

But this is no primitive rain forest. In its thickness and intimacy and low-doorway height it is medieval, a fantasy of sorcery, a primary human space mysteriously abandoned, alive with age. Its primacy and continuity and modesty are naturally connected, since as an entity the wood seems to have accepted, from the outset, its limitations. Rather than trying to reach too high or too far in any one direction, rather than trying to assume territory or increase of its numbers, rather than acting like a forest—which it profoundly is not—it has achieved a kind of immortality or self-perpetuation through an internal and necessary understanding of its special place on the landscape, its special configuration within the weather, which can be extreme, and its especial knowledge of the wind, which is constant. It is like a great old architectural event from out of the deep past, haunted by survival.

This is a wood of trees in the middle of a landmass sea, with a variable sea wind, facts that not only discipline the expansion of the wood's margins but help shape its actual vertical growth. It is as if the wood were at the ocean's edge, with the wind always landward. Out of resistance, therefore, the trees, an acreage of them, are bent, from west to east, at a height of ten to fifteen feet—angles that are further emphasized by the angle of the eastern incline of the valley they grow out of. As it pours down the opposite side of West Dart Valley and crosses the ribbon of the West Dart River, the wind seems to pick up power with the potential of a wave. This is a Dartmoor wind, from across the ocean cliff faces and open distances of Cornwall and Devon.

No wonder the branches elongate on a line parallel with the earth until their weight forces them back toward the tips of their roots. Among such trees there can be no lift toward the theology of the sky, no possibility of ascension. The wind, as the most active and visible agent of change on the moor, drives the branches downward and inward toward the wreck of the granite, lichen-covered boulders the trees seem to cling to. Tangled as they are—branch returning to root—and hoisted out of the warping angles of the stones, the tree-shapes suggest any number of things, not the least of which is a cloister, a series of cloisters, or interiors, where the voice of the wind is the spirit in the wood.

# 2

You have to go there, though, in the boning chill of winter, when the green leaf has given up and left the wood essential.

It is February yet dry enough for a long walk that normally, at this time of the year on the moor, could be daunting to the amateur. Dartmoor is the great dark stain on the English mystery-writer's map in *The Hound of the Baskervilles*, complete with the prison (Princetown), Grimpen Mire (Fox Tor Meir), and Baskerville Hall (Park Hill, Ipplepen), places all within gloomy proximity of one another (and Wistman's Wood). The whole of the moor, which takes up much of South Devon, resembles in outline the state of Ohio, heart-crossed by two vein-like main roads that meet at a spot called Two Bridges. Wistman's Wood is a tall walk north of this juncture.

Dartmoor is Britain's largest open moorland, rising, in parts, to two thousand feet and descending, in sharp valleys, to a variety of quick streams. It is a landscape constructed largely of tors and bogs, ancient trackways and waterways, clitters and cairns, conifers and great empty stretches. Sometimes the open areas build gradually, sometimes the uplift is sharp and dangerous, and often the marshy patches and mires are bottomless. The moor ponies—residual from Iron Age tin mines—the Blackfaced sheep, and the Highland cattle that wander freely are all subject to disappearance through misstep. People, of course, can carry maps and follow marked trails.

This is wild, lost country, filled with secret spaces, swept by the same winds and crosswinds. The winds are rivers over the surface. Deciduous Wistman's Wood, sitting as it does on the upper, climbing slope of a wide valley, seems to have its own individual wind, calibrated for mystery, in spite of the would-be science that has tried since 1620—the year of Plymouth Rock—to categorize, measure, identify, and account for its presence. Even a recent monograph published by Devonshire's Nature Conservancy Council has trouble avoiding the look and feel of the place: "Leaving aside subjective impressions among the more romantically minded of desolation, weirdness, mystery or even evil, the aspects of the wood that impressed to varying degrees were (a) the stunted growth of the trees; (b) the contorted growth of the trees, with sinuous branches hugging the contours of the rocks; (c) the prolific growth of mosses and other epiphytes; and (d) the impression of great age of individual trees and of general decay. These features invite study."

The tourist guides, which depend on glamour of any kind, have no trouble of course with the desolation, weirdness, or mystery of the wood. According to the *Michelin Guide to The West Country*, that is its attraction: "The wood is low-lying, the oaks stunted, primeval; their living trunks, growing out of boulder-strewn slopes, are draped in gray-green lichen. The trees appear to be self-perpetuating yet there are no saplings, nor are there any animals or birds within the wood. It is all very reminiscent of an Arthur Rackham illustration."

What saves the attraction of the wood, however, from being too attractive is that for humans the distance from Two Bridges is longer than its two miles—a narrow, treacherous, soggy distance. In the wrong season—and nearly every season is the wrong one—you have to practically wade there. And you have to walk as much against the angles of the landscape as against the weather. As for the sheep and cattle and wild ponies—the clitter takes care of them. The Wistman boulders are too large and contiguous for any hint of pasture and too slippery with lichen for hooves, and the boulders are everywhere; they really are the ground under the trees. As for the birds, they are missed; but the wood is too thick and its floor too ungiving and cold for much coming and going, nesting and feeding. The iron in the wind may be part of it too. Nevertheless, the birdlessness of the place elevates its sense of suspension and isolation, its cloistering, its attic height, its place above and beyond the reach of claims and commitments, its place as a room, a dream of rooms, removed and out of time—the far place Keats may have had in mind when he referred to his imagination as a monastery in which he was the monk.

# 3

The mix of the adult and child in us is well met here, in both the wood's isolation and anachronism. Part of us longs for solitude and part of us needs mystery, part of us loves surprise and part of us pushes risk. But to be lost in the allegory of our fears, to be cut off inside the solitary confinement of the self, to be alone with only the wind—that takes the fantasy too far. Wistman's Wood is the abbey cloister gone to seed, the dark Grimms' fairy tale bled even raggedier at the edge; it is also, and mostly, a strange and beautiful and real place in which the ambivalent mind is set free to be of two minds, at least. The wood is a true tangle and mist. Even in its upper-netting, at about twelve or fifteen feet, the air seems caught, immobilized, and color-changed, the way the light fills the air in a terrarium. On the ground, where the enchantment of the light seems to begin and where the stones are so piled and overlapped that every crack and seam is a clog of moss and moor-grass and root, the density amounts to an absolute stillness, a stillness that doubles as a principle of order and the stability of gravity. Like the wind, the stones help to misshape the trees while freezing the contortions. It is as if gravity were a heavy, slow wind too. The scene is at once disconcerting and reassuring.

But you have to go there in the chill of winter, when the tangle and the mist have a different darkness from the green dark of spring. In June, says novelist John Fowles, "the oaks are just coming into leaf, long after their low-land kin, in every shade from yellow-green to bronze." Fowles's long essay,

"The Tree," published in the early 1970s, is the first articulate response to the compelling beauty of this ancient wood. His spring descriptions serve to underwrite the darker winter tones. The branches, for example, "grow to an extraordinary extent laterally; are endlessly angled, twisted, raked, interlocked, and reach quite as much downwards as upwards." The branches, he goes on, seem "to be writhing, convulsed, each its own Laöcoon, caught and frozen in some fanatically private struggle for existence."

The granite floor of the wood, he adds, is "like a tilted emerald sea . . . fairy-like. It corresponds uncannily with the kind of setting artists like Richard Dadd imagined for that world in Victorian times and have now indelibly given it: teeming, jewel-like, self-involved, rich in secrets just below the threshold of our adult human senses." The whole place, the whole tree and stone tangle, is "an infinitely rare fragment of primeval forest . . . comparable with a great Neolithic site: a sort of Avebury of the tree, and Ur-wood."

Fowles is writing with a poet-novelist's vision; he is building analogues, Wistmans of the imagination. He is sitting in his writer's room recollecting in tranquility, re-creating within his walled garden space the wild spring space of the wood. He is in two places at once, and both, in his mind's eye, are the same place. He is writing, in fact, in the best sense, a fiction of his memory of the place, with all the knowledge of botany and interest in mystery he can muster. At one point in his narrative he states flatly that there is no wind; at another moment he hears, though he cannot see it, a hedgesparrow, a sparrow that claims, in "prestissimo bulbul shrill. . . . My wood, my wood"; at yet another he senses, in the distance, "the rush of water in a moorland stream . . . like the snore of the raven."

Fowles is remembering a more decorative, Victorian, Richard Dadd wood than the wood in winter. In winter, with the darker turns of temperatures and winds and with the exposure of the networks of the branching and the moon-scars on the stones, the forlorn, skeletal, and Ur-like qualities become enhanced, if not transformed. The green mask is gone. And the closest thing to birdsong is the wind in the thorn. The wood is now the dark tower, our monk's cell, a corner of the maze of our childhood dreams, dreams that we wake up from yet somehow want to sleep back into. The wood is now—and still—bewitched, but witch-ugly. This is the wood alive in winter. This is the great lapsed orchard in moonlight that seemed to rise to the bedroom window; this is the black tree in December that followed you at dusk down the road. This is the animal that slept standing, breathing into the cold white fog.

Outside, on the moor, it is February, ice in the wind and in patches, like ponds, everywhere on the grass. The sky is violet to white. Since the enclosure of the wood is warmer than the open air, the drifting mist gets caught in the netting of the trees before it dissipates. The heavy, smoky vapor hangs like cloth and adds to the intimacy, something that the open moor, with its high bleak tors and Sphagnum moss bogs, bitterly discourages. But sitting here on one of the big green-gray stones, under a big swatch of fern, the limb of the oak it drops from running the length of several other stones, you begin to realize the value of withdrawal, the value of being small again within the larger tangle, within the puzzle, among the protective white-out colors of the cloud. You begin to realize the value of being invisible, stained by everything you touch. And you begin to realize that the imagination really only powerfully works—as a full spiritual reality—from disappearances and absorptions, emptinesses and ambiguities, poverties and denials, from winter spaces.

# 4

The trouble with the spring condition of the world—at least for the pensive man, as Stevens terms him—is the degree to which it calls attention to the flesh, the carnal, to rebirth and fecundity, to what Fowles refers to, in his Wistman's essay, as "the wood's astounding internal fertility." The green world is a garden and the green man, a vegetation god, is impossible to kill, since he is a renewable resource. The green man is hardly pensive; he comes at us, as Fowles himself points out, from the green chaos of our unconscious, from our primary sexual being. He comes at us wrapped in the richness of the leaves, definite with purpose and desire. He is beautiful, if intimidating, with desire. But the mind and heart of winter speak from a wholly other ontological condition, a wholly different set of ambiguities and complexities from those of spring.

For camouflage is different from disappearance.

If the distinction can be made at all, if the archetype of Wistman's Wood can be made valuable in terms of its spring as opposed to its winter bearing, the creative distinction must follow the differences between the allegory of our material being and the allegory of the spirit. The spirit will not be obscured, it can only be absorbed.

Sitting on the brow of one of the big gray stones, within the very interiority of the winter wood, in which the grays dominate the soft moss and fernal greens—the stones rising, into perspective, at a hundred subtle levels, the long, dark, lichen-covered branches running in stasis sometimes only inches above the stones—in which the dead matter of the mortal seasons lines every cranny and depression, in which the air is visible with chill, like a window you can write your name on—sitting here in the middle of this wood in the middle of Dartmoor, in the least time of the year, it comes to you how reassuring this naked space is, how unburdening of the wastes of the spirit, and how clarifying to the imagination. It is a place you can leave and take with you; it is a human, ordered space, free of the density and dominance of the alien green chaos.

Wordsworth, in one of the most insightful passages of *The Prelude*, remembering the Christmas of his father's death, speaks of the bleak music of this time, and the many other winter moments leading up to that year, as "spectacles and sounds to which/I often would repair, and thence would drink/ As at a fountain." He is remembering himself out on the winter moor, remembering the "visionary dreariness" of other spots of time, other deaths and images of death, foreshadowing his ninth Christmas. Keats, in his letter about "To Autumn," speaks disparagingly of the chilly green of spring and sees the real riches in the warm winter browns of the season of winter mists. An elderly Emily Dickinson, writing at the end of her life, in "#1670," announces that "In Winter in my Room/I came upon a worm/ Pink, lank and warm," and in her dream even flies to a distant town to escape it. Whatever her carnal condition, at any passage in her life, there can be no doubt that winter-in-my-room defined her continuing ontological condition as a writer. And Wallace Stevens, for all of his obsession with color and cacophony, says that the poet must have a mind of winter, since there is no change, or even chance, of death in paradise.

The workshop of the imagination is the writer's room. For a poet like Sylvia Plath the interior workspace of the imagination became more and more a winter, a naked, a clarifying space, a space in which she felt, for richer or poorer, more and more subtracted. The winter wood, finally, became her power, as the later poems permit the cold white space to purify the text and allow the lithic pensive tone its winded silence. She disappeared into the tangle. She understood that in order to work, the spirit must be always shedding its leaves and moving among stone, among the ruins of the green and golden season. In order to absent itself the spirit must find absence, the emptiness resonant with memory, a Tintern Abbey, a stubble-plain with rosy, evening hue.

The room in ruins—that is what a spot in Wistman's Wood is in winter. The winter wood reminds us of our poet origins, of the spiritual space and longing even in the child, who follows us from place to lost place. The winter wood reminds us that dark and windswept memory is more vital than a green thought in a green shade and that the setting of that memory is in the moment in the space that represents the truth. Sitting in the room you write in, you sit within the tangle and the winter mist. The leaves have long since blown into the corners. You sit there with the hard language and memory in front of you and you feel yourself disappearing. Wonderful. These fragments I have shored against my ruins.

1993

WHISTLER'S NOCTURNES

*Greaves: The stars are fine tonight.*
*Whistler: Not bad, but there are too many of them.*

"An autumn evening was closing in."

Like a night piece, the opening chapter of *Our Mutual Friend* offers us an image of indeterminacy, obscurity, water darkness: the shadow-life of two figures in a rowboat, like fishermen, working with the tide of the Thames, the great iron bridging of Southwark looming behind them. They are, we find out, a father and daughter, but their identity, in the abstractions of the dark, is more apparent than their business, which is the harvesting of floating suicides and murders risen from the bottom of the river. "How can money be a corpse's?" one of them asks. The question is rhetorical, spoken into the void just under them. The ghoulishness of the scene, from the viewing angle, is softened, even absorbed, by the weight of the air above the darker weight of the water. The unities of color and figure against the larger forms of bridge and stark Victorian buildings are practically photographic, yet quietly dramatic, like a tone poem.

Whistler was no more fond of Dickens than he was of most narrative orders in the world, but he loved the River Thames, particularly in the way it seemed to gather and hold and finally swallow the last light of the day, particularly in the way it created density, atmosphere. At such an hour he loved to be rowed along its thick surface between the festival lights of Cremorne Gardens, on the north bank near where he lived, and the long fields and woods of Surrey to the south. More often than not he sketched, took notes, black and white chalk on brown paper; often, as his critics would agree, he drew in the dark, the twilight having abandoned him. Such sketches, of necessity, looked to be little more than clues to the organization of the space—sometimes a sort of row of houses, sometimes a gantry and crane, with a boat in the water for balance, sometimes the Chinese platform of the gardens. Often he used the memory method of closing his eyes in order to test what he remembered seeing. "And when the evening

mist clothes the riverside with poetry, as with a veil, and the poor buildings lose themselves in the dim sky, and the tall chimneys become campa-
nili, and the ware houses are palaces in the night, and the whole city hangs
in the heavens, and fairy-land is before us—then the wayfarer hastens home;
the working man and the cultured one, the wise man and the one of pleasure, cease to understand, as they have ceased to see, and Nature, who, for
once, has sung in tune, sings her exquisite song to the artist alone, her son
and her master—her son in that he loves her, her master in that he knows
her."

Purple though they may be, the words are Whistler's, part of his important *Ten O'Clock* lecture, delivered in February 1885, some years after the
boat trips and the river *Nocturnes* were completed. The artist turned writer
was, typically, in his antagonistic mode—oratorical, defensive, antibour-
geois, arrogant, and right. "Industry in Art is a necessity—not a virtue—
and any evidence of the same, in the production, is a blemish, not a quality;
a proof, not of achievement, but of absolutely insufficient work, for work
alone will efface the footsteps of work." Or: "Listen! There never was an
artistic period. There never was an Art-loving nation." Or: "To say to the
painter that Nature is to be taken as she is, is to say to the player that he
may sit on the piano. . . . The holiday-maker rejoices in the glorious day,
and the painter turns aside to shut his eyes." The lecture was yet one more
try at finding an audience for an artist who had long since turned from popular realism—even in his portraits—to nature as an urban and/or interior
landscape.

For Whistler the nocturne was a concept as much as it was a perception,
as much an idea as an image. He could take it almost anywhere and, in
addition to paint, could use any number of painterly means. ("Paint should
not be applied thick," he had said. "It should be like breath on the surface of a pane of glass.") Along with the better-known nocturnes concerned
with Cremorne Gardens and the bridges and buildings near them, there is
*Nocturne: Trafalgar Square, Chelsea—Snow*, and there are the watercolored
*Amsterdam Nocturnes*, a variety of nocturnal studies done in pastels and drypoint, and the "floating" *Nocturnes of Venice*, all etchings in a series of proof.
And, of course, there is the original nocturne, *Nocturne: Blue and Gold—
Valparaiso*, done in 1866, which breaks with compositional (and Occiden-
tal) realism by placing the objects (ships at harbor with lights) and the action

(a distant confetti of fireworks) at the "back" of the painting, running something like a dock, monolithically, from the immediate foreground up, a presence that occupies about two-thirds of the space. In all, the *Nocturnes* comprise a period of just under twenty years.

Much has been made of the many influences on Whistler, as a draftsman and as a painter. The influences are said to range from the use of crosshatching and the receding dark tones of Rembrandt to the full and luminous figures in Courbet to the flat, two-dimensional purities of Japanese ukiyo-e to the one-eyed optic reality of the photographic lens. The list is long—Whistler moved in a total world of art and was, for better or worse, one of the founders of Aestheticism. So it seems inevitable that influences as different as Hiroshige and Turner (Turner had been rowed up the Thames by the father of the brothers who served as Whistler's boatmen) should find a resolution in an artist as committed as this one—for whom art existed for its own sake. It is the power with which he understood what was possible, based on what had already been done, that came to distinguish his best work—the *Nocturnes*—from the familiarity and security of the linear, that allowed him to discover the moody "interior" of his subject. Tone is often the term associated with the atmospheric Whistler ("Character! What is character? It's tone that matters!"), but it seems a precious honorific compared with the accomplishment of the nocturne in *Black and Gold: The Falling Rocket*, which Ruskin had name-called a pot of paint flung in the face of the public, and the unsurpassed beauty of the etchings of the Venetian palaces. Tone—another term for the treatment of the purities and impurities of light—may have been a distillation of influences, but by the 1870s, when the *Nocturnes* really begin, the tonal depth of the work is transforming. Ironically, as one of the first in a series of Anglo-American artists, Whistler fit in nowhere, not in Paris with the budding Impressionists, or in London with the dominant Pre-Raphaelites. He was outside, and an outsider; the best of him was disappearing into the resonance of the work.

Asked, at the trial in his suit against Ruskin, to define a "nocturne," Whistler, monocle in place, replied simply, "I have perhaps meant rather to indicate an artistic interest alone in the work, divesting the picture from any outside anecdotal sort of interest which might have been otherwise attached to it. It is an arrangement of line, form and colour first; and I make use of any incident of it which shall bring about a symmetrical result. Among my works are some night pieces, and I have chosen the word Nocturne because it generalizes and simplifies the whole set of them." He had for years been titling his art against the resources of content: if they weren't arrangements, they were harmonies, and if neither of those, they might well be symphonies. The intention, obviously, was to separate the work from its possible story-value and subjectivity, to make an object instead of announce an emotion, to subtract the immediacy of the moment from the plots of time. He was likely less interested in analogies to music (about which he knew next to nothing) than to constructions of metaphor—he was looking for a synesthesia of color and image that would evoke . . . but what—a correspondence? More than anything else, as one critic puts it, Whistler is a compositionist. And true, even his figures in rooms become parts of those rooms, arrangements in color, while whole houses and buildings and bridges became absorbed into the ordered constituencies of mood and atmosphere. Solid forms seem to dissemble, lyrically, in front of us, as if they had become part of the air, softened into grays and darks. We could argue, for example, that a painting like *Symphony in Grey: Early Morning, Thames*, a nocturnal companion, is a completely self-contained piece, completely self-referential; that, as a matter of fact, it is painted on fabric—decorative material—and that it is composed of four bars of alternating monotones— "blue" and "grey." Yet to look at this painting is to look at silence, the moment in and out of time, as Eliot put it; it is a way of looking into something other, the way metaphor offers us the collateral of content, the correlative of the inner life. In spite of its cool pearl tones, *Symphony* is meant to suggest what solitude and privacy, sotto voce, look like.

If you compare the original *Nocturne* of the harbor at Valparaiso to the Thames *Nocturnes* of the early 1870s to the *Chelsea Nocturnes* at the end of the decade to the watercolor *Nocturnes of Amsterdam* of 1883–1884 to the etchings of Venice, the degree of dissolution is amazing. It is not just that the foreground is losing to the background; rather that the monochromatic and tonal values of the ground are absorbing, advancing on those at the front—structures, if you will, are being deconstructed within the composite of the text, within the space of the moment, a blue dark dissolve. Compositionally, that is what the *Nocturnes* seem to be about: the subject evaporating into the object of the painting. It is no accident that the settings of the overall sequence of the *Nocturnes* juxtapose a harbor to a river to a sea (Bognor) to a snow-covered square to canals to the waters of Venice; it is not surprising that medium itself deconstructs from paint to watercolor wash to drypoint. Whistler wished to effect a simultaneity, a oneness, of color and composition in which a single quality of a hue would organize, harmonize, and, subtly, limit the shades around it. Naturally, the shapes, be they buildings or bridges or boats, would have to follow, as if they were only points on the scale of the order of disappearing color.

In the Valparaiso painting the ships are still relatively distanced from their shadows on the harbor surface, and shoreline and skyline are clearly delineative in the faint firelight from the rockets. In *Nocturne: Battersea Reach* and *Nocturne: Bognor*, both blue and silver renderings, the water and horizon lines are beginning to meld with the abstracting of the objects, which are like props, while the color of the water is unreflective, nearly opaque, like a gravity that is holding everything, including the sky, in place. The *Chelsea Nocturnes*, especially those of the Cremorne Gardens, resist dissipating into darkness by noticing sources of light, such as the Chinese Orchestra Platform or Ashburnum Hall; the most famous and infamous of all, the painting of the falling rocket, lights up the smoky panels of dark like a birthday. *The Falling Rocket* is interesting in the way, against the drapery of the background, the fireworks are expiring rather than exploding; again, the gravity of the black water, the Thames, pulls the scattered fire of the debris down— falling, gone. The antithesis of *Nocturne in Black and Gold: The Falling Rocket* is the snow nocturne, set in Trafalgar Square, Chelsea, 1877. The shapes are ghostly, anonymous—two winter trees stage right, one recessive in the middle in the open space between the low blocky buildings—and in their "absence" are made visible by the snow, both in the air, thick as mist, and on the ground. The snow, in fact, is the air, and is moon-bright, so much so that the emotional effect of the painting, entirely reflective, is warm, brown; in the distance the faint window lights, muted yellows and a red, suggest the warmth of a home; while the sky is a blue slate, wide as a wall. By the early 1880s, in a painting entitled *Nocturne: Silver and Opal—Chelsea*, the forms are nearly totally lost, save for a suggestion of two pilings for the Chelsea Bridge. The brushwork has never been less disguised, the horizon line more invisible. If this is fog, you can feel its texture, you can sense at once its scary substance and insubstantiality; the bridge might appear at any moment or the magical air might swallow everything in abstraction.

It is reported that when he was working on the *Nocturnes*, Whistler never admitted sunlight into his studio, which seems to make only obvious sense. The *Amsterdam Nocturnes*, though, begin to illustrate the turn toward more intimate, interior space. There are four of them, three set on canals, one on ice. The medium, watercolor and wash, unlike the breath-on-glass application of paint, has begun to take over. By moving his "camera" closer to the dominant forms—the window-lit houses along the canals, the building behind the ice-skaters—Whistler forces the sky almost entirely out of the picture and brings the background to the fore. The only presence preventing the washed blue-brown forms of the buildings from overwhelming the whole scene is the water, which, in the clarity and calm of the night canal and on the slick surface of the ice, repeats the forms and their pumpkin lights rather ominously. Japanese ukiyo-e translates as "pictures of the floating world." Whatever influence those Edo prints had on the early Whistler had likely, by the 1880s, been long internalized, but there is no doubt that water, as an abiding presence and value, had become indistinguishable from the dark. All along, from the Valparaiso painting on, water, with its mysterious weight and depth, had built and held the night in place. The dark, for Whistler, had become the stuff of water, a floating sheen, a mist, a fog, a snowfall, an idea of dissolve, in which the potential reality of the form, the shape, the man-made structure, had to be close to nullified in order to be transformed. "The whole city hangs in the heavens," Whistler had said, when in fact, at nightfall, it begins to float and evaporate. This is as true of the people enjoying Cremorne Gardens (few of them as there are) as it is of the boats at the side of Chelsea Embankment—floating, evaporating. The houses along the Dutch canals become, therefore, part of the water; they seem to rise from the canals, like natural saturated substances. Like night-blooming lilies. Unlike Monet and other Impressionists, however, Whistler's ambition was not to paint the subtleties of the withdrawing of light, among other country values, but to paint graduals of "the fell of dark," the floating dark, the urban evening pastoral.

Whistler realized how difficult his task was. Asked, at the Ruskin trial, if he thought *The Falling Rocket* is a finished work, he responded, "It would be impossible for me to say so. I have never seen any picture of night which has been successful; and this is only one of the thousand failures which artists have made in their efforts at painting night." He was being more than a little coy, since success in the art market in London at that time depended on theme, definition, and closure of the well-tailored line. The "failure" of his *Nocturnes* is at the heart of their achievement, as their consistent artistic motif and subversive technical need are their "illegibility," their vulnerability. This failure is at its best, and most profound, in the drypoint etchings of Venice, of 1880. Printing, as opposed to painting and watercolor, permitted Whistler to create something impossible with paint—the chance to develop the mood and tone of a single work without altering the matrix of the basic line and arrangement of the scene. By simply varying the amount of ink and color left on the surface of the plate, he could go from twilight to "musty dusk," as Valéry calls it, to full dark. For example, in the nocturne of the view of the entry into the Grand Canal, the sailing vessel, which is our point of focus, gradually recedes into the drawing as the degree and depth of the ink is increased. By the last of, say, four prints, the boat has become even, in perspective, with the forms of the distant city on the horizon, because ever more slowly, in the sequence, the darkness of the water, balanced in the sky, has enclosed it, in recession.

The most beautiful of the Venice etchings is the sequence of the palace—brown ink for a warmer, more humid nocturnal appeal, black for a cooler, stranger appeal. To avoid the calendar-art Venetian views, Whistler had chosen sites within the city, a habit he had acquired in London. Ever the *flaneur*, he decided once again to use his transformative imagination via the memory method, making the eye more than a camera, choosing a vision over a view. It is one thing to work deep tonalities and blends with paint or wash, it is another to achieve translucency through the drypoint of the line. The *Palaces* is not more complicated, architecturally, than any of the other *Nocturnes*: it consists of views of two buildings, the one on the left slightly in perspective, the one closer on the right facing out, like a wall on stage. But the *Palaces*, in texture, is deeper. An alley of the larger canal runs between them under a bridge that is tucked to the back and serves as the connection for the palaces. Half the picture is the canal, and the structures, unlike those in the *Dutch Nocturnes*, are actually in the water. The door arches and the windows and a balcony do more than relieve the blankness of the façades; they activate the drawing and provide negatives of lights by generating shadows, by being shadows, particularly the grillwork of the balcony. As the prints become inkier (in black), the motif of the shadows takes on dramatic, perhaps decadent, possibilities. The nature of any nocturne is to become darker, if only psychologically. By enriching the inkiness of the print, Whistler was able to manipulate the meaning of time passing, the dark coming on. In this case, the "floating" city does more than float; it appears to be suspended between two worlds. The strokes feel less drawn than cut, from up to down, and the effect, in each of the prints, is striking, like hard rain on a window. One senses the artist's hand on the instrument. The palaces, as such, feel "lighter" than the water, into which the vertical and heavy lines of fog and mist are converging. Even the balcony, a darker interior, seems "weighted" toward the water, its shadow ready to run down the building. There is something of the black orchid here—as if the palaces themselves had created night. In the last and darkest spring, a small light, like a lantern, finally comes clear, an anonymous sign of life on the bridge.

In no other work of Whistler's is the perishability of things that matter so deeply rendered. Stone is nothing, the waters of the dark are everything. *Nocturnes: Palaces* is more than an image; in Yeats's symbolist phrase, "it calls down among us certain disembodied powers." It is a sign of what is missing, a symbol of absences, of what is past and passing. It is Whistler's most spiritually open moment. All the *Nocturnes*, whatever the medium, are Modernist—nonrepresentational, atonal, abstract, ambiguous, self-contained, urban. And they force the artist to subordinate the self to the terms of the correlative. But more than metaphor is sustained in the *Palaces*: the isolation of the man, the artist, has peaked as an obsession. Not even the dark is enough, because that is merely the absence of light. If it is true "generally," to use his word, it is true here especially that Whistler needs a refraction, a natural and inevitable presence that will transform without obliterating, a presence that will allow us to see in the dark. In water he had found not only his refracting means but the meaning of the nocturne itself—how at the moment of perfect stillness the dissolution has already begun.

1985

SEASON OF MISTS

On September 21st and 22nd, 1819, John Keats writes four letters to four of his friends—one to his colleague-poet John Hamilton Reynolds, a second to his literary benefactor Richard Woodhouse, a third to his former neighbor Charles Dilke, and a fourth to his housemate and sometime traveling-companion Charles Brown, who has gone off to Ireland and left Keats in Winchester in a state of serene "solitarinesse." A major theme running through all these letters is that Keats has decided he must put past him his "idle minded, vicious way of life" and "no longer live upon hopes"— meaning money from poetry—"and take up my abode in a cheap lodging in Town"—meaning Westminster—"and get employment in some of our elegant Periodical Works." He adds, in his letter to Woodhouse, that "I shall carry my plan into execution speedily." He asks Dilke, who has recently moved into Central London to be near his son in school, to find him "any place tolerably comfitable." He announces to Reynolds that he has "given up Hyperion—there were too many Miltonic inversions in it . . . I wish to give myself up to other sensations." And he confesses to his confidant and collaborator, Brown, that "It is quite time I should set myself doing something . . . I had got into the habit of mind of looking towards you as a help in all difficulties."

The motivations for "the plan I purpose pursuing" are, of course, financial. The difficulties are: one, until recently Keats has been "in fear of the Winchester Jail" for debt, but a saving advance from his publishers has forestalled his creditors; two, on September 10th Keats receives his first news of his brother George in America and it is not good, since George has invested nearly all his funds, on the word of John James Audubon, in a barge now at the bottom of the Ohio River ("Mr. Audubon is a dishonest man," Keats writes later); and three, the Covent Garden money-maker, *Otho the Great*, that he and Brown have just invested tireless hours in cobbling together, will not, he has been told, be produced for at least two years, if then. Yet in spite of these "anxieties," as he calls them, Keats, in this season of late summer, early fall, has reached a calm in his life, a maturity, and is, for whole parts of the day, happy. With new clarity he has taken stock and with honesty assessed his situation.

True, he has had to interrupt his solitude to dash into town to see if something can be worked out for George. True, this sudden journey back to London has put him in a position of feeling alien in the city in which he was born and educated ("I walked about the Streets as in a strange-land—"), though his sense of estrangement has much to do with Fanny Brawne, whom he has not written to for six weeks, and here he is within walking distance of Hampstead. True, he feels like "a dead lump"—he has been absent from London longer than ever; it is still summer and everyone is away. True, if he is to have a life and a future, with marriage and responsibility, he will have to join the world (and London) in a way he has thus far avoided. No wonder twilight and Winchester look so good, no wonder his days there—perhaps more valued because of interruption—seem halcyon, no wonder his solitude right now is so welcome. "I am surprised," he writes in his letter to Reynolds, "at the pleasure I live alone in."

In so many ways this month of September is the watershed for Keats. So much of the basis for his equilibrium lies in his inherent sense of arrival, his knowledge of the fact that he has come to a place in his life and his work that is both the future and the end—a place at once of fullness and emptiness. "It strikes me to night that I have led a very odd sort of life for the two or three last years—Here & there—No anchor—I am glad of it," he writes to Reynolds, and adds, prophetically, "They say men near death however mad they may have been, come to their senses." The closing of the summer and the onset of autumn may have something to do with this feeling of transition and rest, the sense of uplift in spite of the practical circumstances that have intermittently plagued his time away from the social and emotional whirl of London.

For a younger man, Keats has lived a remarkably filled life; there is a great deal of bad news backed up behind this present moment of acceptance and even reconciliation. His and his brother's inheritance, such as it was, has dwindled in no time from pound to pence; he realizes that writing poems, including romance narratives, is no real way to try to make a living; his Covent Garden adventure is stalled; and his relationship with Fanny is at best—certainly since he could not tempt himself to travel to Hampstead the weekend of the 10th when he had gone to town on George's behalf—ambiguous. His health is on-again, off-again, too, with a well-established sequence of sore throats, nervous indigestion, and periods of such low energy he has already written an "Ode on Indolence." Too many people in his family have died of the same causes and too many times, in large as well as small ways, he has challenged the cold English climate—first on his Northern walking tour with Brown the summer before, which he had to cut five weeks because of illness; second, in his insistence on riding around the countryside outside the coach in order to save money.

Nevertheless, for the time at least, he has achieved a sort of peace, having set himself apart from his problems. By October, he may well label the rest of his life—a year and a half—his "posthumous existence," but for now, in the golden and clean chalk air of Winchester, he has arrived at a state of mind in which he feels he can be decisive and can, if needs be, say farewell. On September 21st, he announces he is shutting down his final attempt to finish *The Fall of Hyperion*, passages of which account for his finest narrative writing. In addition, he makes offhand reference in his letters to Reynolds and Woodhouse (to whom he quotes the first fair copy) that on his Sunday walk, on the 19th, he was so taken by the chaste weather and the beauty of the season that he "composed upon it." Actually his setting of the scene for his poem "To Autumn" is well enough known but bears repeating: "How beautiful the season is now—How fine the air. A temperate sharpness about it. Really, without joking, chaste weather—Dian skies— I never liked stubble fields so much as now—Aye better than the chilly green of the spring. Somehow a stubble plain looks warm—in the same way that some pictures look warm—this struck me so much in my Sunday's walk that I composed upon it."

Composed, and composure, is the word—stillness, calm, fullness, a state of mind possessing what Keats himself once termed "negative capability": meaning the ability to be "in uncertainties, Mysteries, doubts, without any irritable reaching after fact & reason." In his letter to Reynolds he had said, "To night I am all in a mist; I scarcely know what's what." Yet this mist becomes, in "To Autumn," the transforming light through which his harvest vision is achieved, a vision saturated with "mellow fruitfulness" and "ripeness to the core" poised against "the stubble-plains" of "the soft-dying day," a vision that in the poem's three odal stanzas plots the day— morning, afternoon, and evening—declines its tones—recognition, celebration, exhaustion—explores its emotion—story, song, elegy—and organizes its work—the flowering of the field, the cutting and storing of the grain, and the venting of the rich void of the aftermath (the emptied-out cornucopia). I think there is a kind of allegory here, in this final example of Keats, who is himself the ultimate example of the eternally young autumnal poet. I think the allegory has to do with ideas of the future, of what follows, particularly as the future is a generalization addressed to the many and a fantasy argued out of history. Particularly the future of poetry.

The allegory has to do with the consciousness of the many as opposed to the imagination of the individual, notions of poetry as opposed to the actual poem. The many, as an entity, do not write poems, the individual does: an individual with a singular destiny, where matters of the future are discovered on a scale of one. The future of poetry, therefore, is always in the hands of the one maker, the destiny of one life. For myself, as an individual, I cannot imagine the future without a sense of an ending, a gathering, a letting-go. The future, insofar as it can be anticipated, has about it the autumnal. The task of the maker, as we go along, is to perfect what is at hand from what has been provided, which is that which we have already seeded and lived through and made, which for Keats, at the most immediate, is the odes of the previous spring and the various personal impasses of the summer.

It is more than interesting that in his first letter of the 21st of September, the letter to Reynolds, Keats makes the free-association comment that "I always somehow associate Chatterton with autumn. He is the purest writer in the English Language." Keats is thinking of one of the minstrel's songs in Thomas Chatterton's *Aella*, where Autumn with his golden hand gilds the fallen leaf. He is also thinking of Chatterton's anachronistic style—not unlike Spenser's—which is an attempt to render language down to a level unalloyed; in Chatterton's case, medieval. Keats does not mention Chatterton's suicide at seventeen, or any possible emotional link between this Tom's death and his younger brother Tom's death in the late autumn of the year before. Purity of language must match purity of vision, not unlike Wordsworth's closing to his "Immortality Ode," where Keats's crepuscular clouds and mists find an antecedent in "The Clouds that gather round the setting sun" taking "a sober colouring from an eye/That hath kept watch o'er man's mortality."

Only emotion endures. If this is an axiom it is, perforce, a very old one, and reminds me of the archeological discovery, some years ago, of the remains of grain and wildflowers in the grave of a Neanderthal child—surely the first poetry, and, not surprisingly, an elegy. "To Autumn," like so many end poems, is an ode whose soul is an elegy. Its very sequence underwrites its psalm-elegy quality—from ripeness to harvest to emptiness—a sequence in time that reprises past, present, and future, like a walk in the country. The Winchester walk Keats took usually started at his lodging on Colebrook Street, proceeded through the yard and walkway of the Cathedral, then down College Street—and under the second-story windows of the room in which Jane Austen had died just two years earlier—and then onto the path along the water-meadows near the River Itchen, and finally, after a mile or so, to St. Cross, a hospice housed among the ruins of an abbey.

In his journal-letter to George, of September 22nd, Keats describes his "To Autumn" walk this way: "I take a walk every day for an hour before dinner and this is generally my walk—I go out the back gate across one street, into the Cathedral yard, which is always interesting; then I pass under trees along a paved path, pass the beautiful front of the Cathedral, turn left under a stone door way—then I am on the other side of the building—which leaving behind me I pass on through two college-like squares seemingly built for the dwelling place of Deans and Prebendaries—garnished with grass and shaded with trees. Then I pass through one of the old city gates and then you are in one College-Street through which I pass and at the end thereof crossing some meadows and at last a country alley of gardens I arrive, that is, my worship arrives at the foundation of Saint Cross. . . ."

Curious that his letters of this crucial end-of-summer, beginning-of-autumn date separate details of the backdrop for his poem, including the first fair copy of the poem itself. He describes to Reynolds his love of the season, to George his seminal walk, and to Woodhouse much of the heartswell behind the need to write such a poem: "I should like a bit of fire to night—one likes a bit of fire—How glorious the Blacksmiths' shops look now—I stood to night before one till I was very nearly listing for one. Yes I should like a bit of fire—at a distance about 4 feet 'not quite hob nob'—as wordsworth says." He also writes out for Woodhouse his near-final draft of the poem.

Season of Mists and mellow fruitfulness,
Close bosom friend of the maturing sun;
Conspiring with him how to load and bless
The vines with fruit that round the thatch eves run;

To bend with apples the moss'd cottage trees,
And fill all fruit with ripeness to the core;
To swell the gourd, and plump the hazle-shells
With a white kernel; to set budding more,
And still more later flowers for the bees
Untill they think wa[r]m days will never cease
For summer has o'er brimm'd ther clammy Cells.

Who hath not seen thee oft, amid thy stores?
Sometimes, whoever seeks abroad may find
Thee sitting careless on a granary floor,
Thy hair soft-lifted by the winmowing wind;
Or on a half reap'd furrow sound asleep,
Dased with the fume of poppies, while thy hook
Spares the next swath and all its twined flowers;
And sometimes like a gleaner thou dost keep
Stready thy laden head across a brook;
Or by a Cyder press, with patient look
Thou watchest the last oozings hours by hours—

Where are the songs of spring? Aye, Where are they?
Think not of them, thou hast thy music too.
While barred clouds bloom the soft-dying day
And touch the stubble plains with rosy hue:
Then in a wailful quire the small gnats mourn
Among the river sallows, borne aloft
Or sinking as the light wind lives and dies;
And full grown Lambs loud bleat from hilly bourne:
Hedge crickets sing, and now with treble soft
The Red breast whistles from a garden <g>Croft
And gather'd Swallows twitter in the Skies—

The revised—and only surviving revised—fair copy, with errors corrected
and final rewritten touches added, ended up in George's hands in America,
who in turn gave it as a gift, in 1839, to a Miss Barker (later Mrs. Ward) of
Louisville, who passed it along to her granddaughter in 1896, who be-
queathed it, in 1925, to Amy Lowell, of Brookline and Boston, and hence
to the Houghton Library in Cambridge. It was published into posterity in

Keats's last book the summer of 1820, when he was too ill to care. Publication, however, in its way, is an inevitable abstraction of the human document. The written poem in the author's hand is the vulnerable human document, not simply because paper is mortal and the words like breath but because, in time, so many hands will have handled it with the opportunity of losing it. Like the letters, "To Autumn" was fair-copied on paper immediately available to Keats, paper he might well have brought back with him from his abrupt September 10th weekend in London, in this case wove paper watermarked "C Wilmott 1818," which means that it was already at least a year old when Keats used it—making it now, under glass, about a hundred and eighty years old. A hundred and eighty years into the future. The beauty of the printed poem, of course, is that it can be reprinted in future editions, editions of the future, ad infinitum, into that perpetuity where the future has no count. The beauty of the handwritten poem is that, like a drawing, it is once-only. Yet a manuscript is not a drawing; it is the singular means to an end, which is duplication. This great poem is written out on paper a little smaller than a standard 8½ by 11, and at this point in time has the look of the usual age-old autumnal yellowing, as if it were a large leaf pressed and preserved.

Does the future die with the death of the individual? Not if he or she writes valued poems. Or is the future what happens in terms of the many after the death of the one? After "To Autumn," Keats's writing life is over, perfected. In spite of all his resolution and intention, he does not, in fact, work as a journalist, nor does he last more than a few days in earnest isolation in Westminster. By the end of October he has returned to Hampstead and Fanny Brawne and by the start of the new year he will have suffered his first full hemorrhage. His posthumous existence will have well begun, that afterlife of the writer when he no longer writes. Sometimes the good news is that there is a future and the bad news is that we will have to live in it. A child born after its father's death is, by ancient definition, posthumous; a book published after the author's death is posthumous. A life lived after the death of promise is also posthumous.

For the individual, artist or not, the future is an end-game, and the future after that, posthumous. In precisely this way, posterity is posthumous. When we speak of the future, nine times out of ten we are speaking in a form of wishful-thinking; the one time out of ten we are probably indulging in fear-fantasy. What the future willfully implies is the forever-ahead, the non-present, the anti-past. The arrow pointing in one direction only. The posthumous is the arrow pointing both ways at once, the past in polarity with the future, the living dead. It is no accident that the mother of the Muses, Mnemosyne, is the goddess of inspired poetry. Like all gods, she is that over which we have no control, since the memory she represents is involuntary, unasked-for, unbidden, but is omnipresent. If the words in Keats's autumn ode are immortal, the paper they were and are eternally written on certainly is not. The words, ultimately, are electric on the air, and their memory is the future—both the memory in the poem and the memory of it.

What will poetry look like fifty years from now? If it does not resemble what we value of the past, we had better not go there. In Keats's era autumn was considered "the painter's season": George Beaumont, Wordsworth's great friend, thought that every landscape should have one brown tree in it. Thus the sense-of-an-ending season, the human season. The season of an emotion that weighs so much like grief, and that fills the heart, yet in Keats's poem lifts the eyes to the gathering of swallows. Odd, perhaps, that the idea of the future as spring and rebirth and forgetting should feel so absent and cold, while autumn feels so rich and warm and memorable. "A Man's life of any worth," Keats had once said, "is a continual allegory," a story of the seasons, of pattern, balance, and arrival; past, present, and future. Then there is the work of the life that lives after.

What will poetry look like fifty, a hundred years from now? What will it sound like? Shakespeare, in one of his very great sonnets, speaks of "That time of year thou mayst in me behold/When yellow leaves or none, or few, do hang/Upon those boughs which shake against the cold,/Bare ruined choirs, where late the sweet birds sang." Thomson, a hundred or so years later, despairs "the leafy ruin . . . the naked tree," yet "Woods, fields, gardens, all around/The desolated prospect thrills the soul." Coleridge, fifty years after Thomson, praises how the redbreast will "sit and sing/Betwixt the tufts of snow on the bare branch/Of mossy apple tree, while the night thatch/Smokes in the sun-thaw . . ." And after Keats, it is Dickinson, in one of her late poems, who perceives how "As imperceptibly as Grief/The Summer lapsed away"; and Frost who is tired of apple picking, since "Essence of winter sleep is on the night"; and Stevens who wants to "Light the first light of evening," in one of his last poems. Autumn, as these poets suggest, is a remembered landscape, a season of memory passed along, inherent in the imagination of closure, a consequence of what the spring and summer amount to, at the edge before winter and the dark. Autumn is the evening season.

I once took the walk that Keats took through the archway at Winchester Cathedral and along College Street out to the watermeadows, spreading from the River Itchen, and then onto St. Cross. The cathedral dominates the town, and walking away from it into the countryside you could still feel the pull of the centuries of gravity that had, season in, season out, worked and weathered its stone—a wonderful contrast with the warm soft yellows and browns and light mist off the river. Naturally, it was evening, and inevitably it was September 19th. From Keats's point of view I was in the future, by nearly a hundred and seventy-two years. I have a sense that language changes at about the same speed as the landscape. The landscape I was looking at was basically, and archetypally, the same as the landscape Keats had walked through on a daily and ritual basis. Some of the path went along behind playing fields and college buildings, of which there were doubtless now more. And I am sure there were fewer trees ("river sallows") and less bramble and hedge than Keats saw, but on the left, looking out over "stubble-plains," in the near-view, there was still plenty of fescue and brome and golden meadow-grass. The River Itchen is a trout stream and always has been. It has changed little. Nor has the grain, the rape or rye or wheat, that had been mostly cut into the distance, west. There were even a few sheep as you got closer to the abbey. There is a famous Gainsborough, *Robert Andrews and his Wife, Frances*, in which the dour white couple are posed under a yellowing English oak, dressed in their finest country gentry. If you can ignore Andrews and his wife and focus, from the viewer's perspective, on the right side of the picture, you will have a feeling for the scene outside of Winchester, looking past the watermeadows, toward the low hills and the sun. It is a vision of the harvest in pure chalk air, the day softdying, with big clouds, crickets, redbreasts, and swallows.

1997

READING AUTUMN

# 1

I guess I'm thinking of two or three poems, maybe more, and of the planet on the table of which they are a small part. In the northern hemisphere of this planet the season would have to be, for me, autumn—all of it, both at the beginning and the ending of the harvest, both a little before and a little after. It would be an autumn you could follow from the American Northwest to the Middle West, down to the Mid-Atlantic and up through the Great Lakes and Pennsylvania, then the Adirondacks and New England and over to England and Europe, a season of "Indian-summer-sun," as Hart Crane puts it, "On trees that seem dancing," a season of spilled apples and rows of shocks of grain, a season of brick dry air in which sound begins to carry the way it will in winter, a season of blown leaves, early frost, early dark, the evening season, the slow sunset season, "the human season," as Keats once called it.

A "Season of mists and mellow fruitfulness," Keats also called it. A season in which autumn is an interior experience. "I stand by a low fire," Theodore Roethke writes, "Counting the wisps of flame, and I watch how/ Light shifts upon the wall./I bid stillness be still./I see, in evening air,/ How slowly dark comes down on what we do." Keats himself preferred, he'd once said, the warmth of "a stubble plain . . . to the chilly green of spring," meaning the fire-sweep of the scythe at harvest. He meant, too, those evenings Roethke is alluding to, of the mind's getting lost in the leaves of the flames of a good working fire. "I should like a bit of fire to night—one likes a bit of fire—How glorious the Blacksmiths' shops look now—I stood to night before one till I was very nearly listing for one. Yes I should like a bit of fire—at a distance about 4 feet 'not quite hob nob'— as wordsworth says."

The corner of the autumn landscape Keats is speaking of and from is Winchester, the cathedral town southwest of London, in Hampshire, in 1819, and just north of the port city of Southhampton and the Isle of Wight, two other places prominent in the seasonal life of Keats. Aside from his first years in Finsbury and school years in Enfield, Keats has never really had a home. Orphaned early, itinerant always, renting rooms with his brothers and later leasing space with or from his friends, he has seemed to be searching.

The crucial criterion for where he might be at any given time is whether or not he can write there—whether the climate, the beauty, the proximity, the society and/or solitude of a place suit him, inspire him. And whether or not he can afford it. Winchester, on almost all accounts, for this late summer beginning autumn, is more or less perfect.

# 2

"This Winchester is a fine place," Keats writes to Fanny Brawne in mid-August. "A beautiful Cathedral and many other ancient buildings in the Environs." Not only is his room large enough for him to "promenade at my pleasure," he has the advantage of "the convenience of a Library," in a university setting "surrounded by fresh-looking country. . . . Tolerably good and cheap Lodgings," too. By mid-September he is writing his brother, George (who is in America by now), that his "promenade" has extended throughout the town and into the open countryside. "I take a walk every day for an hour before dinner and this is generally my walk—I go out at the back gate across one street, into the Cathedral yard, which is always interesting; then I pass under the trees along a paved path, pass the beautiful front of the Cathedral, turn left under a stone door way—then I am on the other side of the building—which leaving behind I pass on through two college-like squares . . . garnished with grass and shaded with trees. . . ."

This little map of early nineteenth-century Winchester (out of Jane Austen) is only a moment in a long, emotionally up and down journal letter (September 17–27) intended to remind George of the sweetness of Mother England and the special civilizing way an English town yields to country, warm "in the way that some pictures look warm." "I pass through one of the old city gates and there you are in one College-Street through which I pass and at the end thereof crossing some meadows and at last a country alley of gardens I arrive . . . at the foundation of Saint Cross, which is a very interesting old place, both for its tower and alms-square. . . . Then I pass across St. Cross meadows till you come to the most beautifully clear river— now this is only one mile of my walk."

In addition to this pastoral interlude, this involved and involving letter amounts to nothing less than an autobiography of the complexity and uncertainties of this time in Keats's life—he has eighteen months to live. The letter ranges from complaints about his literary standing ("My name with the literary fashionables is vulgar—I am a weaver boy to them") to anxieties concerning his love life ("A Man in love cuts the sorriest figure in the world") to what he has been reading ("lately Burton's Anatomy of Melancholy") to remembering the summer before's walking tour of Scotland ("The finest thing is Fingal's cave") to reporting on his health ("I have got rid of my haunting sore throat") to speculating on the nature of physical change ("Our bodies every seven years are completely fresh-materiald. . . . We are like the relict garments of a Saint") to realizing that, even in so short a career so far, his writing has become "more thoughtful and quiet" ("I want to compose without . . . fever").

# 3

The letter also includes—in fact, begins with—an apology from Keats that all he could extract from their guardian, Richard Abbey, is a promise to send George more money as soon as possible, which is a month-and-more prospect in the ocean-going mails. George is bankrupt. Keats receives this news on September 10th and immediately interrupts his Winchester idyll to return to London in order to try to raise funds. He has no money of his own and is himself "in fear of the Winchester jail" for debt, so the manipulative Abbey is his only option. His five desultory days in London are themselves a separate story. He returns to Winchester on the 15th exhausted, having ridden again, as is his habit, on the outside of the coach. It's cheaper, if chillier. If the town-and-country walks he's been taking up until now have sharpened his appetite, the Winchester walks after he gets back from his mission to help George will soften the emotional edges. Writing letters, especially long ones, is a kind of walking as well.

Keats's letters generally have for him a therapeutic function, as the ten-day journal letter to George suggests. Filled with speculation, distraction, worry, complaints, theory, discourse, frustration, fear, loneliness, luminosity, great beauty—the letters stand as the world out of which the poems gain fuller life. The week he's writing George he's writing four of his closest friends. To Charles Brown, his confidant and collaborator, he confesses, "It is quite time I should set myself doing something, and live no longer upon hopes. I have never exerted myself. I am getting into an idle minded, vicious way of life, almost content to live upon others." He asks Charles Dilke, his close Hampstead neighbor, to help him find "any place tolerably comfitable" when he moves back into central London and gets "employment in some of our elegant Periodical works." To Richard Woodhouse, his best literary benefactor, he states flatly, "I am all in a Mess here—embowell'd in Winchester." He also rues the fact that "things won't leave me *alone*." But in spite of his "otiosus-peroccupatus" state, he encloses in his Woodhouse letter a lyric, an ode he's written just two days ago. And to John Hamilton Reynolds, his colleague-poet, he adds, "To night I am all in a mist; I scarcely know what's what—But you knowing my unsteady and vagarish disposition, will guess that all this turmoil will be settled by tomorrow morning."

*Settled* is the word, in a state of settlement, in a state of contemplation, resolution. "How beautiful the season is now—How fine the air. A temperate sharpness about it. Really, without joking, chaste weather—Dian skies—I never lik'd stubble fields so much as now—Aye better than the chilly green of the spring. Somehow a stubble plain looks warm—in the same way that some pictures look warm—this struck me so much in my Sunday's walk that I composed upon it." The Sunday Keats is speaking of is the 19th of September, a day in the midst—let alone the mist—of days of his heavy correspondence. This comment to Reynolds is matched by the poem, the "composition," he encloses in his letter to Woodhouse. In addition to *settled*, another word that covers Keats's clarity of purpose as well as serenity of means in the middle of the whirl of his personal and familial pressures is *composed*. You could argue that the walks themselves, his Winchester walks, aid and abet the poet's ability—his "negative capability"—to separate himself from his troubles long enough to write as if they didn't exist. You could even argue that the letters, like the walks, have a cathartic effect until the effect wears off. I would argue, though, that the season itself, the arrival of autumn, the idea of autumn, is very much at the heart of the calm Keats needs to compose— so much so that *calm* itself becomes part of the subject.

# 4

Calm, in "To Autumn," translates into those warm and temperate values Keats values in his description of his walks. The "stubble plain" evokes the happy result of the autumn harvest, the gathering and garnering of the grain, and recognition of "the maturing sun" that fills "all fruit with ripeness to the core." Mists and mellowness, warmth and temperateness, sweetness and ripeness constitute the images here, along with the grain-gold and rosy hue of "the soft-dying day."

To Autumn

## I

Season of mists and mellow fruitfulness,
  Close bosom-friend of the maturing sun;
Conspiring with him how to load and bless
  With fruit the vines that round the thatch-eves run;
To bend with apples the moss'd cottage-trees,
  And fill all fruit with ripeness to the core;
    To swell the gourd, and plump the hazel shells
  With a sweet kernel; to set budding more,
And still more, later flowers for the bees,
Until they think warm days will never cease,
    For summer has o'er-brimm'd their clammy cells.

## II

Who hath not seen thee oft amid thy store?
  Sometimes whoever seeks abroad may find
Thee sitting careless on a granary floor,
  Thy hair soft-lifted by the winnowing wind;

Or on a half-reap'd furrow sound asleep,
  Drows'd with the fume of poppies, while thy hook
    Spares the next swath and all its twined flowers:
And sometimes like a gleaner thou dost keep
  Steady thy laden head across a brook;
  Or by a cyder-press, with patient look,
    Thou watchest the last oozings hours by hours.

### III

Where are the songs of Spring? Ay, where are they?
  Think not of them, thou hast thy music too,—
While barréd clouds bloom the soft-dying day,
  And touch the stubble-plains with rosy hue;
Then in a wailful choir the small gnats mourn
  Among the river sallows, borne aloft
    Or sinking as the light wind lives or dies;
And full-grown lambs loud bleat from hilly bourn;
  Hedge-crickets sing; and now with treble soft
  The red-breast whistles from a garden-croft;
    And gathering swallows twitter in the skies.

Enough has been written about this great ode—and the spring odes, too, for that matter—to fill the granary, the cider-press, and more. The poem may be entitled "To Autumn," but it's actually looking toward autumn from the edge and ending of summer, a late summer "o'er-brimmed." It was written on summer's last weekend and acknowledges "That full draught" that is "the parent of my theme," as Keats puts it in the other notable work concurrent with the autumnal ode, *The Fall of Hyperion*, which is an improved and updated revision of the failed epic *Hyperion*, from the year before. Keats writes and retouches "To Autumn" in a couple of sittings; "The Fall of Hyperion" is written into the remains of a brilliant fragment of five hundred-plus lines. Both poems, however, represent Keats in his newer, cleaner, "Grecian mode." He had said in his journal letter to George, "Some think I have lost that poetic ardour and fire 'tis said I once had— the fact is perhaps I have: But instead of that I hope I shall substitute a more thoughtful and quiet power . . . I want to compose without this fever." The walks in the "Environs" of Winchester have helped him achieve that

quieter power, and the season has softened the fire, though the sad truth
is that Keats is at one with autumn in the worst way as well. The September after this Winchester September, he will be on a boat headed for Italy,
to die and, apparently, to disappear.


# 5

Because it so perfectly embodies the voice of its speaker without directly
referencing the speaker—except as an implied interpreter/interrogator—
"To Autumn" is often lauded as Keats's purest poem of resolution, standing, to quote Walter Jackson Bate, "transparent before its subject." Aileen
Ward, Keats's other important American biographer, writes that the "poet
himself is completely lost in his images, and the images are presented as
meaning simply themselves: Keats's richest utterance is the barest metaphor." The union of structure and texture in the poem is indeed unsurpassed: the way in which the rhythm of a day's harvest pastoral painting is
created, in triptych, before us, following its fulsome "hours by hours" from
the dew-starred morning to the drowsy noon to the resonance of the "sinking light" of sunset; and the way in which the painting's perspective enlarges, stanza by stanza, from the cottage and "cottage trees" to the low-lying
fields and hills to the softly animated "skies" themselves. So inevitable is
the scene—or more precisely, scenes—it is as if the poem itself were speaking into a mirror in the still, calm voice of the gathered harvest.

But it is the tone—the vocal tone, the color tone, the imaginative tone—
that interests me about this great poem. Its autumnal tone, if you will. We
think of the concept of the correlative in terms of establishing a direct connection between self, speaker, subject, whatever, and the object, the image, the evoked event. "To Autumn" instead correlates self and imaged
"event" indirectly, since the voice of the speaker and the voice in the poem,
in this case, are indistinguishable, as if there were no speaker in the usual
sense, but rather, synesthetically, an eye that hears what it sees—an eye
instead of an "I." The collective correlative of the exhausted goddess, the
spilled store of gathered grain, the half-reaped furrow, the swollen gourd,
the fume of poppies, the wailful choir of gnats, rendered in terms of

mourning, soft-dying, and ripeness to the core—all these details and many more and the attitude brought to bear on their moment derive from a process, a sequence, of witness and surrender, acceptance and reconciliation. No wonder the poem feels tragic; no wonder it seems to arrive so completely at resolution. Its cornucopia runs over.

"Negative capability," the famous phrase Keats has conjured a couple of years before "To Autumn," might serve as an insight of the ideal perspective from which to view the vision of the poem. And perhaps all successful correlatives are negatively capable, like electric wiring. But I find its application here too much from-the-neck-up and not enough from-the-heart-down. Feeling is what we are talking about, the intelligence translated through the senses and the senses understood and translated through the eyes. If we think about the whirl of emotional, financial, personal, and mortal issues surrounding Keats at the time, it seems amazing that he could write poetry at all, let alone compose with mastering composure. One school of thought, certainly, is that writing, regardless, is a form of escape, based on the assumption that poetry in particular is fantasy. On the other hand, Stevens tells us that if poetry is a supreme fiction, that makes it an ultimate reality. Eliot draws the distinction between the mind suffering and the mind creating, though he never says how, exactly, this is achieved—he seems to offer the distinction as a definition of the true artist.

Keats's brother, George, is off in alien America, broke, with a young family, and desperate; Keats himself is penniless and jobless, despite bravura plans and hopes; Keats's love life is an oxymoron; and in the wake of his brother Tom's consumptive death less than a year ago, Keats is aware he is not well with similar symptoms. There is a connection, I believe, between Keats's personal problems in his last full September in England and the "impersonal" art of this last complete great poem. As a symbolist, Keats has been, in his best work, "impersonal" from the beginning; that is what most distances him from the narrative impulse in Wordsworth and the conversation poems of Coleridge, and what distinguishes him from the didacticism of Shelley: the sense that a poem is a transformative act invested in the object, that the subject of the poem is the object brought wholly into its own free space. The emotion comes to life from the empathic contract with the object and is made vital by the separation from, yet identification with, the object. The spring odes may be written with more "fever" than a maturing Keats would find interesting, but the dynamics of his relationship to his material are essentially the same. The spring odes may make more of an announcement of their respective speakers while "To Autumn" makes its speaker into a kind of announcer fond of rhetorical questions, but the presence of the poet is the same. The difference between the spring odes and the autumnal ode is tone and the degree to which the writing is divested of anything not immediately and perfectly in the picture.

# 6

If negative capability has real artistic function—as opposed to being a critical apparatus—it connotes the ability to both separate from and identify with whatever all at once. Its tensile strength is in direct proportion to the difficulty in exacting art from circumstance. "To Autumn" may seem more impersonal when in fact its quiet power and subtle tension come from the difficulty Keats must have had in entering the imaginative space of the poem without projecting his personal, the-world-won't-leave-me-alone troubles. His daily Winchester walks must have helped. But sitting down to write the poem is another matter. Keats must have entered some sort of circle of light, autumnal light; the tension within the space must have been tremendous, enhanced, if possible, by the very problems that defeat lesser writers. The muscle of our being reacts in much the same way: first the resistance, then the relaxation, and the greater the one the greater the other. That tension, in my opinion, underwrites the strength of the rich syntactical intensity, even imagistic and rhythmic density, of the poem. That tension underscores the tone that some readers have found tragic and some readers have found sublime. That tension attenuates by extending the feeling of delayed gratification of closure before the held moment of the "gathering swallows" at twilight.

Can a lyric of thirty-three lines achieve such spaciousness? It's hard not to retro-read Keats's own impending tragedy into this luminous poem. Such a reading, however, substitutes the first-person pronoun for the painter's profound eye. Yet if you think of the poem as a painting only in the sunset hues of, say, a Claude or Poussin, with the backup detail of a harvest scene in a Gainsborough, you focus some of the stillness and solidity as well as the dramatic "blocking" but miss the dimensions of what the poem displaces: you miss the resonance of its widening voice ("thy music too"); you miss the size of its subversion of or separation from an implied narrative; and you miss its "patient" symbolist progression within an eternal autumn. You miss, in a word, what a great sublime painting effects more than any other form: the illusion of simultaneity, in which, in this instance, the heaven of autumn—its mists, its ripeness, its harvest, its drowsiness, and its warmth—is realized as a whole, self-contained, is represented as one "gathering" picture at the very verge of breaking, falling, ending, darkening. The near-burst suspension of things is at the heart of the poem's tacit tension, the way the filled vessel of what has been acknowledged, reaped, and gathered travels beyond the particulars and is lifted, in total, to another level. The feeling of sublimity, right from the start, has to do with this impression of the poem traveling out of its rich, drowsing, melancholy body—no, that's wrong—this impression of the poem as having already traveled, at the outset, from one body into another embodiment is what lifts it, is what gives the poem its deeply spiritual tone.

# 7

Something about the season helps. The accumulating scene of "To Autumn" is a working landscape whose pastoralism itself is interrogated, and the muted nature, the "mellow fruitfulness," of its world should not mitigate the rigor of what the "ripeness" means: it means work, and like the pattern of the day and the length of the season it has a rhythm of cutting and gathering and garnering, of which the exquisite near-exhaustion of the scene is the consequence. This is not about fever, therefore; it's about reflection, about thinking, as Keats often did on his walks in front of a blacksmith's fire. The reader feels the exhaustion as well, that sense we have of receivership, of that "greeting of the spirit" Keats once spoke of. When we meditate we invariably sit or stand in front of a visible or invisible fire, a low fire, like a setting sun in its grain-gold autumnal shades. We leave behind, in that moment, the litter of our dailiness; we may even throw it into the fire. We are calm, and if not yet, we'll get there. It's a held moment, a moment of suspension, and if we're lucky it's a moment that allows us to see what otherwise would have been obscure. In its luminous, and illuminating, twilight, autumn is the human season. To me, the most brilliant aspect of "To Autumn" is that nothing in it exists, save for its "music," without the human, yet the complete sublimation of the human hand in the poem is what gives it its sublimity. The harvesters are gone; we are the harvest, we are the fire.

And even if the haystacks and granary cribs and apple stores are only the half of it, nature, in its "leafy ruin," its "golden grove unleaving," sustains its own involuntary harvest, a harvest perhaps all the more powerful because, like "the soft-dying day," it acts on us rather than the other way around. It keeps its own clock and rhythm. The intimate sublime of the changing leaf surpasses us and thus compels us. In his "Autumn" section of *The Seasons*, James Thomson envisions the pastoral and natural worlds as undifferentiated "Woods, fields, orchards, all around"—this "desolated prospect," he says, "thrills the soul." The thrill is in the discovery of desolation, in the impact of the idea of ruins, in the inspiration we find in absences, and in the connection we make between the abundance of the tree of life and, in the same long sentence, its slow stripping away—"bare ruined choirs." If autumn's twilight tree weren't so beautiful, winter really might be unbearable, "When yellow leaves, or none, or few, do hang/Upon those boughs which shake against the cold." That may be part of the warmth Keats finds in the "stubble fields"—the humanity of the harvest as opposed to the neutrality of naked trees. Yet at the end of the day it's all one, the winnowing season up against the cold winds, wall to wall.

# 8

That hard edge, though, tends to be attenuated in October and November, extended in time to the extent that autumn often seems the longest season, the season of farewell, departure, memory, resonance, the piecemeal ruin of what is passing, so that when winter finally arrives it slams the door. Before that, autumn is like watching a slow, lovely fire go out, in a room filled with comfort and a window still open, "A Quietness distilled."

1540

As imperceptibly as Grief
The Summer lapsed away—
Too imperceptible at last
To seem like Perfidy—
A Quietness distilled
As Twilight long begun,
Or Nature spending with herself
Sequestered Afternoon—
The Dusk drew earlier in—
The Morning foreign shone—
A courteous, yet harrowing Grace,
As Guest, that would be gone—
And thus, without a Wing
Or service of a Keel
Our Summer made her light escape
Into the Beautiful.

This concentrated, autumnal ode by Emily Dickinson is as pure a poem as she ever wrote—pure in its imaginative terms, pure in its sublimation of the "fever" that sometimes pushes her work, pure in the tone it "distills." Her best poems, regardless of apparent subject, are written during the Civil War, a distant but audible trumpet in Western Massachusetts. This poem comes at the end of that period, in 1865, compared with 258 ("There's a certain Slant of light"), 280 ("I felt a Funeral in my Brain"), 341 ("After great pain"), 465 ("I heard a Fly buzz"), and her longest lyric, 640 ("I cannot live with You"), all circa 1860–1862. And although none of these poems seems remotely related to the war and its consequences, it cannot be possible that the tragedy in the air in most of the rest of the country did not drift north to remote Amherst, and did not fail to influence the unacknowledged source of grief in this period of her work but helped create a space, post-war, in which to reconcile. Number 1540 may be about the natural seasonal cycle cum autumn, but more to the point is the autumnal tone that builds from its "Grief" to its "light escape/Into the Beautiful," its sense of grace. The linking of language from beginning to end—from "lapsed away" to "imperceptible" to "Quietness distilled" to "Twilight long begun" to "Sequestered afternoon" to "Dusk" to "Harrowing Grace"—is itself a plot, in increments, of linguistic and imaginative reconciliation.

Written in the autumnal year of World War I, 1917, W. B. Yeats's "The Wild Swans at Coole" also reconciles with change and the future—"when I awake some day/ To find they have flown away." The quietness distilled here is defined as that self-reflexive stillness, as both adjective and adverb, just as the stillness itself is defined by the breaking of it by the alternate paddling and wheeling "in great broken rings" of the swans' "clamorous wings." Images of stillness and references to "still" as continuance ("Unwearied still") appear in four of the poem's five stanzas; they help organize the silence, the mirror calm of sky and water, against which the swans "drift" and fly, and within which the speaker sees and hears more deeply. The trees, says the speaker, are in their autumn beauty; naturally, it's twilight, "October twilight"; the paths are dry, the water "brimming . . . among the stones"; and the swans, "those brilliant creatures," are "Mysterious, beautiful," all fifty-nine of them. Counting is the speaker's way of paying attention, and of measuring the mortality implicit in the scene. Leaf by falling leaf, it seems, he is aware. Melancholy may enhance the tone of the experience of what the speaker is listening to and looking at, but clarity, a certain bell-clarity ("The bell-beat of their wings above my head"), underwrites the heart of the poem and warms the elegance of its distances. The speaker realizes that like the leaves and the swans he too is interchangeable. The counting goes on, regardless of who's counting, just as the longing so given to the season is eternal.

# 9

My heart aches, "my heart is sore," says a lovelorn Yeats. Autumn will make a ruin of the heart, but it will also fill it. It's off the subject to suggest some of the intersections meeting in "The Wild Swans at Coole," including the off-stage presence of actress-activist Maude Gonne (no pun intended), the precursor presence of symbolic swans, the allusive presence of war, and the aesthetic presence of the Celtic Twilight (symbolist mist). But one thing for sure, Yeats, like Dickinson and Keats, *sees* and by his own eyes is inspired, scene and setting, since autumn is a place to come to, not so much to escape war and personal conflict but to put them in perspective, the perspective of a larger, transcendent rhythm, removed in time from time. Robert Frost's "After Apple-Picking" is written at the beginning of World War I, and at the beginning of Modernism, but they seem worlds away from the ambivalence, exhaustion, and, in the end, emptiness blessing Frost's poem. Frost is as much an existentialist as the next modernist, "over-tired/Of the great harvest I myself desired." Nor is his autumnal insight any less ambiguous, since

> I cannot rub the strangeness from my sight
> I got from looking through a pane of glass
> I skimmed this morning from the drinking trough
> And held against the world of hoary grass.

The early announcement in the poem that the speaker is "done with apple-picking now" serves to intensify what this post-harvest state of being amounts to: a body burdened by its own desire, filled, and desiring to be empty. It's the in-between of these desires that makes him, like Keats's Ceres, so drowsy and dreamy. The keenness in the air of the season is here turned in on itself—sleep, or better, sleepiness, becomes the twilight vision, the dream vision, through which Frost's speaker can see: The harvest's excess is also its emptiness, and both states are as undesirable as desired . . . "oozings hours by hours."

The Dickinson in Frost not only feels the ache of the "instep arch" from standing hours on the ladder but knows the potential pleasure, the excess, of the fantasized "ten thousand thousand fruit to touch/Cherish in hand, lift down, and not let fall." Yet the fruit will fall, regardless, picked or not. This vision of the cup "o'er-brimmed" is completed by the reality of the cup spilled, and so the richness of the harvest season becomes its ruin—its warm "stubble fields," its "bare ruined choirs" of the orchard. To drowse, to see in an altered state that includes, at once, the richness as well as the ruin is to reconcile with the season after apple-picking, winter. Autumn's leaner, winter-edge, on the December, after-apple-picking side of "To Autumn," maintains this tone but with sharper focus and a change of light. Late autumn is about the value that endings give to things, the living value that winter bestows.

# 10

"Is there an imagination that sits enthroned/As grim as it is benevolent, the just/And the unjust, which in the midst of summer stops/To imagine winter?" Stevens asks this question in the midst of "The Auroras of Autumn." It's asked in the typically abstract language of the senior Stevens, but it means to address the complete nature of what autumn is: transition, contradiction, resolution, the opposite of "breeding/Lilacs out of the dead land." It's a rhetorical question, since the strength of the imagination is to imagine winter in summer—that is, autumn—and the greater the tensile strength in the polar separation of the seasons, the greater the negative strength, the more sublime. For example, the great summer-in-winter meditation, Walt Whitman's late autumnal ode, "Crossing Brooklyn Ferry," written in December, while the light is still white gold before it turns to snow. The negative capability here applies to setting as much as season. Imagine the scene of the harvest as a harbor and the "tall masts of Mannahatta" as the trees, backed up by the "beautiful hills of Brooklyn" and the emerging skyline of Manhattan. Imagine the honey-white light of a December evening and ferry crossing of the East River, "the sun half an hour high," sparkling in the air and dazzling on the water. Imagine the travelers themselves—those crossing the river now and those who have crossed it and will in the future—as part of the harvest, part of the change and renewal, upon whom "the dark patches fall."

No poem in American poetry, perhaps any poetry, more movingly articulates the "impalpable sustenance" of disintegration of self in terms of all of that which is not self than this hundred-and-thirty-two-line contemplation. For Keats, it's as if the self disappears a priori into the poem; for Dickinson the self is the interrogator and mortal witness; for Frost the self is the dreamer, between waking and sleeping, fulfillment and loss. For Whitman, though, the self is in process, in *medias res*, in both space and time, river and crossing, and whose realization is possible only through the "dumb, beautiful ministers" of the urban natural world he has envisioned. For Whitman, the city, "mast-hemm'd" Manhattan, is nature, and the medium of passage is light, late autumnal, penultimate light, and life-bearing water, light-refracted water, "the float forever held in solution," and each of these—light and water inseparable—is manifested in detail throughout the poem—in the "scallop-edg'd waves of flood-tide" to the "fine spokes of light, from the shape of my head, or any one's head, in the sunlit water."

Again and again, detail by accruing and returning detail, Whitman comes back to the "eternal float of solution," water as light, light as water, in order to demonstrate the ritual imaginative dissolution required to join that "which none else is more lasting," which is a harvest of all that is palpable in the poem, including ships and seagulls, buildings and hillsides, ferry and passengers, past, present, and future, all of them, great or small, furnishing their parts toward the impalpable, which Whitman calls the soul. The suggestion is that the fullness of being that autumn represents and the corresponding emptiness (dissolution) it simultaneously creates are not only cyclical, seasonal, but predictable, thus eternal, a kind of afterlife to spring's rebirth of life. Light and water are ancient symbols for these passages, but by reinventing them in an urban pastoral Whitman gives added dimension to the sublime. "Crossing Brooklyn Ferry" is a crucial act of imagination, whose substance draws its sustenance from the time of the year and the angle of the early December light on the East River, facing away from arrival and against the setting sun.

# 11

Exactly to the Sunday one year after he writes "To Autumn," Keats makes his own crossing, entering what he calls his "posthumous existence," his autumnal afterlife. Along with a friend, and now fellow-traveler, Joseph Severn, Keats is on a small brig, the *Maria Crowther*, heading down the Thames for Gravesend to the open sea and then to Italy. It's September 19, 1820, with the prospect of a warmer winter climate seen as a possible remedy for what ails him, which is a subject of some conjecture. Clearly he is ill, and has been, in degrees of declension, for a long time—certainly since the first near-fatal hemorrhaging the February before. Because of storm delays, rough seas, indifferent food, crowded conditions, and further bouts of hemorrhaging, plus a ten-day quarantine once they reach the many "mast-hemm'd" Bay of Naples, the voyage—if such a clumsy crossing can be called a voyage—is excruciating, leaving Keats to wonder why he's left England in the first place, if only to die so far away. It will be Keats's twenty-fifth birthday, October 31, before passengers and crew again touch land.

Keats's and Severn's destination is Rome, the Eternal—if you will—City. It's a hundred and forty miles north along the Mediterranean coast from Naples. In too many ways the journey by small, slow, hard-bottomed carriage over a rutted road will reprise their painful three-week sea-journey. The ride in the vettura and the overnights in the "villainously coarse and unpalatable" accommodations, however, will be in dramatic contrast to the nature—both human and otherwise—they encounter on their sixteen-miles-a-day passage, a passage that for Keats becomes a descent. The coastal road means stopping at such places as Terracina, Mesa, Torre de' Tre Ponti, Velletri, and Albano; it means moving in and out of sight of the sea, among lush hills of olive trees and Lombardy poplars and stone pines. November rains have visited the coast in the week right before they've started, so that now, suddenly, the weather has improved to the point that blue skies, blue views, and warmer temperatures have taken over. "The pure air," Severn will note later, "was exhilarating," and at the walking pace of the speed at which they're traveling, they have plenty of time to breathe and drink in the atmosphere. Pale Keats is managing as best he can in the bob-and-weave of the ride. To give him more room Severn decides early on to amble beside the carriage.

Severn is a young painter. The subtext of his companionship of Keats is that the art community in Rome may advance his artistic career by supporting his chances for a Royal Academy traveling fellowship. But that is in the future. Right now it's his painter's eye that helps to bring the slow trip north to life. Two or three sights dominate Severn's memory when, many years later, he writes his memoirs. One is the giant aqueducts, the great land bridges for water, that the ancient Romans have engineered, just as they have engineered the well-worn road they are traveling. The aqueducts give the effect of ruins, of great twilight structures lost between worlds; if Severn had thought for a moment, he might have linked their fragmentary look to certain scenes of desolation in Keats's Hyperion poems, where old Saturn sits like broken statuary awaiting the change of gods. There are even, intermittently, left-over gibbets for the crucifixion of thieves, though their status as ruins is somewhat compromised by the ragged bones of bodies still adorning a few of them. Then there is the example, as they approach the Campagna, of the cardinal, in full regalia, who along with the aid of his footmen is shooting songbirds out of the sky. "He had an owl tied loosely to a stick," Severn writes, "and a small looking-glass . . . annexed to move about with the owl, the light of which attracted numerous birds. The whole merit of this sport seemed to be in not shooting the owl. Two footmen in livery kept loading the fowling-pieces for the cardinal, and it was astonishing the great number of birds he killed."

Such sights serve an ironic texture, completely exotic to these two bright young Englishmen. The looming stone bridges over land, the hanging crosses, the Catholic clergyman, himself dressed in and named for the color of a bird yet shooting them for sport—these human parts have an otherworldly, grotesque, transitional feel to them, alien—at least to an outsider—to the Italian Arcadian autumnal landscape. To Keats, whose consumption has severely weakened him and given him the look of his "palely loitering" knight-at-arms, such strangely real yet surreal encounters must reinforce how far from home he is. As if he has entered a demi-mortal world. On the other hand, the freshening sea wind and new November warmth have brought the wildflowers back, of which, Severn says, there is a "profusion." He doesn't say which wildflowers, though at that time of the year yarrow, Queen Anne's lace, and tansy would be popular, and maybe hawkweed and goldenrod, all off-whites and yellows. And for fresh color, if they are near the sea or among the marshes, an occasional marsh rose. The Campagna, too, trying to redeem its reputation for evil air (mal'aria), produces flowers. Perhaps if Severn had stayed with Keats in the carriage he would have enjoyed the profusion as an observer. But since he is walking, and wanting to cheer his friend, he decides to pick some of the flowers and to fill "the little carriage." Severn reports that Keats "never tired of these . . . they gave him a singular and almost fantastic pleasure that was at times almost akin to a strange joy."

# 12

He picks a lot and for several days, placing and replacing his bouquets around the ailing poet until the vettura is "literally filled . . . with flowers." Though no one mentions the obvious—including the biographers—by the time they reach the outskirts of Rome, Keats is in his funeral carriage. From this moment on the story is, in the words of one commentator, "a masterpiece of disintegration," culminating, in three excruciating months, in Keats's death. They enter Rome through the Lateran Gate, pass the Colosseum—yet another autumnal ruin—head north for a mile or so and arrive at the Piazza di Spagna in the late afternoon in the middle of November. Keats's Roman doctor, a Scotsman by the name of James Clark, who, like many in the English colony, lives on the Piazza, has found rooms for them a bird's walk away at number 26. Suffice it to say that if too many of the images from Keats's life, particularly near the end, become emblems of foreshadowing, such as the flowers he arrives in Rome surrounded by, then the famous little room to which he becomes confined and in which he dies will more and more resemble his living tomb. He must have become fairly familiar with the "festoons of Roses" adorning his ceiling, for example, enough so that at one late point he tells Severn that he can already feel the flowers growing over him. Even books and letters he will not open begin to take on the autumnal "odor of mortality."

Winter in Rome is a twilit season, a kind of crepuscular, chill fall. There are rains and there is morning fog and in the evening an almost invisible mist. But in between, on the best days, the soft gold light brings out the texture in the Travertine stone and the old color in the rosso Romano and yellow ocher buildings. Autumnal colors, fading tones. On those rare days when they do get out, in late December, early January, when the air still has some warmth in it, Keats and Severn "stoll on the Pincio . . . particularly because it was sheltered from the north wind." Keats also, occasionally, rides, but "at a snail's pace," with Severn matching stride by walking shoulder to shoulder with the horse. Once the companion, Severn is now the nurse, ever conscious of the weather that seems to be sustaining his friend, weather that can be "warm like summer" or "lovely . . . like the Italian spring in winter." Keats, for his part, must be thinking he's entered an afterlife for sure, a place in beautiful mid-light between nothingness and the palpable something whole life is. Outside, in "the balmy air," the bits and pieces of Rome he manages to see must seem imaginary, like a floating Arcadia, while inside, in the half-dark, staring at the painted roses on his ceiling, Rome must feel like a mausoleum, a space—as he writes in *Hyperion*—that "where the dead leaf fell, there it did rest."

2002

# DIRTY SILENCE

Delivered at a symposium on contemporary poetry, *After the Flood*, on November 17, 1979, at the Folger Shakespeare Library in Washington, DC.

*Tell X that speech is not dirty silence*
*Clarified. It is silence made still dirtier:*
*It is more than an imitation for the ear.*
*—Wallace Stevens, "The Creations of Sound"*

# 1

Stevens never quite tells us what his silence made still dirtier is, but he does suggest later in the poem that it is the visible made a little hard to see and the audible a little hard to hear. The actual lines are addressed to a poet X, who is the villain of the piece, a man too exactly himself, a man too much in the way of the poem, and they go something like this:

His poems do not make the visible a little hard

To see nor, reverberating, eke out the mind
On peculiar horns, themselves eked out
By the spontaneous particulars of sound.

I would like to be able to say to you this morning that *dirty silence* is an accurate gloss of free verse and that blurred vision, accompanied by the spontaneous particulars of sound, played on peculiar horns, is, collectively speaking, the very language of free speech. That, of course, would not be true. Stevens's answer to the issue of "naked poetry" is his blank-verse answer to the issue of dirty silence clarified: "We do not say ourselves like that in poems." Dirty silence may not be a pure oxymoron; nevertheless, it is a metaphor describing a certain kind of tension necessary to the "music of a poem"—to use another Stevens phrase—if by music we mean a poem's total vocal and visual rhythm.

We have been hooked for so long on the two-party system in poetry, on the argument between so-called formalism and so-called free verse, between reactionary and radical, conservative and visionary, that we have tended to look at the American version of the art as political—the Dickinsons and Frosts and Stevenses and Wilburs on one side of the aisle, the Whitmans and Pounds and Williamses and Lowells on the other. And every so many years, sometimes in as little time as four, each side has nominated and tried to elect a president of poetry. Indeed, the debate has gone on so much from the start of our entry into the "modern world"—in the period right after the Civil War—that our national poetry often appears to exist less as a historical experience and more as a continuing contemporary condition, less as a linear development of action and reaction (as in the linkage of a Spenser-Milton-Dryden-Pope-Wordsworth, et al.) and more as a series of concentric circles, within a single cylinder of time, with various figures placed at pole and antipode.

Critics fond of the overview have tended to see this debate as a dialectic rather than as a strict dichotomy—especially in terms of proper English as our ghost language. If my configuration of circles is correct, such critics have more often than not placed egalitarian Emerson at the center of gravity. Because if as a Transcendental theologian, Emerson appeals to our vanities about our vital relations with nature, it is as an astute and pragmatic reader of poetry that he appeals to our vanities about verse. You will remember his famous complaint against "a recent writer of lyrics" (Emerson's own poet X) for whom "the argument is secondary, the finish of the verses primary." Emerson declares that "it is not metres, but a metre-making argument that makes a poem,—a thought so passionate and alive that like the spirit of a plant or animal it has an architecture of its own, and adorns nature with a new thing." He continues that "the thought and form are equal in the order of time, but in the order of genesis, the thought is prior to the form." Even as a poet Emerson cannot avoid essaying. There is that high beginning moment in "Merlin" in which he states:

> Thy trivial harp will never please
> Or fill my craving ear;
> Its chords should ring as blows the breeze,
> Free, peremptory, clear.

An architecture of its own, free, peremptory, clear. Lest it sound as if I am putting words in Emerson's mouth, it should be obvious that he is not, no more than was Stevens, promoting a free verse over a formal one. He is, however, drawing—in theory at least—a line between mere verse or "lyricism," as he calls it, and real poetry, poetry tied inevitably and effectively to its intellectual and emotional sources.

If Emerson and Stevens seem to be talking out of both sides of their mouths at once, they are. To make the full generalization: they would seem to want us to write formal verse as if it were free, and so-called free verse as if it were formal. A familiar, if not always possible, aesthetic assignment. Yet as references in the history of our critical thought concerning rhythm in poetry, I would choose these two fundamentalists over Pound or Williams just because they absorb rather than disavow our national debt to an inherited language and a distinctly inherited rhythm. I would choose them, as I would choose the reader in Eliot or in Roethke, because they are far less interested in the political debates between poets than in the formal dialectics within poems.

What Emerson's meter-making argument offers us is a coherent basis for reading both, say, a Whitman and a Dickinson; and what Stevens's dirty silence offers us is a coherent metaphor for reading the conflicting evidence of our contemporaries.

The poems of Whitman's, for example, that many of us feel most satisfied with are those that inhere to a stable rather than a shifting center—poems that hold the line, in Poe's phrase, toward a single, illuminating effect—that supply the reader with the connecting rhythm and closure of a presiding metaphor. As wonderful as "Song of Myself" is, for me it remains an anthology, a manifesto, a great rangy text, compared to the greater gifts of "Crossing Brooklyn Ferry" or "This Compost"—two poems that develop themes of disintegration and regeneration through the terms of their inherent and limited raw materials; two poems that confront us indirectly rather than resort to the poetry of bravado; two poems that allow the accent to rise as well as fall. Organic or invented, Whitman, at his most interesting, works hard toward singular unity, wholeness; he does not attack the architecture for the sake of being free, peremptory, and clear.

Dickinson too has suffered from stereotype. If too many of her poems scan to the tune of "The Battle Hymn of the Republic" or "The Yellow Rose of Texas," the fault may lie with our hearing of the essential 4/3 hymnal line. The fact is that in her finest work Dickinson struggles against her

apparent need for metrical closure and metaphysical purity by opening and
shutting the line unexpectedly and by mixing up her metaphor as if she
were taking, on the spot, psychological shorthand. Number 640, for instance,
is a direct address to the Reverend Charles Wadsworth—a painful, beautiful love poem, and, at fifty lines, her longest. It is the poem that begins

> I cannot live with You—
> It would be Life—
> And Life is over there—
> Behind the Shelf
>
> The Sexton keeps the Key to—

and concludes by breaking the poet's hymnbook quatrain pattern with a six-
line emphatic stanza, four rhyming lines of which drive the same nail in.

> So We must meet apart—
> You there—I—here
> With just the Door ajar
> That Oceans are—and Prayer—
> And that White Sustenance—
> Despair—

In one of her last poems, number 1670, Dickinson pursues the key sexual
rhyme of Room/Worm/warm/home/Form/swim/him/dream through four un-
even stanzas in such a way as to let the dream, the pursuit, the transformation of a worm into a snake in her chamber, take over. By insisting on her
repetitions and clipped lines, her quick surprises, Dickinson frees the form,
freeing it to become her real antagonist.

   I am not, by the way, sponsoring a simpleminded law of contraries, in
which the form is supposed to act as an anchor to content, content the
current trying to carry the boat out to sea. I am talking about the dialectic
of form itself, an argument of the energies within a poem. It may be true
that Whitman needed a father figure—literally, as in his love of Lincoln, or
figuratively, as in his use of a presiding metaphor and meter. It may be true
that Dickinson needed a demon lover and that the underlying energy of
her poems is suspended sex. But these are issues for the biography of con-

tent. They do not address directly enough the poetry of the poem. And neither am I attempting to describe a Chinese jar moving perpetually in its stillness, though it is true that I believe words move only in time, and that, after speech, they reach into the silence, make it still dirtier.

I am trying to pay attention to a phenomenon that has preoccupied our poetry from the beginning. The first phrase of Eliot's landmark essay, "Tradition and the Individual Talent," reads, "In English writing. . . ." He does not say, "In writing in English. . . ." I know I am waxing the point a bit, but what he says is *In English writing*. Then he goes on to define poetic relationships that exist outside and against that tradition—English writing in the American English language. Our American meter-making arguments with our English antecedents are too long and too well documented for me to worry with here; but I do want to stress that our witness of what our language is and what a line of poetry means comes from a culture, king, and country that we rejected. Yet as we could not invent an absolute alternative we did adjust one. We discovered a whole new landscape, new skies, a different sense of time and space, extreme natural wealth, Indians, and eventually more and more Europeans. When Williams was asked by an Englishman, "But this language of yours, where does it come from?" Williams snappily replied, "From the mouths of Polish mothers." Whatever the anxiety of influence within the rich Romantic tradition, there is in our American poetry a present tense conditional with the past, a past that, like it or not, provides us with a ghost language, a ghost form, a ghost rhythm, be it sonnet, elegy, or ode, be it epic or pentameter rising; a past that has left us with a shadow line and line of thought. From Whitman to Williams, the argument has really been a matter of a difference of diction and syntax, a language of our experience, a language within a larger mother tongue. In lieu of an original language for poetry, we have been perennially forced, with Emerson, to realize a new dialectic of rhythm—Anglo and American, monarchical and democratic—if by rhythm we mean movement, if by movement we mean form.

Yet, as my own comments suggest, we have tended, historically, to talk about form in the limited terms of the movement of a line, and from that assumption we have tended to speak of lines adding up to something: the bottom line. Whether it is Emerson looking for its counterpart in nature or Pound telling us to compose in the sequence of the musical phrase and not in the sequence of the metronome or Williams asking us to believe in a variable foot as well as a triadic "stanza" or Olson claiming all the white space of the page; whether we are discussing biorhythms or breath pauses, caesuras or enjambments, accents or syllabics—we have focused on the science of the line. We have tended to speak of form in poetry in terms of the way we write or type it, across the page, and according to the determinations of line break. We have, in fact, and more often as critics and theoreticians than as poets, tried to beat the Tradition at its own game. We have tried more than once to make an American line. Of course, considering the achievement of our ancestry, we have had little choice but to deal with what is primary . . . Poetry, as form, is a problem of movement across a measured space. But as form, that is not all it is.

Still, I am reminded of a little panegyric of Pound's celebrating the American virtues of Whistler, who, like Pound, was a sometime Londoner. The third stanza goes:

> You had your searches, your uncertainties,
> And this is good to know—for us, I mean,
> Who bear the brunt of our America
> And try to wrench her impulse into art.

I hope you could hear the measure of this quatrain—four lines of ghost pentameter, half of which are sure iambic. There is even a little assonant rhyme going on, in couplets. And the poet even manages to interrupt himself ("for us, I mean") without interrupting the "music" of the line. Indeed, it is a technique, this talking back against the metrical potential of the line, that Pound was to later perfect in that matrix of meters, *The Cantos*. It is a technique that feels particularly American: speech barking back at song.

## 2

The trouble with concentrating the discussion of rhythm in American poetry on the line is that it continually shifts the balance toward the weight and measures of the form we have inherited and away from the idiom in which we live and move and have our being. Even a poet as fed up as Williams, in a poem as gorgeous as "Asphodel, That Greeny Flower," ends up substituting the artifice of his triadic formula for that of another. His formations impose upon rather than reveal variations in rhythm. "Of love, abiding love/it will be telling/though too weak a wash of crimson/colors it . . ." is one kind of clear music, whereas the lines that immediately follow support a different music— "There is something urgent I have to say to you. . . ." Free verse ought to be flexible enough to handle such juxtaposition in kind, without the form aggrandizing. Williams's metrical good sense transcends the stair-stepping of his stanzas; his lines read through the silence of his line-breaks. Thus, "Asphodel" reads better than it is written, better than it is affixed to the page. Ironically, the harder Williams works against the regularity of the stress, the more he emphasizes its place in his poem.

If 1855 and 1912 are the important dates in the history of our struggle with the conception of the line—from Whitman's long yawp to Pound's announcement of an "absolute rhythm"—then sometime in the middle 1950s through about the presidential term of John Kennedy (1960–1963), we began to extend our aesthetic to include the whole length of the sentence. Whether we are talking about Projective verse or Beat or Confessional or Deep Image, and whether the phenomenon has received much critical attention, the fact is that along about then we began to divide up into category and constituency, armed against the academic, and ready to try to deal with the poem as a whole—as a discontinuous rhythm, often with the verbal surface at odds with the content—whether it was composition by field, poetry by protest and confession, or poetry as the interpretations of dreams. We began to look beyond the inherent demands of the line toward the total spatial and temporal needs of the poem. We began to read past the rhythms moving across the page to those moving down as well. We began to read the language as having a will of its own. Olson's "The Kingfishers," for instance, wants to find a way of including the poet's whole big body, a way of responding to the full, the literal moment—mind, heart, hair, and all. Lowell once spoke of how he arrived at the "form" for the family poems of *Life Studies*: they were written, he said, with as much formal containment and packed verbal surface as any of his earlier lines; he simply chopped them up. He did not have to tell us about the difference the chopping makes, or the difference the content of crisis forces. And "Howl" is one long sentence long, a litany of loss in a list of losses, held together by a left-hand, anaphoric rhyme of *who's* and a right-hand answer of commas, all built on the single, wonderful statement, "Carl, while you are not safe I am not safe." As for those poets rediscovering the image—with the exception of his prose-poems—a poet like Bly seems to want to be able to operate outside the rhythm of narrative terrestrial time altogether in favor of the poetics of an inner, imaginative space, so as to create a kind of light striking the page.

There is no such thing as a definitive American line because there can never be any fixed way of writing the free-verse line. Our argument with our forebears is really an argument against metrical and linear closure. As the examples of Whitman or Williams or Lowell or even Dickinson might show, it is not so much that our poetry has rejected the ghost forms we inherited but that the needs of our experience make demands, in every generation, that we explode those forms. But of course we can never exactly blow them up, not as long as we live within the same inherited language, the same accents and patterns; we can, however, move through them, past them, distending or extending them. (That is what idiom is all about, the language of an identity; language as "the music latent in the common speech of its time.") Free verse has about the same meaning for us as free speech: though we would never shout fire in a crowded theater, free speech is our birthright and responsibility.

And that is why the silence is getting dirtier and dirtier. As the line turns toward the completed sentence, the sentence turns toward the total linguistic structure and texture of the poem, its total rhythm, toward spontaneous particulars and particulars of sound. If the phrase "free verse" has any useful meaning, it lies in its emphatic sense of the poem as an open entity, moving by assonance and consonance, moving by rising as well as falling rhythm, moving by image and rhetoric, and moving, most of all, by surprise. On the other hand, if the dialectic between the unit of the measured line and the unit of the full sentence were to be relaxed, it would still be necessary to maintain their tension if only as a stay against just "one person talking to another," to quote Eliot again. From John Ashbery to James Wright, a generation of poets decided that apprenticeship is one thing but forms of closure could lead to solitary confinement. Ashbery and Wright, in fact, force us to read them whole poem by whole, for their "single effects," or miss them in their entirety. Their ears are tuned to the sentence—certainly to the completion of image and thought, but clearly also to the richer, intimate disclosure of the discovered emotion.

The chief distinction between the verse line and the free-verse sentence is the distinction between a poetry that continually returns and one that continues, that turns, then goes on. Whatever adjudications have to be made between persona and person in a poem, between the suffering and the creating—as between relative relationships the speaker has to his or her raw material—in American free verse since the 1960s we are asked to move from line to storyline in such a way that the interchange be imperceptible. Line break becomes line turn, line continuum, a sentence. As the vocalization of the line occurs *within* it, the endings of the lines begin to add up to something visual, yet something we see through. This kind of voicing over the integrity of the line into one sentence, toward the totality of the poem, is often hard to hear, not because the verse is really prose but because the verse is accumulative, acquisitional, special, and, if it is of the quality of a John Ashbery or a James Wright, understated—leaning toward or away from the predictable, the regular, never quite on the expected mark.

Our free verse, then, is fictive music, both literally and figuratively, developed through the art of the individual idiom. Its narrative values depend, implicitly, on its lyric imperatives. The story in the sentence becomes the story of the sentence.

But all of this at best addresses the energy and the rhythms withheld or released in the poetry of the syntax. The sentence itself goes on. In depending on the sequence of subject-verb-complement, free verse depends on cause-and-effect connections, and therefore emphasizes, sentence to sentence, temporal plot over spatial pattern. If pattern is what we hear in verse, "plot" is what we are asked to listen for when the verse is "freed."

On Wednesday the queen died and on Friday the king died, says E. M. Forster, and we have straight-on narrative; but on Wednesday the queen died and on Friday the king died of grief, we have plot. Pattern is how we draw the line from here to there; plot is why. In emphasizing why over how, free verse further depends on its ability to dramatize, to bark back continually at the song, as when Ashbery, in "Wet Casements," tells us that he "can't have it, and this makes me angry" or when Wright tells us, in poem after poem, "Don't blame me, I didn't start this mess."

That remarkable tension between how and why, the lyric and the dramatic, between lingering and needing to go on, between the horizontal rhythm of the line and the vertical rhythm of the story, with the balance always favoring the movement down, is what gives free verse its gravitational authority. The verse itself, the lyricism, lives in the phrase, the clause, while the freedom lives in that language that completes the sentence, that extends and connects it to the next. (W. S. Merwin, for example, a poet who has played with the abridgement of the line and the syntax of the sentence better than any of his contemporaries, writes of "St. Vincent's" that "its bricks by day a French red under/cross facing south/blown-up neoclassic facades the tall/dark openings between columns at/the dawn of history/ exploded into many windows/in a mortised face." The line breaks are intended to excite as much as complicate the differences between ending, enjambing, and continuing—to make us move swiftly through the emphasis of phrase to the total structure of the stanza. The tension between breaking and entering the new line is supported by the need to go on, to complete, to make whole: a whole thought, a whole perception.) In that growth lies the dramatic voice, the voice unwilling to simply sing, but nevertheless demanding to be well heard. Yet a voice not simply speech. In the achieved free-verse poem we hear the formalization of a process, as well as a progress: we hear form itself, as an idiosyncratic language, being achieved. And the form speaks, in its dialectic of poetry against itself.

# 3

Perhaps, though, we should look at the bright side, think of our formal problems less in terms of a busy dialectic and more in terms of a happy correspondence. Last year the young American poet, Robert Hass—a figure somewhere in the aesthetic middle ground between a contemporary poetry committed to the tight line of the image and one reinventing the longer, more flexible line of narrative—published a book entitled *Praise*. The second poem, "Meditation at Lagunitas," goes as follows:

All the new thinking is about loss.
In this it resembles all the old thinking.
The idea, for example, that each particular erases
the luminous clarity of a general idea. That the clown-
faced woodpecker probing the dead sculpted trunk
of that black birch is, by his presence,
some tragic falling off from a first world
of undivided light. Or the other notion that,
because there is in this world no one thing
to which the bramble of *blackberry* corresponds,
a word is elegy to what it signifies.
We talked about it late last night and in the voice
of my friend, there was a thin wire of grief, a tone
almost querulous. After a while I understood that,
talking this way, everything dissolves: *justice,*
*pine, hair, woman, you* and *I.* There was a woman
I made love to and I remembered how, holding
her small shoulders in my hands sometimes,
I felt a violent wonder at her presence
like a thirst for salt, for my childhood river
with its island willows, silly music from the pleasure boat,
muddy places where we caught the little orange-silver fish
called *pumpkinseed*. It hardly had to do with her.
Longing, we say, because desire is full
of endless distances. I must have been the same to her.
But I remember so much, the way her hands dismantled bread,
the thing her father said that hurt her, what
she dreamed. There are moments when the body is as numinous
as words, days that are the good flesh continuing.
Such tenderness, those afternoons and evenings,
saying *blackberry, blackberry, blackberry.*

It is unlikely that you heard many line breaks. I hope, however, that the rhythms in and of the sentences were audible, if not always certifiable; and I hope that the overall formal plot of the poem, from exposition to complication to climax, could be followed. Hass calls it a "Meditation," which traditionally has been that chance to think aloud, brood, speculate, wander a bit, and possibly arrive at a conclusion. However we are to look at it, as an action or as an argument or both, there is something intellectually and emotionally serious at stake here, something obviously painful, local, real. The poem reads deductively, going from generalization to the supporting evidence as if we were being instructed, yet it is clear that the experience at the center of the poem has itself brought the speaker to this Pacific place—to ruminate, to set priorities. And the poem is framed by its "philosophy," yet it is also clear that all the new/old thinking about loss has been changed, affected, intimately transformed by the time we hear the word blackberry repeated in the last line. And the poem is arranged in four discrete units, paragraph-like, rather than in announced stanzas, yet, again, it is clear that transitions are being offered and that the order, once headed, seems inevitable.

The title, "Meditation at Lagunitas," would have us believe in the fiction that the speaker is actually standing by the ocean thinking about loss, telling us he is thinking about loss; when in truth, to round out the tautology, the speaker is exemplifying, showing us that he is there thinking about loss—demonstrating, dramatizing the fact, speaking from the condition of loss. He even notices a clown-faced woodpecker for us—to reassure us. I worry the point because the greater fiction is always the form itself, the revealing, realized emblem. By dramatizing, by creating a setting for his sense of loss the speaker is formalizing it. But I will have more to say about that later. For right now, "All the new thinking is about loss./In this it resembles all the old thinking." These two lines of wit and confidence, this thought-rhyme, will be the last two so juxtaposed, so end-stopped in the poem. For the remainder of this first verse paragraph the speaker will deliberate back and forth, sometimes ten, sometimes twelve, sometimes sixteen syllables, building by parallels of pronoun and antecedent, working down to the poem's essential perception—"a word is elegy to what it signifies"—a bottom line with the first full integrity of a concluding statement. A bottom line indeed. The passage goes again:

> All the new thinking is about loss.
> In this it resembles all the old thinking.
> The idea, for example, that each particular erases
> the luminous clarity of a general idea. That the clown-
> faced woodpecker probing the dead sculpted trunk

of that black birch is, by his presence,
some tragic falling off from a first world
of undivided light. Or the other notion that,
because there is in this world no one thing
to which the bramble of *blackberry* corresponds,
a word is elegy to what it signifies.

If you can imagine it, the right-hand margin is somewhat angular, in keeping with but not overstating the anxiety of the thought that links *loss* and *erases* and *tragic falling off* and *no one thing* and *elegy*. Nearly all of the eleven lines are divided by caesura or comma, or interrupted by periods. The final, the summarizing, line of the passage turns out to be, of course, the best balanced, "elegy" positioned against "signifies." Save for the starting "couplet," the passage is a single, extended sentence, with the emphasis on the apparent rationality of perception opposed to notion. And though it is hardly a syllogism, the passage does play seriously with the logic of loss. This is the "music" of its speculation, its theory.

And it would seem, having stated all the issues, that the initial form is satisfied. A little speculation with illustration. But since the center of the poem and the reason for its having been written involve an emotional and sexual encounter that superficially bears no necessary connection to the beginning, a way must be found to get there, to link up. In this case, through a third person, a friend.

We talked about it late last night and in the voice
of my friend, there was a thin wire of grief, a tone
almost querulous. After a while I understood that,
talking this way, everything dissolves: *justice,
pine, hair, woman, you* and *I.*

If we listen closely we can hear plot developing, as the terms for loss begin to complicate, enlarge, magnify. In just these four and a half lines, Hass achieves the status of a protagonist, a presence no longer simply engaged in thinking but in talking out his thinking about loss. He gets in and out of the discussion so quickly we barely have time to notice how fully he extends his thesis. There are four references to the concern that there is in this world no one thing to which the bramble of *blackberry* corresponds:

first the pronoun *it*, which sends us in reverse order back through the passage we have just made; then *thin wire of grief*, the tone of voice of the friend; then the speaker reminds us that we are, in fact, *talking this way*; and finally *everything dissolves*—presumably into words—*justice, pine, hair, woman, you* and *I*. Half the poem is over, and we have, in the meditating mind and mediating voice of the speaker, moved from thinking of loss to talking in the terms of you and I; and a woman. It has been a declension directed at the heart of things, the memory in the poem.

> There was a woman
> I made love to and I remembered how, holding
> her small shoulders in my hands sometimes,
> I felt a violent wonder at her presence
> like a thirst for salt, for my childhood river
> with its island willows, silly music from the pleasure boat,
> muddy places where we caught the little orange-silver fish
> called *pumpkinseed*. It hardly had to do with her.
> Longing, we say, because desire is full
> of endless distances. I must have been the same to her.

Easily the poem's most lyrical moment, these lines move with the grace of their attention—one long sentence of experience, three short sentences of comment. Motion, with modification. The long sentence, the central sentence, turns and turns and turns, with less need of pause than continuation. The sense of the unit standard of the lines would have them breaking something like:

> There was a woman I made love to
> and I remember how,
> holding her small shoulders in my hands (sometimes)
> I felt a violent wonder at her presence . . .

Remarkably, Hass observes this standard fairly closely, even though many such closely observed lines could go flat very fast. The issue is that he works against the habit of the thought and possible metrical unit to make the good sense more interesting sense, to let us ease into the emotion with him. He also wants to emphasize visually, as well as vocally, some of the other names into which "everything dissolves": woman, holding, sometimes, presence, river, boat, fish. Freeing and breaking his lines for their best sentence sense, their plot-complicating sense, allows the poet to discover his stresses within the phrase or the clause, while the voice-over of the speaker, the actor in the poem, is free to carry us through the line and storyline to completion. Hass's speaker brings us out of our river dream, with its island willows and silly music from the pleasure boat, rather abruptly. It—again, the opening pronoun—it hardly had to do with her, he says. The truth of this is softened a bit by his asking us to remember that longing is full of endless distances. Therefore it must have been the same with her. But, the speaker adds,

> . . . I remember so much, the way her hands dismantled bread,
> the thing her father said that hurt her, what
> she dreamed.

Like so many in this poem, the lines here keep tucking in, with "bread" and "what" and "dreamed." Bread and a thing said: they may be the source of dreaming, but the consonant ending of *d* and *t*, the rhyme of *bread* and *said*, drive home the hurt for both speaker and lover. The speaker concludes, in something close to a quatrain, that the bread is the body, just as the word is inevitably, elegiacally, flesh, and flesh, word. A fair exchange.

> There are moments when the body is as numinous
> as words, days that are the good flesh continuing.
> Such tenderness, those afternoons and evenings,
> saying *blackberry, blackberry, blackberry.*

If this poem is successful it is successful because it moves convincingly from the easy wit of thinking about loss to a condition of fullness, tenderness, and feeling the loss; from the melancholy of the word to a belief in the body; from blackberry as a sign to blackberry as speech. Yet vocally, and emotionally, the poem grows through the internal strength of its sentences, through a music worked out within the completed sentence structure. The line is determined more by its aural good sense than by its sense of measured sound. As the primary combining and cohering rhythm in the poem, the sentence naturally extends into the verse paragraph, the paragraph into the poem.

Nevertheless, "Meditation at Lagunitas" is one stanza in duration, a single, continuing embrace of its tensions—and not just those tensions between the line holding and the sentence going on, between the visual and vocal rhythms, and not just between the word and its corresponding flesh, and not just between the idea and the emotion. This piece seems to want to travel the distance from meditation to love poem, from one temperature to passion. It seems to want to be organized around alternating parts of its speech, a longer passage to short, longer to short; that is, eleven lines to five, thirteen lines to four. It seems to want to achieve resonance if not closure, to complete its *blackberrying* yet remain open-ended. The poem is plotted, certainly, from, through, and to something. And it does move within a time frame of causal relations, from thinking to talking to remembering to realization, from here to there, through a list of synonyms for loss—until loss itself is transformed.

One of the advantages of fixed or invented forms is that they secure the reader in space as well as time; line by line they reassure the reader of an order, past and passing and to come, within the void of the page. So in a sense, no matter how we vary those forms, so long as they are surefooted we are potentially aware of the whole of the poem, its plan, and its commitment to closure, from the start. We can sit back and enjoy the music that much more. We can anticipate.

Free verse is famous for reassuring no one of anything, least of all the reader. Yet when it is done well, its ambition, and its ability, I would like to think, is to find a form as secure in its space on the page as it pretends to be in the time it takes. The point is important because it permits us to see free verse less as a creative accident than as an earned achievement, less as attempt than as perfected art.

All the new thinking is about loss because of those afternoons and evenings when the body was as numinous as words, moments and whole days of the good flesh continuing, saying this is that to which the bramble of blackberry corresponds. That sentence is the plot in summary—in reduction, the cause-and-effect, temporal, ongoing rhythm of the whole. But it is not the poem as a whole brought to bear. It is not the form, achieved.

One of the worst poetry clichés, reintroduced as an aesthetic in the 1960s, was that this dominant mode, free verse, should represent the spontaneous overflow of powerful feelings without much exercise in recollecting them in tranquility. Even Lowell, from out of the tranquilized 1950s, would later describe his experiential *Notebook* sonnets as "the loose ravel of blank verse." The notion that free verse must be either naked or dressed for dinner does not deal with the dialectic of the phrase itself. It can be free of its verse only to the extent that it keep the faith, in sounds that are a little hard to hear, with sights a little hard to see. Its lyric values are amended by the voice, the voice normally in the middle of its dramatic circumstance. It is a voice at once preoccupied with expressing and advancing the story, of moving across the space, yes, of making us pay attention, but also necessarily committed to moving down the page, of keeping our attention. The interval of the phrase and clause may be the basic unit of its lyricism, but the sentence is the rhythm given meaning, the line a way of getting there. The parental, the ghost form may be more apparent in some free-verse poems than others: regardless, the nominal music will be invariably speech barking back at song. And the simple weight of the bottom of the page will favor passage over pause.

But there is a bottom line. Stevens ends his poem, "The Creations of Sound," by offering that "We say ourselves in syllables that rise/From the floor, rising in speech we do not speak." I read these lines as referring to a language so intelligent with the source of the poem that the language seems a priori to the art, so that the poem would perform as provided with its speech rather than having learned it en route to its last line. The formalization of free verse would consist then in its ability to speak from the floor from the first line on—and to continue, line by sentence, to free the voice from the imitations for the ear.

And that is why Robert Hass's poem is a meditation of a meditation. At the point of entry of thinking about loss, he has entered the form. He has set tone, he has reached at once into the silence. His medium, his agency, will act as his means; it will even allow him to write a sort of love sonnet within a whole, it seems, other story. The fiction of American free verse is not so much that the demands are any less formal but that they are finally any different.

1981

SENTIMENTAL FORMS

The idea of the sentimental in poetry is concurrent with the eighteenth-century notion of sensibility. That is, the ability to express, and press, one's apparent emotional life is inextricably and from its literary beginnings tied up with the ability to empathize, to identify with the other. Looked at another way: in order to make the emotional exchange complete we can identify only with what we can project. At sixteen, Wordsworth wrote a little poem entitled "On Seeing Miss Helen Maria Williams Weep at a Tale of Distress."

> She wept.—Life's purple tide began to flow
> In languid streams through every thrilling vein;
> Dim were my swimming eyes—my pulse beat slow,
> And my full heart was swelled to dear delicious pain.

The poet is clearly falling in love with his own powers of identification, his ability to answer the sight of tears with the potential for tears. Indeed, his empathy is exaggerated into the presumptuous. Because his own heart is deliciously full he can project a whole hyperbole of emotion, something like bathing, from purple to languid to thrilling. As Helen Maria Williams is herself being observed responding to "a Tale of Distress," there must be some exponential law of emotion involved. The fourth line skips an extra beat: grief itself is the subject here—grief observing grief observed.

If all the emotional problems of poetry were as obvious as this one, we would have little trouble separating the man from the boy. Yet the moment sensibility itself is an issue—"when the writer is defending that Humanity which is not satisfy'd with good-Natured Actions alone, but feels the Misery of others with inward Pain, it is then deservedly nam'd Sensibility" (*The Prompter*, 1735)—the moment we begin to think about what and how we feel, the moment we begin to construct correlatives for what we call our inner lives, the moment we imagine our emotion, at that moment we have acknowledged an ambiguity. We are naming and judging our experience, we are thinking about feeling, constructing the self-conscious heart. In that single, especial sense Stevens is right. All poets, since Rousseau, are Romantics, thinker-feelers—subjects as well as sources. At what point does the empathetic contract become pathetic; at what point does indentification become indulgence? A sixteen-year-old Wordsworth is a far different Romantic from the later poet who says, "Our birth is but a sleep and a forgetting." To contemporize the argument: if we accept Galway Kinnell's suggestion that the richest poetry expresses a "tenderness toward existence," we must also accept the risks of emotion in possible excess of the perceived experience. Whatever our sympathies, we cannot have empathy with ourselves, and whatever our empathies, we cannot afford, in art, sympathy for others. Empathy treats the object of affection as an equal, sympathy assumes the role of a superior. If we accept J. D. Salinger's suggestion that sentimentality is "giving a thing more tenderness than God gives to it," we must accept certain inherent limits on how much emotion we are allowed to invest. For all we know, God may be neutral and the idea of tenderness itself is sentimental.

God does not speak in iambs, or if He does He does not measure the length of His line. We are so used to blaming content for the sins of form that it may be impossible anymore to accept that the formal indictment of speech as poetry is, from the perspective of the spheres, ultimately sentimental—caring for a thing more than God does. Villanelles were originally comedic forms; sonnets have forever been vulnerable to the valentine; and the sestina, the most formal romance a poem can have with poetry, must invariably exaggerate as it repeats six-and-a-half times its six end-words. The aesthetic problem with any fixed form, ballade to triolet, is to rescue form from itself—to bring it back into the emotionally believable. But this is the aesthetic problem for any poem, fixed or free.

Had young Wordsworth written "She wept.—Life began to flow through every vein;/Dim were my eyes—my pulse beat slow,/And my full heart was swelled with pain," he would have corrupted his quatrain, his form, in favor of a straighter emotional line. He would have also lost something, a kind of buoyancy, a kind of generosity, a kind of conviction. His purple adjectives want to extend, elaborate, and interpret the value of the moment. Their value, in fact, is to value the moment. Grief is good here, something to be demonstrated and responded to. The question is not, finally, whether a poem, or any work of art, is sentimental, but whether we will be able to afford its emotional commitments—commitments that in and of themselves grow as inevitably as the form, inevitably with the form. Whatever else content is in poetry, it is at least the manifestation of something without the poem within the poem. We are told that there are those poets whose last appeal is to form and those whose last appeal is to content. There is no way to avoid content in poetry, there is every way to fail at form. If sentimentality, as an act of tenderness, is an attempt to confer significance, to place a value, form is as much a tenderness as the "content" it sustains. But no reader wants to read a lie, and if he feels the poet is playing with himself by indulging the music or the image or the facts of the poem, if he feels the poet is playing with his audience by indulging the emotion of the poem, he is going to cry foul. Insofar as art stands outside nature, it is potentially sentimental. Insofar as art stands outside its own abilities to authenticate and make us believe, it is permanently self-indulgent.

We had the experience but missed the meaning, says Eliot. It is that return, that need to re-create by creating, whether recollected in tranquility or anxiety, that exposes us to our deepest lives. Se we find in the reformation of experience a meaning. If that is treating experience with a tenderness in excess of its original value, we may as well give up poetry for science. Without the conference and council of art, experience may not have an original value. The art of poetry is the art of arbitrating between memory and means, so that form will be forced to understate what, by implication, it overvalues. Wordsworth's little poem merely imitates and therefore participates in the sweet grief it has evaluated. His adjectives and emphatic accents mimic rather than transform the emotion. Form cannot afford to be incongruous but neither can it simply agree with experience. We look for that language that will allow us to love without requiring that we yield. When James Wright, among the most influential poets of tenderness of his generation, offers us "The Prayer of the Sour Old Doctor of Philosophy in the Temple"—

> Oh lovely Italian face,
> Listen to this one:
>
> One slim red-haired shadow
> Awoke and rose up in Puerto Rico,
> And the silken insides of her plumeria flowers
> Bloomed in the moonlight.
> She heard a voice:

119

"Come to me in New York, I am dying for you."
She arrived, and he screwed her
Into plenty.
He gave her one little red-haired loneliness
Screaming and bleeding down her slim thighs,
And he gave her one little pot-head
Rotting on Riker's Island.

And now the slim red-haired shadow
Is dead of cancer at twenty-one
In the South Bronx.

Oh lovely twelve year old,
Speak to me of Spring.

Then leave me in Winter, at home
With the alone.

—we have to say, with all affection, that the poet has exceeded his emotional authority. The discrete diction of "her plumeria flowers" blooming in the moonlight and screwing "her/Into plenty," of "one little red-haired loneliness" and "one little pot-head" cannot rescue the expressed sympathy, and sympathies, of the speaker, a speaker who, at the outset, has tried to tough out his tenderness in the posture of telling a joke—"Listen to this one." The fact that the poem is addressed to the "lovely Italian face" of a twelve-year-old only further exaggerates the emotion. Because Wright delays his stake in the material until the very end he has to substitute "sensibility" for presence, the mentality for the personality of feelings, with the result that his example reads like an object-lesson. Formalizing the poem as a prayer appears to be an attempt to finesse our response in advance. The speaker seems willing to remain at the outlines of emotion ("Speak to me of Spring"), as if pity itself were the protagonist. It is no surprise, then, that the final couplet slant-rhymes into cliché two of Wright's favorite words, "home/alone." The form here, in which the speaker will announce but will not act, is almost a parody of what is possible. As free verse, the poem has the whole page and more at its disposal. Instead it toys with its "little red-haired" story ("Rotting on

Riker's Island/ . . . dead of cancer at twenty-one/In the South Bronx") without surrounding it with sufficient reason for caring. The sour old Ph.D. in the temple expects us to take him at his word. Form that exposes emotion to the extent that Wright's work does—formal phase or free— must pay for what it pays out, every line and followed through. Otherwise, we are being asked to operate in an emotional vacuum and believe what we are told. The tenderness of any poem depends on the skepticism of a full form filled.

In free verse especially the full form means full disclosure—sometimes of the story but always of the emotion. "The Prayer . . ." is a recently published poem, one that all too easily expects to fulfill the poet's personal sense that "one must have the character of a great man who loves women, children, and the speech of his native place, and the luminous spirit that lurks frightened in the tortured bodies of the sick and the poor." If this sounds like a description of Charles Dickens, that is no accident. Wright is the great empathizer of American poetry, a master whose work as a whole has redefined the emotional life available to a poem. The old Ph.D. praying may lack the context of his convictions, but convictions he has. In a more representative voice, and one that well anticipates future work, Wright continues the innocence abroad that distinguished *Two Citizens*.

*By the Ruins of a Gun Emplacement:*
*Saint Benoît*

Behind us, the haystack rustles
Into the summer dusk, and the limber girl's knees
Alone are barely visible among the rust
Of grape leaves. We are one face
Gazing into another, dim.

What shall we do if the round moon comes down
The river alone,
And strolls up out of the Loire
To make once more his command of these pastures,
Orchards, and the many bypaths for wandering,
Takes them for his own once more, his own
Paternal fields?

121

As the lovers scuffle
In the drying coins of the dewfall behind us,
I can close my eyes and see the tall young
Noble the moon, pausing
A mile or so down river, inland
Maybe three quarters of a mile
By the sandpit pond. There, no one at nightfall
Pauses alone with his wine. There, no one
At dewrise but only the moon
Lifting deliberately, between the long slim
Fingers, the startling faces
Of night creatures. Who are they?

I met a snail on a stone at Fleury,
Where, now, Max Jacob walks happily among the candles
Of his brothers, but still do not know
The snail's secret.
I do not even know
What we shall do if the round moon comes down
The river and strolls up
Out of the Loire
To take once more your startling face up
Among his drowsed swans,
All three, whose names,
Dewfall and Nightrise and Basilica,
Napoleon stole from Spanish horses
A dusk long ago, before the last time

Somebody gouged a trench along the Loire.

We often speak of form as if it were something else, something separable from its source and destiny. Even as one body being filled by another the gothic inclination is to seek out a corpse, to disinter. Form is a performance, an enactment rather than an entity. For a poet like Wright form means having "pity/For the pure clear word." And for a poet of particular pathos it means having pity for the pure clear emotion. Form is a way of going, and coming back. "By the Ruins of a Gun Emplacement" is surrounded by the history of poetry—from "ruins" in the poetry of Warren to

Eliot to Browning back to Byron, all the way back to Horace—and by the history of itself—the gun emplacement being of World War II vintage. Max Jacob, for example, the French poet and friend of Apollinaire, was arrested at Saint-Benoît and later died in a German concentration camp. While the reference to Napoleon stealing names from Spanish horses only widens the circle. The poem is also surrounded by the poet's preoccupations—dusk, the moon, and, best of all, a great river. Ohio, Mississippi, Tiber, Loire, wherever he is Wright finds a river and creates a form in that unique category, the love poem-elegy. River and form are equally bent. The first time he asks, rhetorically, "What shall we do if the round moon comes down/The river," it is posed as a question, the second and last time it comes out as a declaration. Saint-Benoît is a place of dusk, at dusk. The moon, that "luminous spirit," that European history, that "tall young/Noble," is the poet's way of moving through the weighted dark toward some inevitable tenderness. The repetition of phrase and image, the free-verse rhythms at ease with the speaking voice, the details, the actual names of things all help suggest the dimensions of the motif while clarifying the emotion. The moon is less Wright's correlative than his correspondent. "We are one face/Gazing into another, dim." As through a glass darkly, the speaker and his wife watch, in a kind of wonder, as the close world around them becomes illuminated—both the world in its immediate "summer dusk" and the world in its larger time of a "dusk long ago." These two citizens are very much, at this moment, caught between times. That is part of why the speaker is apprehensive about "the moon/Lifting deliberately, between the long slim/Fingers, the startling faces/Of night creatures." In the anonymity of first dark they are night creatures too, among ruins.

Were this poem about Saint-Benoît and certain vague emotional attachments, "the rust/Of grape leaves," it would be little more than the indulgence of a Postmodern Georgian. The gun emplacement, however, is the hard evidence of context. The two citizens are the literal evidence of the emotion. The particular and certain knowledge of the poem is the knowledge that the moon may come down the river and stroll up out of the Loire "To take once more your startling face up/Among his drowsed swans." And we are one face. It is the history of a death that finally preoccupies this poet—not Max Jacob at Saint-Benoît but Max Jacob under stone at Fleury, who walked with his piece of the moon, "among the candles/Of his brothers." It is the moon knees of that "limber" girl that are answered in the "snail's secret." And it is the snail on the stone of Max Jacob's grave and the grave itself that are magnified into the three named swans and a trench gouged along the Loire.

Wright's gift to us is his ability to identify and identify with the sources of emotion. His poems are among the most generous we have because they risk again and again the tension of the form not finding what will suffice. "By the Ruins of a Gun Emplacement" is a love poem in the form of an elegy, an original sentimental occasion. Along with the moonlight, it celebrates the dusk, the river Loire, the dead, and the clarity and depth of a single experience made more singular by what we thought was familiar. Most of all it celebrates our "one face/Gazing into another, dim." This early and most isolated reference complicates the imagination of the rest of the poem. *Once more, once more*: between the living and the dead, between dewrise and nightfall, dewfall and nightrise, the basilic face of the moon is constant, like a muse, like a source of poetry that finds you out. The moon, that old history of an emotion, that old death mask, becomes more than Wright's inspiration; it is the antagonist who keeps the poet honest, who allows him to praise what we might otherwise reject. The moon is the source of tension here, for lovers and elegists. The idea is to enlarge the emotion of love with the possibility of pathos—to find, in form, no difference.

Nothing really happens in the poem. Except for the notice of the "scuffle," the moon is the only *event*. The action is internal, revelatory, disclosed as revelation, of one face showing itself to another. The landscape and the setting feel otherworldly, not just foreign. As the pastures and orchards and bypaths open up, as the river runs out, the poem must declare, in its last full stanza, its connections. Like the moon, the two citizens are, at this moment, between the summer dusk of the lovers and the long dusk of Jacob, Saint-Benoît, and Fleury. I still do not know, I do not even know, says the speaker. In the knowledge and acknowledgement of that doubt we are asked to enter the form of the emotion, its substance—we are asked what to do if the moon should come down the river, that long grave, "To take once more your startling face up/Among his drowsed swans."

1978

WHAT CEREMONY OF WORDS

*Resoluteness*
*Simplified me . . .*

"Her attitude to her verse was artisan-like: if she couldn't get a table out of the material, she was quite happy to get a chair, or even a toy. The end product was for her not so much a successful poem, as something that had temporarily exhausted her ingenuity." This comment by Ted Hughes, in 1981, in his well-known introduction to *The Collected Poems*, must have come as a surprise to many of Sylvia Plath's readers. Still nearly twenty years after her death, the notion that the poet of suicidal imperatives must be as committed to form, right up to the end of her career, as she appeared to be committed to content must have seemed secondary or at least beside the point. The poet who could begin her last poem with the knowledge that "The woman is perfected./Her dead/Body wears the smile of accomplishment" had surely transcended the duller duties of the artisan. Yet until the last year of Plath's life, March to February, her poems have none of the cold confessional, frenetic, lean, somebody's-done-for, apocalyptic drive of that sad time. Instead, they reveal a poetry preoccupied with the inventions of rhythm, pattern, and an emphatic, sometimes excessive aural sense of the way words bond within the line or sentence. They reveal a poetry in constant preparation for the next move, the next place to be—whether it meant slanting the rhyme, divesting the stanza of a scheme, or opening the poem to the indictment of immediate experience.

Perhaps those who preferred "the autobiography of a fever" in *Ariel*—Robert Lowell's phrase—were arguing against some of the first golden writing that appeared in magazines in the late 1950s, writing that could sound like:

Through fen and farmland walking
With my own country love
I saw slow flocked cows move

> White hulks on their day's cruising;
> Sweet grass sprang for their grazing.
>> ("Song for a Summer's Day")

Or perhaps they had in mind some of the formula writing that appeared in *The Colossus*, the table-chair-toy writing of the craftsman, so elaborate and insistent that even in "Black Rook in Rainy Weather," one of her strongest early poems, the abcde//abcde pattern of rhyme survives for seven stanzas. Elaborations of the labor of poetry tend to be the rule before 1959, the labor of apprenticing, so much so that John Frederick Nims could speak, in his review of *Ariel*, of the "drudgery" of the first book. What distinguishes Plath, though, from other budding formalists of the time is that she worked to invent forms rather than fill them. Aside from the obligatory school-girl sonnets and villanelles and sestinas, there are very few traditional forms in her career. She was always inventing, contriving, conjuring. Form was something she could create, even repeat; it could mean passage to the next poem, and to the experiment. Those who found *Ariel* profoundly different from the work that preceded it could have looked back, for formal guidance and anticipation, to "Mushrooms," the last poem written for the first book.

> Overnight, very
> Whitely, discreetly,
> Very quietly
>
> Our toes, our noses
> Take hold on the loam,
> Acquire the air.

And before that to "Moonrise" ("Death whitens in the egg and out of it./I can see no color for this whiteness./White: it is a complexion of the mind."). And before that to "The Thin People" ("Empty of the complaint, forever/ Drinking vinegar from tin cups: they wore//The insufferable nimbus of the lot-drawn/ Scapegoat . . ."). And before that to a small piece of a poem entitled "Resolve"—

Day of mist: day of tarnish

with hands
unserviceable, I wait
for the milk van
the one-eared cat
laps its gray paw—

of which these are the first few lines, written in 1956. Cat's paws, thin people, and mushrooms are obviously not the issue here. The predominant mode of *Ariel* is couplets and triplets, and the short line, stanzas of psychological shorthand, of the quick take, the hook. Whatever the difference on the scale of pain the poems of the last year represent, they had models for their making, antecedents for their craft.

If *Ariel* was, and has been since, worshiped for its perceived confessional content, its doom images, its words-torn-from-the death-flesh heart of experience, worshiped for poems, in Lowell's phrase, that "play Russian roulette with six cartridges in the cylinder," it is also a book justly celebrated for its powerful and poignant testimony—at the nerve end and at the cutting edge—of a life that became simply too vulnerable. At its best it survives the "O-gape of complete despair" by the sheer discipline of its art. But we need accept neither the cynicism of Hugh Kenner, who maintains that "all Plath's life, a reader had been someone to manipulate," nor the anxiety of A. Alvarez, who speculates that "it is as though she had decided that, for her poetry to be valid, it must tackle head-on nothing less than her own death," to question assumptions about the nature of Plath's achievement and the position her most famous book holds within the perspective of her *Collected Poems*. What concerns me, as it has concerned others, is that the biography and autobiography, *The Bell Jar* and the letters, the rumor and the psychoanalysis not displace the beauty and triumph of the range of her art. Whatever "confessional" means to poetry to which it is too often ill-ascribed, it is first of all a kind of journalism, a reductive label intended to *get at* something in the work, something of publicity value. It is about the news in a poem, its gossip. With the names and the dates in place, it would paraphrase, extrapolate, the projected psychological content, not unlike the theme-mongering sometimes promoted in the academy. Except that it would not be looking for ideas but intimacy, the dream-data, the midnight or dawn compulsions; it would turn poetry into the prose of therapy. And it would fantasize the poet as victim and the domestic and daily terrors of the world as villain, chief of which is the paradigm of the lost or bad parent. "We suggest that a pattern of guilt over imagined incest informs all of Plath's prose and poetry. When Otto Plath died of natural causes in a hospital on November 2, 1940, he might just as well have been a lover jilting his beloved." Whether the critic here is right or wrong is not the issue; the issue is that Plath's guilt is irrelevant to the good reading of her poems. Not that we need to see her poetry in isolation or in a vacuum, but independent of tabloid vagaries and mythic pretensions. The life in her poetry is a transformation, not an imitation. Its terms and its struggles are acted out within the form, within the crux and often crisis of form. "Daddy" may or may not be light verse, as Plath herself once suggested. It is certainly less confessional than it is persona writing—intoxicating, relentless, allegorical, and, finally, dark. It is patently ironical, and nearly Swiftian in its satire. "Lady Lazarus" may or may not be a signature poem, but it is far too close to being a parody of the poet as suicide and the publicity of suicide to be confessional. Taken straight, beware, beware, it is only funny, or worse, bald angry. The fact that these poems too have antecedents in earlier work ("Daddy" as far back as the rhythms of "The Disquieting Muses"—"I learned, I learned, I learned elsewhere,/From muses unhired by you, dear mother"; "Lady Lazarus" as far back as the gothicism of "All the Dead Dears"—"This lady here's no kin/Of mine, yet kin she is: she'll suck/Blood and whistle my marrow clean") implies that even angst requires strategy and preparation in order to be effective, especially under the pressures of the psychological extreme. They are both crafty poems, with histories to their craft. Nazi lampshades and Meinkampf looks, vampirism and witchery are part of the planning, among the buttons pushed. Plath did not suddenly become a poet with such poems or with the publication of *Ariel*, nor did she become a success at the moment of her death. She worked hard at an art for which she had the gift for a good ten years.

We can run a search for the Medusan imagery or plead a case for the Yeatsian cosmology, we can concentrate on the "Sivvy" poems (mother) or on the beekeeper poems (father), we can read her as a romantic or as a precipitant expressionist, we can locate influences as different as Theodore

Roethke and Wallace Stevens. We can, in the long postmortem, see her as Esther Greenwood or as Lady Lazarus, daughter or mother, supplicant or applicant, sinned against or sinning. We can place her in history or alone with her ambitions. We can test Plath's work, in other words, in any number of ways alternate to the trials and errors of confessionalism. And we have. But where is there room, in the various critical/biographical approaches, for the unforced visual quality of "Departure," written in 1956 and included in *The Colossus*; where is there room for the aural power and density of "Blackberrying," written in the early fall of 1961 and excluded from *Ariel*— among the assumptions about her content and the "staticky/Noise of the new"; among the attractions of violence, both sentimental and rhetorical, where is the notice, in Keats's word, of Plath's capacity for *disinterestedness*, her ability to be at one with or disappear into the richness of the text?

At one level, "Departure" looks to be not much more than a sharply focused study, in brilliant painter's terms, of a fishing village, Benidorm, along the Spanish coast: table and chair work, even though the concretion of images generates especial energy.

> The figs on the fig tree in the yard are green;
> Green, also, the grapes on the green vine
> Shading the brickred porch tiles.
> The money's run out.
>
> How nature, sensing this, compounds her bitters.
> Ungifted, ungrieved, our leavetaking.
> The sun shines on unripe corn.
> Cats play in the stalks.
>
> Retrospect shall not soften such penury—
> Sun's brass, the moon's steely patinas,
> The leaden slag of the world—
> But always expose
>
> The scraggy rock spit shielding the town's blue bay
> Against which the brunt of outer sea
> Beats, is brutal endlessly.
> Gull-fouled, a stone hut

131

> Bares its low lintel to corroding weathers:
> Across the jut of ochreous rock
> Goats shamble, morose, rank-haired,
> To lick the sea-salt.

The sea, the coastal territory, "water striving to reestablish its mirror/Over the rock," will become central, even stock figures in Plath's work right to the end. In this poem, perhaps the first purely realized of her early pieces, a poem fairly free of the self-conscious and compacting busyness of a great deal of the writing at this time, the sea and environs represent the antagonist, the life principle. They help make it possible for the object world itself to become the subject, because unlike the majority of the popular writing starring the first-person singular Plath, this piece mutes the position of the speaker to simple motivational status—resignation. "The money's run out.//Ungifted, ungrieved, our leavetaking." What shines in the real eye is correlative nature. True, in its own way, it is a natural world that could hardly be called neutral—what is not kinetic is vitally colorful—but neither is it parceled into the raw examples of what become, later, psychic fractures. This "quick" study reads whole, it pays attention, directly, to detail—the green figs and grapes, the cats in the unripe corn—and without editorial help allows the details to develop and complicate the moment on their own. The half-serious line "Retrospect shall not soften such penury" permits the poet her chance to project: from that rhetorical line the images go up in volume and increase in intensity. The simple fact of penury and the need to move on, the poem's motivation, force a growth in strategy—the eye can no longer just see, it must interpret. Interpret the biography behind the poem.

This is the way in which, in the logic and psychologic of the structure, brass and steely patinas, nature compounds her bitters, the natural corroding weathers of the rest of the experience, leading all the way back to the flat report that the money's run out. Nothing in this poem, therefore, is imposed from outside its world. Its lines of clear delineation and projection come from within what is immediately and dramatically established, as in any well told story. Compare the longer, softer rhythms of the first three lines to the same length of work in the last two stanzas; once the money's gone (penury), the rhythms turn tighter, much more consonantal, and abrupt. Thus we know, in the plot of things, why the prosody has changed, and we know, by the time the sea is brutal endlessly, that something serious is at stake without the speaker having to promote her cause. Later, of course, by 1962, what is at stake in Plath's best poems will take on absolute proportions. By then they will have acquired so much external life, such an autobiographic force-field, that it will seem difficult to judge whether a particular poem has created sufficient self-reference not to depend on the author's prose therapies.

"Departure" represents a psychological landscape (seascape). It is as well an accurate rendering: it begins and ends *inside* the picture, within the framing warmth of the fig trees and the harshness of the sea-salt. Its otherness is the object, and objective, world, but also natural, chronological, alive. A few years into the future, Plath will write, along with "Mussel Hunter at Rock Harbor," "Tulips," and "Last Words," one of her finest poems of that narrative, objective category in which the line-into-sentence is extended in time, and connects and continues fully enough to fill the white space— her "wide" poetry, as one observer puts it. "Blackberrying" rests somewhere between the beating of the outer sea of "Departure" and the Devon coast of "Sheep in Fog," where the "hills step off" into whiteness. It certainly rests between them "stylistically," between the clearly delineated shapes and solids of the older poem and the spare, poetry-as-absence surrealism of one of her last.

> Nobody in the lane, and nothing, nothing but blackberries,
> Blackberries on either side, though on the right mainly,
> A blackberry alley, going down in hooks, and a sea
> Somewhere at the end of it, heaving. Blackberries
> Big as the ball of my thumb, and dumb as eyes
> Ebon in the hedges, fat
> With blue-red juices. These they squander on my fingers.
> I had not asked for such a blood sisterhood; they must love me.
> They accommodate themselves to my milkbottle, flattening their
>     sides.
>
> Overhead go the choughs in black, cacophonous flocks—
> Bits of burnt paper wheeling in a blown sky.
> Theirs is the only voice, protesting, protesting.

I do not think the sea will appear at all.
The high, green meadows are glowing, as if lit from within.
I come to one bush of berries so ripe it is a bush of flies,
Hanging their bluegreen bellies and their wing panes in a Chinese
     screen.
The honey-feast of the berries has stunned them; they believe in
     heaven.
One more hook, and the berries and bushes end.

The only thing to come now is the sea.
From between two hills a sudden wind funnels at me,
Slapping its phantom laundry in my face.
These hills are too green and sweet to have tasted salt.
I follow the sheep path between them. A last hook brings me
To the hills' northern face, and the face is orange rock
That looks out on nothing, nothing but a great space
Of white and pewter lights, and a din like silversmiths
Beating and beating at an intractable metal.

Eliot is fond of referring to the "aural imagination," the ability of the language to transform the music in and of the image in the process of its pronouncement. Valéry speaks, in his notebooks, of the language within language. And Rilke says that "if a thing is to speak to you, you must regard it for a certain time as the only one that exists." "Blackberrying," it seems to me, brings together the best vocal and most effective visual impulses in Plath's poetry. It gives the speaker her role without sacrificing the poem's purchase on the actual impinging natural world. It enlarges rather than reduces. Its ceremony comes from one of the poet's most disguised sources, the small moment, the domestic life. ("Mushrooms," the poems for her children, the poppy poems all share, for example, a sense of size, even though they derive from objects and experiences small and diurnal in scale.) "Blackberrying" likewise isolates the action to the job at hand, and to the story line. But unlike the sound and image effects of poems better known, this one is not driving nails, sawing on one Orphic string, or ritualizing an extreme psychological state. No question that at the point of entry the reader is tested: either accept the muscular terms of the poem or stay out. Timed in the present progressive, it opens in motion, in saturation, incan-

tatory. We are led immediately, in hooks, down a blackberry alley, where a
sea, somewhere at the end of it, is heaving. The impression is one of tun-
neling, of being drawn into and through narrow, yet thick space. All the
senses are crowded, even exchanged ("Blackberries/Big as the ball of my
thumb, and dumb as eyes/Ebon in the hedges, fat . . ."). What is remarkable
is the way Plath, in shifting the context of the blackberries from container
(alley) to contained (milkbottle), intensifies the feel of claustrophobia.
Once the berries are in the bottle—"they squander on my fingers . . . they
must love me"—they flatten their sides in order to accommodate; they, in
effect, choke on the space. It is a brilliant telescoping and projecting and
resolving of the speaker's "going down in hooks," and is prepared by a stanzaic pattern of free verse that allows the middle lines to fill before breaking at emphatic (sea/Blackberries/eyes/fat) hooks in the sentence. The
credibility and vitality of the movement of the full stanza, however, are
validated by what will carry the rest of the poem—Plath's skill at creating
aural equivalents, images that gain their first power from their hearing. The
first line, for instance, though one of the least apparent "imaged" in the
poem, still manages to effect a strong visual pull by letting "nobody in
the lane" be picked up and quickly reinforced by "nothing, nothing" only
to bump, abruptly, into "but blackberries." It is a line of wonderful subtraction by addition, the content filling the needs of the form. This same
sense of abutment structures the remaining stanza. By repeating and paralleling the word "blackberries" three strategic times, Plath makes, in effect, a single alley-and-hook sentence down to the last two and a half lines.
Then, like a stepping-off of periods, she shuts off with three full stops, each
a little longer in coming than the one before. This vertical rhythm is what
pacing in a poem, and music in poetry, is all about.

If the enclosures of the alley and milkbottle help organize the experience in the beginning stanza, the plan of the whole poem becomes obvious
by the second. The cloister opens to the overarching sky, and by the third
stanza to the open sea. This Devon landscape-to-seascape is right out of
Hardy—nobody in the lane, far from the madding crowd. In just the time
it takes to get from the blackout, blackberry close of the alley, where we
can hear the great source "heaving," to the "high, green meadows," over
which go birds that are "bits of burnt paper wheeling in a blown sky," we
realize the speaker is being pulled along, compelled. The mimetic language

is becoming denser, a little waxy—"the choughs in black, cacophonous flocks." The first three lines of the second stanza, in fact, press their vocalization, their repetitions of sounds—"protesting, protesting"—about as far as they dare, leading the poet to counter the buildup, as she does everywhere in the poem, with a flat, declarative notice, in this case, that "I do not think the sea will appear at all." Two of the longest lines Plath ever wrote appear at the end of this stanza. They make a kind of couplet, coming out of one of the poem's best balanced lines:

> I come to one bush of berries so ripe it is a bush of flies,
> Hanging their bluegreen bellies and their wing panes in a Chinese
> screen.
> The honey-feast of the berries has stunned them; they believe in
> heaven.

Looking ahead to the denials in the forms of the later work, we can appreciate the fecundity here, not simply in the fullness of the image of the berries, but in the progression of the idea of the berries—berries, flies, bellies, wing panes, honey-feast, heaven. And the berries that have been blue-red juices so squandered on fingers they must love me are now the honey-feast of flies that believe in heaven. This is the countryside of health; the speaker's senses are sated. There is uncharacteristic generosity in this writing *sans* the sometimes characteristic rhetoric. There is giving-over to the world, to the natural world, to the life outside, beyond the nerve ends of the self. Giving over, however, does not mean giving up. "The only thing to come now is the sea," announces the speaker at the start of the last stanza. She emerges, as into a sense of light, from the winding sheep path, from the high meadows, from the blackberry alley, with the wind, the open wind, suddenly blowing its phantom laundry in her face. The close, interior dimensions of where she has come from in order to get here, having been called by the clues of the heaving of wind on water and overhead, having picked her way—of all tests—through blackberries, have brought her, one last hook, to the edge, the north face.

Plath's position at the end of "Blackberrying" is a reading of her position for the remainder of her life leading up to the "edge" of her last poem. "We have come so far, it is over." Here, however, at this full and apparently open moment, looking toward the complementary, fantasy coast of Brittany (another "Finisterre"), it is not over. The sea may be "beating at an intractable metal" and the speaker may be looking out at "a great space," but this climactic image, as psychologically as it is actually audible, underscores the rich, insulating presence of the whole of this writing. Nearly every line risks the heavy hand that has marked too many of her narrative-nature poems: the clogged consonance, the alliterative tattoo, the aureate weight of the diction. Yet the insistent winding path of its structure (the movement from the blind and sensual alley to the meadow sighting of bird flocks and flies to the vulnerability of the dissociative mind confronting the intractable) and the absorption of the speaker into the flow of the action (though she is the actor, she is led) help keep the language of "Blackberrying" on the line and ensure that the incantatory effects result from the inwardness of the experience, from even the threat of the experience. The images of the Chinese screen and the metal of silversmiths, as opposed to the homely milkbottle, may seem extracurricular to the landscape of the poem, but they are as much a part of the transformation as are the choral features of nothing, nothing, protesting, protesting, beating, beating. These images are projections; their dimensions get their measure within the text. If the speaker, ontologically, is as cut off by the white and pewter lights and the din of the silversmiths as she has been by the opacity of the blackberries and the bush of flies, perhaps we have come back to the "nothing" in the last stanza for a reason. Her condition, throughout the poem, is static, in a dark that is blind and in a light that is blinding. It is the blackberrying itself that is the motion, the active principle. But it is more than a motive: it is the act of the lyric form answering itself at every turning, every *ing*, making the emotion an enclosure.

"Blackberrying" is high rhetorical style compared to the great majority of poems that finally make it into the posthumous *Ariel*. Only "The Moon and the Yew Tree" and "Tulips" suggest its density of texture, though in tone they both better approximate the "light of the mind" of what became a very strange and luminous book. If Valéry is right, that form in poetry is the voice in action, then Plath was obviously in some debate as to what her true voice was: the poet of riches or the poet of austerity, the poet of connection or the poet of the quick cut. It is a formal debate inherent in her career, declaration or denial. To her credit, she allowed the debate to become dialectic, allowing the energy of the argument to produce rather than paralyze the work at hand. Nevertheless, by the end of her life—the last year, year and a half—it is clear that the poetry of absence, "words dry and riderless," is the rule. So much so that almost every good poem in the manner of

> Axes
> After whose stroke the wood rings,
> And the echoes!
> Echoes traveling
> Off from the center like horses

turns into an *ars poetica*, an address of and to her art. Which is to say that concomitant with the struggle for life is her struggle with the form her passion wished to take. Poems as superficially variant in subject as "Words" and "Sheep in Fog" and the incomparable "Ariel" share this interest in self-reflexive, self-defining purity of purpose, and each chooses the expressive terms of "indefatigable hoof-taps" ("Words") and "hooves, dolorous bells" ("Sheep in Fog") to enact the purification. "Ariel" is, of course, Plath's singular and famous example of the form completely at one with its substance, the language exactly the speedy act of its text. The point for the poet is obvious: "How one we grow,/Pivot of heels and knees." The speaker thus becomes as much Ariel as the horse, and together they become the one thing, the poem itself, "the arrow,//The dew that flies/Suicidal, at one with the drive." The run from stasis in darkness into the red eye of morning is a miraculous inhabiting, in which the natural and referential world dissembles, blurs into absence, to the point that the transformation of the horse and rider can become absolute. "Something else//Hauls me through air. . . ." In seconds, she is a white Godiva, unpeeling dead hands and stringencies, then, almost simultaneously, she is foam to wheat, and at that freeing instant, in terror or in ecstasy, the child's cry melts in the wall. "Ariel" is as close to a poetry of pure, self-generating, associative action as we could hope for, as if the spirit, at last, had found its correlative, had transcended, in the moment, memory. Mallarmé once speculated that the ideal poem would be "a reasonable number of words stretched beneath our mastering glance, arranged in enduring figures, and followed by silence." This is generic enough to account for a lot of symbolist writing. It certainly accounts for the black-eyed berries that cast dark hooks and the deafening pewter lights at the edge of the open sea.

Plath did not live long enough to sort out a form that could negotiate between the enclosing rhetoric of a "Blackberrying" and the absolute, exposed language of an "Ariel." Likely she would have never needed to. Likely this "third" form is a wished-for integration of personality, the healing of fracture. For me, though, the writing near the end is not up to the discipline of "Ariel," and feels instead a little starved, anorectic. Such writing may be accurate of the state of her soul, but it is beyond the perfection of her art, the perfection that "Blackberrying," in September of 1961, and "Ariel," in October of 1962, individually represent. Here is a poet who could either project into the landscape or internalize it so as to disappear; she could both narrate and configure experience. In either case, she was committed to the transforming powers of the art, emblems of a life outside her own. Putting the "blood sisterhood" of "Blackberrying" beside the red-eyed cauldron sunrise of "Ariel," we can begin to see that behind the separate masks, all the masks of her good poems, there is a unity, an integrity, and an integrating of imagination, so that whatever the hammer-splittings of the self, behind the sad mask of the woman is the mind and heart of someone making transcendent poems. To the extent that Plath is "artisan-like" is the extent to which she is whole. Beginning in the fall of 1961, she will have written the truest symbolist poetry we have had since Hart Crane, and before him since Dickinson.

1985

LYRIC YOGA

# 1

I blame, in part, my sometimes inability to sit still on those hours of hardwood silence endured at meeting. They felt unendurable, I'm sure, because, at nine or ten or twelve years of age, sitting still for long stretches is antithetical to a child's nature and because breaking the silence by speaking in front of a lot of people, especially people as alternately dour or fired up as Quakers, is worse. Even the adults, I remember thinking, must be speaking up in order to relieve the body's boredom. I don't believe that by college meeting got more comfortable—not that comfort was its point—so I finally stopped going and ultimately chose to meditate and articulate by other means: in solitude and at the typewriter.

What I took away from Quaker collective meditation was the good sense of stillness—not so much its length in time as its presence within the space of things, which translated as the need for reflection, a sense of order and mindfulness, and a way to reach the insights of contemplation, the deep interior moment. The Quaker concept of the inner light became an opportunity for self-interrogation, self-witness. Giving witness, I later remembered, was exactly what meeting was all about. And stillness and its silence were the place where you could arrive at an understanding of mind and heart, even if you kept it to yourself.

Stillness within the self, within the silence. Being alone is what writing is about. Writing is giving witness. In my attention-deficit years, sitting in meeting in relative motionlessness inside a cave of Quaker rectitude was difficult enough; the thought of having to stand—worse than in school—and speak from whatever shallow depths of my being I could muster was paralyzing. My tongue turned to wood, hardwood. When I started, seriously, to write I learned that being alone with blank white paper was no less intimidating, no less a publicity. I also learned that stillness was inwardness and a way to prepare to speak, the deep dream and daydream the content of the words. Writing became the restlessness answering the stillness. To the degree that sitting still, moving inward, having insight are virtues of meditative silence, the complexity of the process also involves finding a form to express the experience. Poetry, for me, was that form.

## 2

Stillness and restlessness, related or separate, have become one of my poetry's themes. More importantly, they have become essential to the way I make poems, the way I sit in a chair and address the page and the way I interrupt myself to pace or think or empty the moment in order to start again. Writing—its concentrations, demands, anxieties, joys, backs and forths—is so intimately tied to the body and at the same time about leaving the body that it's sometimes impossible to distinguish into twos its singular experience. Which is why most writers' time at the desk means getting lost in time. The physical body becomes the host for the spiritual traveler. In this sense, stillness comes to represent the body, restlessness the imagination.

One, however, could easily argue the matter the other way around. That is the beauty of polarity. Restlessness is the body's inclination, stillness the spirit's great desire, not unlike T. S. Eliot's famous Chinese jar moving perpetually in its stillness. The body sits at its angle of repose or angst and allows the mind to do its work, just as the fingers translate, even transform, what the mind speaks. Are the words on the field of the page more physical or spiritual realities, actual or ontological, or is one merely passage to the other, not possible without the other—in effect, a simultaneity? This is, of course, a rhetorical question. We are told, in various philosophies, that the alphabetical letters I'm writing right now simultaneously stand for something, like agreeable math. But if the letters are obscure, the handwriting poor, the typing sloppy, the words on the computer screen ungrammatical, the sentences in makeshift paragraphs confusing, what is represented except an attempt at communication? Writing, literally, needs to be artistic; writing, figuratively, must be art. The subtleties, the tones, the implications, the nuances, the edges and angles, meanings and possibilities are otherwise blurred, distorted, dumb.

The act of writing may be a restlessness. The result is its stillness, a text fit for both contemplation and revelation. Writing perfects the writer; it also completes longing in the reader. Writing and reading are stillness and restlessness closed into a whole performance. In "Thirteen Ways of Looking at a Blackbird," Wallace Stevens states right out that he doesn't know which to prefer,

The beauty of inflections
Or the beauty of innuendoes,
The blackbird whistling
Or just after.

For the writer, subsumed in the silence of making something, there's little difference between before and after, memory and the moment, the instant and its resonance. The inflection is the innuendo. The restlessness can only speak through stillness, just as the fullness must first be empty.

Your whole life you are two with one taken
away. The inadequate air and fire,
the inadequate joy, the darknesses
of the room so gathered at the window
as to fly, wing on wing on wing open
against the glass, opening and closing,
bone, blood and wrist. But nothing happens but
exhaustion and evidence of the eyes,
the red-gold cloud-break morning beginning

with the objects that floated in the dark
draining back to the source, floating back to
the surface tension of things, those objects
struck the way the first light starts suddenly,
then slowly in relief across the room,
the window's shadow garden come back one
last time once more from the leaves. Waking now,
the door half-open, open, the doorway's
blindness or blackness silence to be filled.

These first two stanzas from a forty-five line poem of mine refer to a series of mornings when I'd wake up with the early light and wait, in half-sleep, for the full sun. The time seemed interminable—a throwback to the internal time of meetings in my childhood—with the graduating shadow-play of sunlight coming into consciousness, while the body lay in recess. Slow waking was also the mind coming alive, making connections, associations, organizing an inferred narrative. The lighter it got, the richer the visual mix. When I thought about the experience later, and over the next many days and weeks, it turned into language, into an imaginative event, based on an understanding of and insight into what started it. Writing became a mediation of a meditative moment: a meditation, in fact, of what became a spiritual experience. The whistling and just after.

# 3

Everything I've so far said about stillness and poetry, about the byplay and polarity of restlessness and stillness, meditation and silence, insight and articulation can be applied to the principles and practice of yoga. This is true whether one is seeking physical or spiritual focus, epiphany or some involuntary combination, whether one is looking for holistic health or the sublimity of beatitude. To say that poetry is a kind of yoga, or the other way around, is to observe the obvious. And yoga is no less susceptible to cliché than poetry is. Yoga has become so generic an American activity and so generally applied that what one means by invoking it may be one thing here and another there. One hears of power yoga, slow yoga, aerobic yoga, movement yoga, dancing yoga; one is distantly aware of Tantra yoga, jnana yoga, raja yoga; and through a graduation of asanas or pure pranayama, one may wish to achieve a state approaching true kundalini. Yoga may be, according to *Psychology Today*, the fastest-growing "fitness training" in America, but you have to wonder what the Bhagavad Gita or the Upanishads or the Vedic hymns would make of yoga as gym art.

B. K. S. Iyengar has commented that "the original idea of yoga is freedom and beatitude, and the by-products which come along the way, including physical health, are secondary for the practitioner." Iyengar has trained many of the contemporary American practitioners of hatha yoga, who themselves are now teachers. Hatha refers to that force within us that, when released, leads to self-transformation, self-transcendence. Yoga postures are part of the means to that end. They include siddha-asana and mountain pose, both emphatic postures of vertical stillness, postures of the body erect between two worlds, earth and fire. It's hard to get away from the body, the form, as the vessel in which the content of the mind, heart, and spirit

146

are lifted; it's hard to get away from the spine as the ascending ladder or the breath as the good ghost of our being. Yoga fails when the body becomes the end in itself; yet yoga is only rhetoric without the body to bear its message. In the short seven years I've been doing yoga, at a kind of good middling second level, I've come to realize that though performing the postures themselves may be the blackbird whistling, the real effect comes just after, when the freedom of the release becomes joy.

Writing poems may or may not be yoga by other means. Poems as such, however, do take on the dynamic interactions implicit in yoga, particularly in the way that form and content, body and mind, turn inseparable. Poems, in this sense, like all art, represent the ideas as well as the ideals of the poses: balance, breath, movement within stillness, clarity, empathy, discovery, inevitability, release, and the quiet sublime of a reference outside the self. The claims of yoga, nevertheless, are only as good as its practice, regardless of any high-minded talk surrounding its teaching. The same is true for poetry, or of any human activity that aspires to grace. When I think about it, Quaker meeting, writing poems, and practicing yoga, as a chronology, have formed a link in helping to create the expressive texture in my life. The experience of the one has found fulfillment in the next—to the extent that meditation and making and "posing" have melded into a single process, in which doing one recalls the others.

We say that the body is a temple, because we know that it's nothing but mortal architecture without the self-regard of consciousness and conscience. The contemplative moment draws us to our sources; we see inside. We close our eyes, in fact, in order to see with clarity. Indeed, the imagination asks us to see with our eyes closed. So we make connections in the dark and thus we imagine what our bodies can do and be, how the breath of the spirit can come and go with perfection, how the ladder gravity of the spine can soar. Poets speak of rhythm and breath as the lifeline of the poetic line; they speak of form as the embodiment of the poem's energy, the bodying forth of its meaning and being. To expire is to breathe out, to inspire is to breathe in. To aspire is to breathe with the mind, to give purpose to the heart's rhythm. The spine is an aspiration, too, since it lifts us from foundations. To imagine what the body can achieve is to invest it with awareness—to begin to make it twice alive: first as a body, then as an embodiment.

# 4

Whatever vision I aspire to in my poems, I'm basically a practical person. That is, I try to live within myself and move through the world with a certain economy: economy of speech, manner, gesture, purpose, and desire. Like many practical people, I hate waste—wasted energy, wasted words, wasted means. W. B. Yeats once defined poetry as wasted breath, but he intended his description as an economical, ironic, understated observation. From a didactic point of view, poetry is wasted breath, since it's wasted into language as lyric, as music itself is wasted into the air. The poetry of yoga wastes its breath a lot like music, since breath—its expiration, inspiration, aspiration—is exercise of the spirit. Waste and renewal, waste and renewal—every pose seems to be working to right the balance between waste and renewal, the balance between giving back to the air and taking back in from the air, as if we were rediscovering the lungs of our original nature.

The first lesson of yoga is how to build an economy of breathing, how to find the best balance between the voice in the air outside and the voice that is great—in Stevens's fine phrase—within us. When that balance is abridged or confused in some way, as it so often is in the dailiness of our lives, we seem to black out a bit, become disoriented, frustrated, depressed; we start to list or stoop and suffer a diminishment. To lift the spirit—quite literally—is to correct from imbalance to balance our breathing, to reestablish its healthy, inherent economy.

In my limited experience, I've found that the actual quality and tones of voice of the yoga instructor have a great deal to do with coming to an understanding of balanced breathing. I've been lucky in that the person I've studied with for the past seven years has one of those voices that speaks from the heart without a trace of hype or strain, someone who, without the appearance of trying, transforms the instruction into images. Yoga, I've come to realize, is almost as much about the right economy of words and imagination as it is about the best balance of breath. Of course, the words are breath, and the body the extension of the breathing. The language of the instructor becomes the student's language, part of the body's honesty with itself. And what is the voice except the pose honestly enacted?

"I saw a yogi remain in the air, several feet above the ground last night at a group meeting"—this detail from Paramahansa Yogananda's *Autobiography of a Yogi*. Levitation, real or perceived, as a true or false economy, may or may not be of value. One has one's own opinions regarding the miraculous. But levitation, as a rich imaginative experience of the body's victory over gravity, is exactly what true yoga economy is about. By victory I mean balance, resistance, polarity with the ground—as even, the poet says, the invisible breath of the spirit must abide the earth. The right human voice, as much a part of nature as birdsong, is words relative to the gravity or levity of their rendering. The yoga body wants to be of that voice, at one with it.

# 5

The sun god Apollo is not only the god of poetry but the god of light and healing. It's good to remember this connection in respect to yoga, which seeks to repair through enlightenment. The Apollonian metaphor suggests the body in darkness needing to be brought into the health of sunshine— perhaps not so much the extreme of noon as the quieter, softer healing light of dawn and sunset, each twilights in their way. Thus the figure of Apollo more than likely suggests the body and soul in shadow needing to be brought to a place beyond ambiguity and ambivalence. What I like most about the Quakers is their belief that the light is already there, inside us, at about one candlepower, meaning that it's a meditative light of understated divinity. For the ancient Greeks and Romans—as well as the Romantic John Keats—Apollo was divine. For anyone seriously studying yoga it's understood that the self itself is part of a divinity, a natural, ecumenical divinity. Like it or not, religious orthodoxy tends to be a strong noon light pouring down on things. Divinity of the spirit is more like Emily Dickinson's "certain slant of light," at early morning and evening, part of nature.

What is especially beautiful about early and late light is how quiet it is. The dark and high noon have their own special invisible sounds. But angular light is healing, and a state of beauty we are drawn to. The third stanza of the poem I quoted earlier has a Lazarus figure locked inside the tomb of his own darkness.

A man was sick, a sickness unto death.
All he wanted to do was lie down,
let the light pick him apart like the dust.
He wrapped himself in his mind, in his own
absence. He did not want to hear the rain,
with its meaning, nor the moment after
rain, nor the sound of Jesus weeping, nor
the dreaming, which is memory, though he
lay a long time cold, head against the stone.

Morning light is a coming into wakefulness, evening light into aware-ness. Probably the best time to practice yoga is when the sun is breaking or setting over water, a plain, or between mountains. Most of us, though, live in cities, where buildings form the landscape. It's tempting in cities to look into mirrors rather than see through windows. But yoga, emphatically in an urban landscape, is about windows, windows above the heaviness of noise and distraction, and closer to the sun's salutation. City or country, among buildings or trees, the poetry of yoga asks us to rise from the dark weight of the night's body or the dead weight of the day's and become alive again, to be lighter in every possible way. And to see with the insight of quiet light.

When I was a boy my father and I would drive up to Canada to fish. The lakes there are famous for their stillness and darkness, their depth and cold. Evenings, sometimes, if we'd made a good catch of pike or pickerel and had a good meal, he'd let me lie in the bottom of the boat off a long line from the shore so that I could drift a little and look at the sky, which seemed like a lake itself, large and deep and pure, with gold and silver twilight ever so slowly, ever so softly about to slip under. The enormous edges of the lake were long since in silhouette and distant, and the summer sounds barely audible, so I had this feeling of floating between the stilled buoyancy of the water and the great silence of the star-filled sky. It was a feeling of immense disappearance, or of joining something larger. Perhaps it was like that feeling we have in dreams of falling or flying, where we are taken out of ourselves, if momentarily. It was a kind of feeling children often natu-rally discover and one that adults often try to get back to.

2001

AUTOBIOGRAPHY AND ARCHETYPE

# 1

When Wallace Stevens writes that you must become an ignorant man again and see the sun again with an ignorant eye and see it clearly in the idea of it, he is focusing on one of the things basic to an archetype, which is its original sense of itself, its almost primordial a priori sense of itself, while suggesting, at the same time, another basic thing, which is an archetype's dependence on recurrence, reenactment, return. He is suggesting seeing the new in the old, the old in the new; seeing that, at once, the archetype is original and familiar, ancient and present, eternal and mortal; recognizing that its ghost cannot be summoned except in a living, particular moment. For the writer, the soul of that moment is the common life we call autobiography, since our identities depend so much on that with which we identify and that which identifies with us.

Yet just as there are no straight lines or corners in nature, there can be no easy lineation between the archetype and named experience. If there is too direct a connection the archetype usually degenerates into allegory. When I say bird flies between the cover of the woodland understory and the exposure of the open field, I'm aware, at some point, that a bird is also a symbol, more often than not a symbol, through its song, of longing, or through its flight, of life's brevity, as brief as a sparrow darting the length of a mead hall. When I say that a tree is a green complexity of time and change, mystery and clarity, I know that trees, by their silent natures and sentinel presences, are the nobility, and that the fountain branching of the elms that once lined both sides of the street, meeting in the middle, describes a vaulted, cathedral ceiling. When I evoke one of my parents, say my father, I want the experience in the poem to be fair to memory and larger than life, since *father* is word as well as specific flesh.

Archetypes, in the abstract, have a genius for generalization. But to be of any use they must be arrived at inductively. Autobiography, as remembered experience, is inductive; in fact, it is the first definition of inductive. Nevertheless, we may have had the experience, says Eliot, but missed the meaning, as if meaning were inherent in, concomitant with, the experience. Seeing, or remembering, is a way to get the meaning, the idea as well as the image, just as experience itself repeats and returns, becomes general, common. Archetype is the machinery through which autobiography achieves something larger than the single life; and autobiography is the means by which archetypes are renewed.

Who am I, we sometimes ask ourselves, to have such a life? We call it a gift, I suppose, because we didn't ask for it. But because it is a gift it has a price. Who am I? "Death is the mother of beauty" is a matrix of archetypes—three very big ideas linked in a logic that makes a powerful one idea, an idea that requires us to see out of the old something new; and out of new connections a first idea. Who am I? is an old archetypal question, to which the answer is—regardless of who I think I am—my autobiography. Or would my biography by someone else better answer the question? Self-biography draws on resources that require us to see the archetypal within the actual, the eternal within the mortal, the parental within the beautiful. And to that extent archetypes are autobiographies of the imagination.

I once wrote, in "My Mother's Feet," that "Someone who loved her said she walked on water." The poem, in its way, is both an appreciation and a panegyric, an elegy to vulnerability. However ancient and mystical walking on water is, when I heard the comment in conversation when I was a boy, I knew that the expression was familiar and the idea rather wonderful but understood that it could also be either praise or putdown. For my mother, from the tone of what was said, I realized it must be praise, praise that as an adult I treat with a certain affection and irony, since my mother's feet were working feet, like a bricklayer's hands. Feet here become the synecdoche of an archetype, just as the action of the feet, in the auditory imagination, becomes the verbal act itself, which is central to the archetype as well—the literal metrical feet of the way the line walks the line and the way the caesura ("Someone who loved her//said she walked on water) marries the act to the internal rhyme. Words linked to words enact the oldest archetypes; they darken the breath with knowledge.

## 2

Stevens further writes that the first idea is an imagined thing—not so much made up as made visible. Insomnia has been an image in my poems from the beginning, an image of the terminal kind, the kind that causes you to wake up far earlier than you should, the kind that becomes like a dawn patrol. If sleep is *terra intermedia* (Jung), then terminal insomnia is an abrupt edge. It is one of those fundamental conditions that lends itself to trans-formation, and that echoes a first idea, an ancient survival mechanism. Lazarus, the ultimate insomniac, is a manifestation of the myth of resur-rection, just as resurrection is the sun rising. Terminal insomnia aborts this natural moment, anticipates the changing of dark to light.

*Lazarus at Dawn*

Your whole life you are two with one taken
away. The inadequate air and fire,
the inadequate joy, the darknesses
of the room so gathered at the window
as to fly, wing on wing on wing open
against the glass, opening and closing,
bone, blood and wrist. But nothing happens but
exhaustion and evidence of the eyes,
the red-gold cloud-break morning beginning

with the objects that floated in the dark
draining back to the source, floating back to
the surface tension of things, those objects
struck the way the first light starts suddenly,
then slowly in relief across the room,
the window's shadow garden come back one
last time once more from the leaves. Waking now,
the door half-open, open, the doorway's
blindness or blackness silence to be filled.

A man was sick, a sickness unto death.
All he wanted to do was to lie down,
let the light pick him apart like the dust.
He wrapped himself, in his mind, in his own
absence. He did not want to hear the rain,
with its meaning, nor the moment after
rain, nor the sound of Jesus weeping, nor
the dreaming, which is memory, though he
lay a long time cold, head against the stone.

You see the wind passing from tree to tree,
thousands of green individual leaves
silver and fluid at the surfaces,
the long nothing narrative of the wind.
The wind is the emptiness and fullness
in one breath, and the holding of that breath,
restlessness and stillness of the spirit.
You see your dead face in the gray glass close,
and see that it is already too late,

that death's blood nakedness clothed white is smoke,
the father standing in the doorway white,
whom you see in part, the way the morning
gathering is part in the slow degrees
of rectitude, a kind of twilight dawn.
Nothing is said, though he knows you love him.
Nothing is said, though you know he loves you.
Longing, as a sickness of the heart, is
invisible, incurable, endless.

I wrote this poem after a series of stark early mornings. I'd wake up at three, sometimes before, sometimes after, and if I was really tired closer to four. At those hours you drift in time—do I wake or sleep?—your eyes closed within a visible stone-gray space, often cold, sunlight still so distant, so under the lip of things, that whatever light exists seems refracted, left over from the day before. This particular time it was probably March, slow spring, sunrise earlier and earlier. I had large windows, with myrtle trees backed up by large hardwoods, in layers of shadow that, with the dawn, advanced to bring the outside in, but at invisible speed. After a while my eyes would open, adjust, and begin to pick apart parts that were being revealed—edges, angles, and known detail, shapes that I knew by heart yet now distorted. And in the long hour before the sun would actually break, the room would change, and change again, a different space entirely.

One thing: across the one-room apartment from my bed there was a doorway leading into a deep walk-in closet, with a door. The door seemed, always, to have its own notion of opening and closing, and in pre-dawnlight, halfway between open and shut, disappeared into the dark, a dark that when you looked at it long enough or caught it, surprised, at an angle, resembled the rectilinear height and width of a grave, as vertical as a man standing. Among all the grays and emerging bric-a-brac of color of the room, the doorway stayed solid; solid black. Lying there, inside time, you had to ask yourself—or it felt like the question had been asked for you—whether this was a void or an emptiness filled.

The idea of the figure in the doorway came to me *after* the stanza in which I project the figure of the sleepless Lazarus, who wants only to lie down. The figure in the doorway had to be a father, my father. For the living, sleep may be a little death, but for the dead, as I imagine it, there is no sleep. Perhaps dreaming, then, is not so much a death-wish as a life-wish, a desire to return, since the dream is a memory of life, its richness, confusion, strangeness, randomness. Lazarus wants to sleep in order to rest; inevitably he dreams his resurrection, his coming back to terms, his reconciliation with the father, who, for me, becomes the life-principle, not less confused and contradictory, but passionate, even potentially violent; while the absent mother is inconsistent, withdrawn, even aloof, manic-depressed, calling from death.

# 3

Muse figures are complicated, and a great part of their complexity is that they tend to choose us rather than the other way around. They are involuntary sources of the work they tell us must be done. Jung characterizes three foundation archetypes: the shadow, the anima, and the animus, and he says that they each have equal numinous power, perhaps combining power: antagonist dark shapes delineated by light, as if one were seeing one's own shadows, whose source of illumination is just off periphery. My father has been, in differing degrees and intensities of magnitude, such a muse—a shadow stained darker in his combination of anima and animus. If Nature is the guarantor of our imaginations, our parents, and those who sometimes take their places, are the collaborators of our emotions. The muse here is an animating principle, an inspiriter, and a conspirator of content. The drunken god in my father, the vulnerable, wounded animal in his heart, the passionate, generous, violent dimension of his mind are all aspects of his

157

divided personality. My mother, the familiar, on the other hand, is like the form in my poems—half-measured, precariously balanced, quietly obsessive. She is the selector and separator, the organizer of space, the civilian, the compromiser, but fragile, and—depending on the content—threatening to fall apart.

My father was like a thief in the night. A house-breaker, intruder, trespasser. He worked long hours, factory hours, and more often than not spent the evening at Bing's or another beerhall, as my mother called them, and then, in a state somewhere between stump drunk and depressed sober, drove home. He was like the horse who knows the way, rain or shine. Almost every night, in fact, he was out in the world, in bar-life. He could not make a quiet entrance, and sometimes he would be suddenly hungry, hence kitchen noises and the usual muffled, corrosive arguments with my mother. Occasionally, though, if it were really late, say two to four a.m., he could enter the house with stealth, in order to keep his secret. I never failed, regardless of the hour, to hear him. Some nights, clearly, he needed to be heard, and the fight that followed was his way of rejoining the group. Some nights he needed to remain the alien, the outsider. Either way, he was the reverse of the rule of childhood: the one heard rather than seen.

The next morning, whatever the hour of his nightly arrival, he would be up at dawn and on his way back to the gray grind and cycle of the day. He was a foreman, which meant that he could be late to work if needs be, so long as he didn't push his luck. And in many ways, except for the burden of his family, my father was a lucky man. People were drawn to him, which was surely one of the reasons he loved bar-life so much: the family of his buddies. Alcohol was the oil of affection. But he was popular at work as well, among the sober business of great machines, tool-and-die, molten steel, cast iron, welding, assembling. He had the humor and innocence of a man who understands men, and he never lied, except to my mother. He had fierce physical strength, the kind other men look up to. As a boy I spent Saturdays at Bing's at his elbow. As an adolescent I worked summers at the same factory, like a distant relative, someone who must prove himself. On weekends, from my childhood until the year I left home, we both worked the garden and the few animals on our small farm at the margin of town. Work was my father's salvation—work for the sake of work as a transcendent virtue: a purifier, rectifier, and, finally, an apology. For my father, work made up for all the other failure in his life, almost. The Depression and World War II probably had something to do with my father's (and my mother's) emotional attitudes and limitations, just as his father had proved to be an overbearing antagonist. Events and parents teach us how large fate is and how small we are. Life taught my mother fatalism, but it taught my father luck. Drinking was his way to live in luck.

By the 1950s my parents, like most adults of the time, had adopted the protective coloration of Cold War repression, a posture that lent itself to latent, implied or otherwise, accepted domestic violence. My father's various frustrations often exploded, especially when the demon was encouraged. Drinking was the prime encourager, but so was my mother, and, by extension, so was I. The bully in my father would take over, and the best you could do to deal with it was to bully back or else melt into the wall. This terrible dance takes its toll. By the time I left home I never looked back. Somewhere in my twenties, however, I began to identify, even empathize with my father—somewhere around the time I turned twenty-three and realized that I had been born when he was twenty-three, a fact of life that would have sunk me. That was the moment I began to wear my father's body.

# 4

I was out of the country, and out of touch, when he died. I missed the funeral; in fact, missed his death altogether until I stepped off the return plane and was greeted with the news. The muse is ultimately a figure from the dead, which is why lyric poetry, whatever its announced subject, is so elegiac. Love, fear, anger, longing, any number of sources of joy or pain may drive the fever, the cool fever, of the poem, but the result, the overtone, will always return—if sometimes in the silences—to reconciliation with loss—if sometimes only in the language. The narrative of the lyric bends to shape some part or all of a circle. In Ohio, when a funeral is successful, they say you could have sold tickets. From what I'm told, you could have sold tickets to my father's funeral. Even those of us who might have hated him also worshiped him, as my mother, once he was gone, was fond of saying. Something about him did compel attention; you felt more alive in his presence. Which is why, as a boy, I loved his company so much. His rough affection was larger than life, certainly, and powerfully, larger than when he would pick me up and carry me under his arm like bread. I remember Nellie Otte, my high school English teacher, asking me about him—many times—asking me to say hello. Your voice, she would say, is just like your father's. She loved me too, I think.

Thus archetypes are never abstractions, whatever general ghost forms they fill. They are our feeling sources, and in the line-up behind the figures in our dreams they loom, like parents, at the end of the line. Perhaps only one parental line can dominate our inner lives, while the other becomes the one we suffer for, as if we were doomed to perpetuate their marriage within our own hearts. In our time we have turned these classic parental sources and struggles into an industry of illness, like a sickness to be solved. But who would medicate the muse? My father and I have colluded to create my limitations; as he is my resource, I am his representative. I don't see myself as having written father poems or not-father poems, tree poems or bird poems, country poems or city poems, love poems or elegies. The heart in my poems belongs to the muse as much as to me—double-hearted, as it were. Or one's heart of hearts. When I hated my father I was dead; when I learned to love him I came to life—though I wish it were that simple. I know that when he died I was free to love him again.

You cannot write alone, no more than you can be alone inside your poems. The muse is not only, in contemporary vernacular, an inspiritor but a facilitator. As the acknowledged or unacknowledged antagonist—that is, the opposition that creates the energy and story of the poem—the muse is both the need and means. It provides the imagination with context, and when all is said and done, the text itself. The treeness of our trees, the birdness of our birds, the pity of our forgiveness, the beauty of our longing, our paralysis, our prevarications, our palaver, all may saturate the colors and textures of our poems, but they are masks over the singular face of the archetype. The famous loneliness of the writer, like the long-distance runner, is just part of the reason we invite the muse; when it is good, when the writing is like breathing, the muse has invited us. That moment near the beginning of Keats's last poem, *The Fall of Hyperion*, when he is struggling to identify "What Image this, whose face I cannot see," is a moment "That made my heart too small to hold its blood." It is a recognition scene. The goddess he is looking at may be Moneta, but the face is his dead mother's, the muse unmasked.

> Then saw I a wan face,
> Not pin'd by human sorrows, but bright-blanch'd
> By an immortal sickness which kills not;
> It works a constant change, which happy death
> Can put no end to; deathwards progressing
> To no death was that visage; it had pass'd
> The lily and the snow . . .

And in that moment in Delmore Schwartz's seminal short story, "In Dreams Begin Responsibilities," when the narrator is sitting in a darkened movie theater rerunning, on the movie screen in his mind, the film of his parents meeting on a boardwalk by the romantic sea—that moment when he stands up in the empty theater and shouts at the screen not to do it, not to meet, not to fall in love . . . that is a permanent heart-dream moment.

The film of my parents meeting shows my father driving across Ohio in his new yellow Ford convertible coupe, two hundred and sixty miles between Barnesville and Piqua. He is twenty-one, the car is a birthday present, and he is about his father's business. It is 1937 and the far side of the Depression. All in all, farming and lumbering have been less affected than urban economies, so my father's car is more a gift of generosity than the glare of ostentation. My mother's mother is a single parent raising two daughters, of whom my mother, at eighteen, is the younger. They run a boarding house, where fate will have it, my father will stay. He is supposed to be marrying, within the year, someone else. Instead he meets my mother, who without ever having driven anything larger than her grandfather's bicycle, wants to try the yellow convertible. She is a Depression child down to her soles, and this car looks like a chariot. My father comes from Welsh Quaker rectitude, my mother from soft Methodist fires. They will, in the years ahead, together and singly, wreck many cars and walk away as if they had never been there. This time, of course, is my mother's first, and most meaningful, wreck. She is barely down the road a hundred yards before she runs dead into a tree, from which she will wear, under her right eye, forever, a small, hardly visible scar.

2001

CHAPTER AND VERSE

# I
## RHETORIC AND EMOTION

# 1

If tone is one way, historically, of describing the voice within and of a poem, then rhetoric is the way tone of voice is achieved. Rhetoric ought to be no more or less than the presence of the poet, made manifest, in his poem. The poet's voice, his way of presiding over his material, whether the intention is to inspire or illuminate, whether the terms are those of a persona or one of a trinity of personal pronouns, is inevitable. The question is never one of the fact of a voice but of the effective control or disclosure of that voice. There is of course no such thing as omniscience in poetry. The point of view is always limited, someone is always speaking. The speech, though, should be dramatic, not pontifical, should be less heard than overheard. More recently the test of a good poem has come down to the relative believability or authenticity of its voice, its rhetoric, often at the expense of more traditional tests. Indeed, too much time spent at the verbal surface could, according to such a reading, compromise the possible depth of statement. At the extreme, craft—insofar as a revisionist art is concerned—has come to be regarded as a Republican virtue. And *rhetoric*, in the pejorative, has come to mean something crafty, a con. Yet looking back just a few years to Black Mountain, the Beats, the 1960s surrealists, the Confessionals, each was identified by a particular rhetoric. Back almost two hundred years, at the point of entry into the industrial consciousness, Preface to *Lyrical Ballads* declared poetry's independence from the neoclassical decorum of the eighteenth century. A little over a century later, André Breton, in his surrealist *Manifesto*, sought to free and redirect the energies of the imagination by *rewriting* its assumptions. Rhetoric, whatever the year and whatever the aesthetic, establishes credentials, identifies voice.

Rhetoric also releases. If there is a general difference among younger poets today, it is a difference of rhetorical sources: those who write out of an emotional imperative and those who write from an emblematic commitment. The latter are represented in the second part of this piece. As to imperatives, Marilyn Hacker ("I still balk at my preference for rhyme.") is as intimate and intense as anyone writing, even if she still disguises herself as a formalist.

> The umber dowagers of Henry Street
> gossip from windows while they rest their feet:
> The Jew on East Broadway sells rotten fruit.
> Last night the cops busted a prostitute;
> broke up a crap game in the hall next door—
> woke up the kids at almost half past four.
> As taken with the ripened fall of words
> against the yard as what they saw or heard,
> their voices scoop the sun like beautiful
> harsh birds, until the cindered yard is dull
> with evening, and the regularities
> of grubby men and children home to eat.
> Two laminated toucans pepper meat
> as sunlight sheaths behind the sumac trees.

The sonnet is labeled "September," the time of the year and certainly a metaphor for the time of day. There is just a little of the Brahmin perspective (Cummings's Cambridge and Lowell's Boston) of being slightly above it all, off to one side, sorting and selecting, judging. An odd but effective angle for the material. The engineering of the poem is everywhere apparent and is supposed to be, and in surrendering point of view to perspective, Hacker has apparently lifted herself out of involvement. Yet the mode of this sonnet is dramatic, a piece of storytelling; rather than argumentative, it is rendered rather than reasoned through. And the wrist-rapping strictness of the rhythm and rhyme, the acceleration of some lines posed against the abruptness of others, and the authority of detail all suggest anything but aloofness. The events of the poem are obviously witnessed or we would not care. By increasing the level of energy the engineering only serves to intensify the rhetoric and our awareness of a voice. The speaker is simply off-stage, with more freedom to play with diction and detail than she might have were she a part of the action. In fact, had the poem been written in terms of an "I" the potential for sentimentality would have been enormous. There are too many other people and too much going on in the poem for the poet to take it personally: the passion would have gone soft. By staying out of it Hacker is that much more believably involved. That is the success of her tone, where the voice is calling from.

Dave Smith takes a longer look in "The Perspective and Limits of Snapshots"—and into the past but only superficially into the pastoral. Here is the first third of the poem.

> Aubrey Bodine's crosswater shot of Menchville,
> Virginia: a little dream composing a little water,
> specifically, the Deep Creek flank of Warwick.
> Two-man oyster scows lie shoulder to shoulder,
> as if you walked them, one land to another,
> no narrow channel hidden in the glossy middle
> like a blurred stroke, current grinning at hulls.
> It is an entirely eloquent peace, with lolling
> ropes and liquid glitter, this vision of traffic
> and no oystermen in sight. Clearly, Bodine is not
> Matthew Brady catching the trenchant gropes frozen
> at Fredericksburg with a small black box. So well
> has he excluded the neat Mennonite church, yachts,
> country club pool, the spare smell of dignity seeps.
> Perhaps it is because of the zoom on the teeth
> of the oyster tongs; perhaps it is after all Sunday.

The action picks up later in the poem, as does the writing. The rhetoric for now is mostly commentary ("It is an entirely eloquent peace"), punctuated with clues ("with lolling/ropes and liquid glitter"). It reads like exposition, as if the poet were setting up the scene, the complication. In fact, the poet is trying to establish his voice, get control of his presence in the poem, in order to mediate between point of view and the story being told. Smith is better with Bodine, whose snapshots he is presently interpreting, than with Brady, whose picture he is remembering: "trenchant gropes frozen/at Fredericksburg" is clogged phrasing and seeing, with none of the economy of vision he is praising Bodine for. Yet in the total—and Smith is a poet who demands to be read on the whole—the effect of the stanza is one of detail not only selected and *seen* but voiced-over, cared for. The side step of the "you" in the fifth line is more anonymous than named; Smith is referring to the reader as much as to himself. The story continues.

> Above the last boat, the flat-faced store squats
> at the end of the dirt road as if musing over
> accounts receivable. No doubt it has weathered
> years of blood spilling. A spotted hound lifts
> his nose above what must be yesterday's trash fish,
> his white coat luminous against deep foilage. What
> Bodine fails to see is the dog turning to lope
> uphill under that screen of poplars, behind fat
> azaleas that hide the county farm and the drunks
> pressed against wire screens, sniffing the James.

"No doubt," the speaker says of the store's "weathered/years of blood spilling." And not content to commit, to interpret the limits of snapshots, he tells us what Bodine "fails to see." The fictional device here is interesting in that, one, it admits the basis for the technique of order in the poem, and two, it fixes the relationship between the speaker and his material. The actual story lies outside the snapshot, as we shall see; and the speaker is really a narrator, a storyteller who needs to read into and past the limits of the "flat-faced" picture. The dog leads us out of the frame into the outside, as-yet-unphotographed world of county farms and drunks in the lockup. Smith concludes his poem with an incident, an incident and truth too large for the perspective and limits of snapshots, an incident added to fulfill the function of the narrator—to complete the still life with context, the third dimension.

> One oysterman thumped his noisy wife (the window
> was accidental) because she had a knife and mourned
> their boy twenty years drowned. If he knew Bodine
> stood at the marsh tip where his boy dove, if he
> were but told a camera yawned to suck in the years
> of his worst sailing shame, he would turn away. He
> would whistle up boys in the dust that is dignity
> and if he could he would spit in his hand and tell
> his nameless black cellmate there are many men
> for whom the world is neither oyster nor pearl.

Now the narrator has made his photograph, organized and interpreted from the parallel, "real" world. Two pictures, then, one, Bodine's, placed inside the other. As in Hacker's sonnet, the actual "I" has been circumvented, but unlike the observer's role in "September," Smith's voice presides as a participant, to the extent that he can believably make assumptions about the inner life of his oysterman. Smith's story has moved through the closed space of the original photograph, commenting and placing clues ("no oystermen in sight//years of blood spilling//drunks/pressed against wire screens") to the surrounding space of the outside world, a world too various and dangerous for the eye of a single camera. The success of Smith's tone of voice is that through his use of a narrator he is able to be intimate without being familiar. He begins at the shoulder of Bodine sighting crosswater at Menchville and ends standing beside his oysterman in a cell. A trip like that takes time, much more than fourteen lines, with a sense of open-endedness and continuum. So Hacker is right in tying up her scene with couplets, however loose the knots, and Smith is right to allow his story the full play of the page. Hacker's means are implicit, Smith's explicit. If occasionally Smith's lines seem to be widening toward prose, then so much the better for his method. He is competing with fiction, after all, in a prose that scans. When he alliterates like a poet is when he is most in trouble. "The spare smell of dignity seeps. . . ." If it does, it should not. The closing incident of the oysterman is the best written because it is the most deeply felt moment in the poem. In its use of repetition and measure, in its directness of phrase, it is as well written, as Pound would say, as good prose.

Both Hacker and Smith work the language hard, often enough to the point where their voices embellish more than they engage the material. For the reader, the tone of a poem is very much based on trust, what he is willing or not willing to believe. No good reader is going to stay long to listen to self-indulgence. Marilyn Hacker, for instance, has a habit of pursuing analogy to the absurd—

> O hurry up, my guts convulse for love,
> though I have only seen your neck, your wrist,
> your lapis eyes worn underneath black lace.
> You will be stone on me, remind me of
> marble and amber, quartz and amethyst

> while I taste my tongue corrode your face.
> This lapidary passion for your face . . .

O hurry up please, it's time. The obsession here could have humor if the reader could find reason to trust a countervailing irony. "You will be stone on me" is good, but it is lost to silly and predictable metaphor (guess the line that follows the ellipsis: "could crystallize into a kind of love") pushed at us in the extreme—and lost to the gratuities of the late, late show: "I taste my tongue corrode your face." The remainder of the sonnet is no better, nor the overwhelming clue of the title, "Stones, Jewels." If the metaphor of the body-into-stone is meant to suggest separation, then it is done much more convincingly throughout the rest of Hacker's book. *Separations*, a second collection, is obviously a title intended to establish far more than the terms of the poet's domestic relations: in the book's best poems, those in which the rhetoric and the emotion arrive together, separation describes her state of being. In "After the Revolution," "The Companion," for example, and in the title sequence, a veritable trauma-drama of sonnets, Hacker achieves the magnitude she is after—a sort of personal moral outrage, levied on scale, with discipline. For all her form and feathers, she is a street poet, a ranter. She is also incredibly professional. So that by the time she gets to the page, negotiations have been or are about to be worked out between the emotional imperatives and the demands of the art. Insofar as it makes a difference she writes free verse in rhyme.

Dave Smith has simpler problems. His rhetoric sometimes outruns the action, as if to compensate.

> It must be
> like entering a world where every breath turns dead
> reckless and pure as gull
> song tuned by nothing but ribbed sealight,
> where hard-headed laid-down fathers rise up slowly
> among crocus and bluebell as if
> only minutes before
> sleep whined like a gnat.

The antecedent for "It" is fiddling, as in a buck-dancer's choice. The language has suddenly fallen in love with its own music, and the imitative effect is literary rather than real. There are four similes attached to two metaphors that are themselves related to an outside, it, referent. Images should provide windows, not mirrors. *Cumberland Station*, Smith's third full volume, is a book filled with large and large-minded poems, most of which are successful, most of which—such as the title poem and "Looking for the Melungeon" and "On a Field Trip to Fredericksburg" as instances—illustrate a remarkably stratified Southern rhetoric building through plot. *Looming* is Smith's own metaphor for the process familiar to seamen that makes "distant objects appear larger, in opposition to the general law of vision, by which they are diminished." When the size of the object is appropriately gauged by the size of his language, Smith's poems tell powerful stories. He wastes himself on a lot of writing-about-subjects ("The Sex of Poetry," "The Palmreader," "Coming Attractions"), playing at wit that rings false. He sometimes succumbs to his influences, Dickey and James Wright. But when he sticks to local business, his Tidewater Virginia sources, his full-bodied rhetoric is unique, even antique.

If Hacker looks formal, Smith appears to be four-square. Both of them read out of fashion. Neither of them, however, seems completely comfortable in the close patterns they have set for themselves. And though the discomfort may be the chief positive tension in their work, the aesthetic order feels more often imposed than inherent. For Hacker it comes down to a predictability of rhythm, for Smith it is the prolixity of the line. They both seem to be looking for some third form, a *vers libre*, to relieve the burden of habit, to open the opportunities toward something not quite prose.

# 2

So-called free verse has been around a long time—all the way back to the Psalms. Still, as a form of poetry practiced by individual poets, it is really an invention of the nineteenth century and an inspiration to the twentieth. It is as various in nature as its practitioners, whether one begins with W. E. Henley, Arnold, or Whitman, or a century later with James Wright, W. S. Merwin, Adrienne Rich, or Galway Kinnell, or even Ted Hughes, to stick to the English-speaking examples. Indeed, variety is exactly the point of free verse. As a phrase the term is as unfortunate as it is inaccurate. It sounds like a revolt against claustrophobic Victorian conformity, when in fact it is an aesthetic alternative generalized along with historic changes in the other arts. Impressionism and atonal music, for example, began as freed verse, as open form. As individuals vary in its use, so do generations. One could doubtless devote an essay, if not a book, to delineating and chronicling the contemporary relationship between the free verse of a given time and the poetry written in fixed forms. Surely they are not unrelated. The Eliot of *Four Quartets* and the Yeats of *The Tower* write out of a similar cultural and historical context, yet totally different aesthetic assumptions. In our time, the paternal generation, almost to the man or woman, has summarized within a whole work the growth from the formal to the "free." Richard Howard's *Alone with America* is a catalogue of such careers, ranging from A (Ashbery) to W (James Wright). The continuum in the work of each of the poets he considers is clear, but so is the change.

One critic has described free verse as a kind of soliloquy, thinking out loud. Perhaps. But it is hardly a speech made up on the spot. It is more likely a profoundly different rhythm, lying somewhere between the discursive and the metrical, between the quantitative advantages of prose and the qualitative of poetry. Free verse is really flexible verse, whether it rhymes by accident or measures a line now and then, whether it is *Life Studies** or *The North American Sequence*, or whether it descends the page in the shape of a riprap. Younger poets, including Hacker and Smith, have taken the rhetorical tradition of free verse and turned it more and more idiosyncratic, in the direction of the personal and associational—not to confess but to share in one another's dream-life. Even the stated "I" is now less specified: what is important is the emotional or emblematic center of gravity, the sense that the poet has consulted his source more directly than himself. (The era of the great egos ended with Berryman.) The tone has become more intimate as the territory has become more detailed, discrete, named. All of this makes for a poetry at once more responsive and potentially irresponsible, as if each event, each experience had its own free verse equivalent in form. The problem being in finding it.

---

*This essay was written before Robert Lowell's tragic death.

Eliot is fond of writing things like, "As for 'free verse,' I expressed my view twenty-five years ago by saying that no verse is free for the man who wants to do a good job," and in the next breath adding, "The music of poetry, then, must be a music latent in the common speech of its time." The two comments complement rather than contradict each other. *Latent in the common speech of its time* reads like a rewrite of something Wordsworth says in his Preface about the voice of a good poem being in a language "spoken by men"—indeed in a language in which there is "no essential difference between prose and metrical composition." The difference, though, as Eliot states, is in the music, though that difference is to be distinguished within a common speech—not in a separate speech for poetry and one for prose. The point may seem commonplace, yet there are a substantial number of poets who still operate in a realm of imperial diction. The patterns of formal poetry, regardless of the variability within the line, tend to emphasize the linear, a going across the page. Hacker's sonnet "September," for all its common speech, offers line breaks of a pentamerous predictable nature, and the rhyme only reinforces the line-length. The patterns in free verse, however, tend to emphasize the vertical movement of the poem, a going down the page. Perhaps the term "music" is really a prosody word limited in its metaphor. "Pace" would better describe the passage by which a free verse poem, whatever the length of its line, breaks and enjambs, stops and restarts its way down. There may be few real differences in diction between free and formal verse (at least there should not be), but there are real differences in rhythm—although, finally, the differences may relate more to rhyme, or rhyme schemes, than to the internal music of the line. So-called free verse should scan too—it might even, in its own off-handed way, rhyme internally, but it must not schematize the rhythm or the possible rhyme. The prosody of free verse is the prosody of assonance, consonance, and surprise.

What has happened in the 1970s is that as free verse has become the norm, it has become refined, more various, and more abused. At its flexible best, it calls less and less attention to the language and more to the body of the action. Ideally, to quote Louis Simpson, its language should be transparent. One is tempted, as others have been, to see the language as the clothing of a poem, ranging in taste from what one wears at Court to what one wears to bed. But the "body," naked or not, "of the action" ought not be limited to the anthropomorphic. Traditional verse, in its most formal circumstance, has typically turned its action into an argument. Free verse, even in its iambic phase, beginning with *The Prelude*, has let the action speak for itself: and invariably narrative has been involved, either as the whole story or parts thereof. As a genre of under a hundred lines, free verse has come to mean the dramatic lyric, an intensified, implicative action. What makes that action convincing or authentic is the tone of its master's voice. Tone is what we are left with once the language assumes transparency.

But there is a mind as well as a body to the action. And together, whole, in terms of voice print, fingerprint, phrenology, and shadow on the wall, they probably should look and sound a lot like the person of the poet. The point of a poem declaring its freedom as verse is that it somehow better represent the individuality—no, the *personality* of things, the metaphysics of the action, and *who* is presiding. Such a poem might represent more than a life in either crisis or transition or introspection, more than a life in simple action: but a moment in or out of time, "while the music lasts," a moment as a synthesis of memory and present tense, of experience and experiment. If the lyric is the fragment of our time, then tone is its authenticating means. The poet would convince us that the piece he is giving us is not from whole cloth but from the total fabric. Without the self-appointed skills the formalist can display, the free-verse poet is especially vulnerable to questions of credentials. The tone of his voice, as it brings together what is happening with why it is happening, as it gives thought to the emotion, as it calls more and more attention to the person behind the performance, must pass some fairly tough tests as to what is true as well as what is beautiful.

So Emerson, Wordsworth's intellectual contemporary, is precisely on the mark, as he defends yet another Transcendentalist assumption: "For it is not meters, but a meter-making argument that makes a poem,—a thought so passionate and alive that, like the spirit of a plant or animal, it has an architecture of its own, and adorns nature with a new thing. The thought and the form are equal in the order of time, but in the order of genesis the thought is prior to the form." Had Emerson regarded his own feeling-life less nervously, he might have at least included the *idea* of emotion as an element equal and a priori to the form, and had he lived after Einstein he might have included space as an order with time. Frost, Wordsworth's heir, and ever practical, looks to rhythm and what it represents, its mind as well as its body, in the category of the sentence rather than the line: "A dramatic necessity goes deep into the nature of the sentence. Sentences are not different enough to hold the attention unless they are dramatic. All that can save them is the speaking tone of voice somehow entangled in the words. . . ." If free verse is beginning to sound like irregular blank verse, with a particular emphasis on its correspondence with its sources, its ability to represent the a priori emotion and thought in a rhythm and texture as close to a sense of the original experience as possible, well . . . this would mean representing *an action*, dramatically, *in sentences*: which would mean representing an actor, the speaking voice, one who would normally participate in as well as preside over the action. Perhaps free verse has become the language of the tribe, and the tone of its intrinsic voice is what we hear coming from the tribe's most totemic, intimate imagination, the speaker in a dream.

# 3

When Coleridge makes his famous distinction between poetry and prose it seems a most precise and precious one. What is, after all, the real difference between the best words in their best order and just words in their best order? A profound difference, of course—all the difference required. Difference enough, in fact, to determine rhythm. And to Coleridge, as to Wordsworth and Emerson and Eliot, *that* distinction—of the "musical phrase," as Pound called it—is absolute. Prose has no prosody. And poetry— though it may not tick like a metronome or decorate or inflate—must make music. For all the approaches to free verse, from Whitman to Williams, from Ginsberg to *The Book of Nightmares*, it has been described more by approximation than definition. It has nearly always remained stuck somewhere between the positive pole of poetry and the negative pole of prose. It has been what they are, hybrid or separate, but not quite. It may turn out that free verse is a third form, a genre unto itself, a pattern apart from, if related to, other patterns. If it is not quite poetry in its formal arrangement, it is certainly not prose in its formal appearance. To paraphrase Coleridge, it may be simply the best action in its best order—an action less dependent on line breaks than on the sentence, yet an action more determined by stanzas than by the paragraph. Yes, and action committed to the rhythm of the story *as it is received*, as it is perceived. An action whose voice is more sensitive to nuance and source, and therefore more vulnerable.

For example, take a "Time Lapse with Tulips."

> That kiss meant to sear my heart forever—
> it went right by.
> And the way we walked out on Sundays
> to the bakery like a very old couple, arm
> on arm, that's gone too,
> though the street had a house with a harp
> in the window.
>
> Those tulips again.
> They think if they keep being given away
> by the black-haired man at our wedding
> I will finally take them in time
> for the photograph. But they are wrong.
> This time I will hand them back or leave them
> sitting in the mason jar
> on the grass beside you.
>
> See how the guests lean after me, their mouths
> slightly open. Only now it's plain
> they were never sure, that the picture
> holding us all preserves
> a symmetry of doubt with us
> at the center, the pledge
> of tulips red against my dress.

This part of a poem from Tess Gallagher's first book, *Instructions to the Double*, may not be typical of the musculature and heavy metaphor so vigorous in so many of her pieces. In a wonderful tossed-off sort of poem such as "The Horse in the Drugstore" (also excerpted), the imagination and music perform more obvious feats of free verse—

> . . . it is enough
> to stand so with his polished chest among the nipples
> and bibs, the cotton and multiple sprays, with his black lips
> parted just slightly and the forehooves doubled back

in the lavender air. He has learned here when maligned to snort
dimes and to carry the inscrutable bruise like a bride.

The Alexandrine length of lines between the quarter rhyme of nipples/lips
is kept fairly busy with its i's and l's and s's, not to mention its bilabials.
The black/back rhyme is neatly buried too, ending the next line. But the
closing two lines best illustrate how image can be blessed by music and still
remain in the speaking rather than a singing voice. "Lavender air" may be
an obvious aural combination; yet when extended, after a full stop, to
"here" it becomes more interesting, especially complicated by the assonant-
consonant sounds of "learned . . . when maligned . . . /dimes." The abruptness of "to snort" is just the appropriate interruption for the long i's and l's
built around it and headed into "inscrutable bruise like a bride." There is
even formality here, with at least five accents a line, the length itself made
longer by units of unstressed syllables. No, "Time Lapse with Tulips" makes
very few of these overt gestures toward the musical phrase—or toward the
high gloss of metaphor, for that matter. Instead, it offers the reader apparently less and ultimately more. It begins, modestly enough, *in medias res*, in
the past tense, and moves after a time lapse, to immediate speculation about
the position of some tulips in a wedding picture, and concludes with the
photograph itself. The poem is unified by situation, then, and more particularly by the framing idea of the photograph. Moreover, as in most poems
in open form, this one depends on the growth of a clear leitmotif—from
the searing kiss itself, a red kiss, to the shape of the harp in the window, to
the central image of the tulips (the pun is surely no mistake), to the open
mason jar, to "their mouths/slightly open," and back to the tulips, by now
red. The "plot," however, the cause-and-effect of things, is what finally
holds our attention. We begin right in the middle of the old mutability
theme ("that's gone too"), oddly enough in the simple past tense—oddly,
because in terms of the emotional life proposed, the events in the first stanza
seem to have occurred after the wedding picture, an event even further in
the past, yet an event spoken of here in the present. We are dealing, of
course, with the time lapse in the speaker's head: the first stanza is expository, a set-up, memory; then the keying-in on the single, suggestive object,
"those tulips again"—again because of the memories at the beginning—
and so the story becomes complicated, what to do with those tulips; and

then, in the last stanza, the story is completed though entirely open to "a symmetry of doubt"—for the guests, the tulips, for the couple, the marriage. The poem teases us with ambiguities, the least of which is whether or not those tulips really are to be in the wedding photo ("But they are wrong"//"the pledge/of tulips red against my dress"). "With us at the center," says the speaker, of the "symmetry of doubt" comes confirmation of the chief ambiguity—"This time," those tulips again, and likely again, on into the indefinite future. "The picture/holding us all preserves/ a symmetry of doubt" is more poetic than actual paradox; it is part of the speech of the poem. But "This time I will hand them back or leave them" is "at the center" of the story. Like the kiss, like the harp in the window, the tulips, beautiful as they are, are destined to change, to reenact the oldest cliché in poetry. There is a difference, though. Of course we cannot fix in time what is fluid, neither can the wedding picture, however well it frames the couple and the guests. The tulips, however, are not exactly in the picture, only the "pledge/of tulips red against my dress." The tulips are in "this time," where they can be handed back or left sitting in the mason jar. Perhaps fluidity simply means a life-time series of photographs of death, and so those tulips, "sitting in the mason jar/on the grass beside you," are as much of that process as "you" are, and as the speaker is. Obviously they are: and that is their "symbolic" value. Red is both the color of love and death.

So far, extrapolated, those tulips are fairly familiar stuff, time lapsed or time out of time. But earlier, right at the start, before we come to "Those tulips again," we are offered "that kiss," that particular one, "meant to sear my heart forever." Of course, dash, dash, "it went right by." Gallagher classifies her realities according to time lapse; she is being coy. It went right by accelerates time considerably. And it suggests that more is involved here than just another chance for *carpe diem*. The poem is very much about the living, not the dead, about the inherent human flaw in human relationships—us at the center of a symmetry of doubt, doubt about life, perhaps, doubt about marriage, yes. Still fairly familiar stuff, that people fail, and that they are failing even at the moment of purest success. The photograph tells us that. What is most individual about this poem is hardly its theme, but its tone, the feel of the thing, its total effect, from the sound of the voice to where the voice is calling from. Again and again, Gallagher breaks up combinations that might remind us of the verbal dexterity of "The Horse in the Drugstore" in order to minimize the music. The last line, for instance, reads sweeter as "the pledge of tulips red against my dress": the whole "last" stanza, in fact, could easily be rearranged down to five lines by simple extensions of lines into fuller units. The same with the preceding stanzas—and without loss to the symmetry of the poem. Certain vowel and consonant sounds would be enhanced by a consistently longer line. But also "enhanced," and also exaggerated, would be the emotional life of the poem. "Time Lapse with Tulips" cannot afford to iron out its edges. Place "it went right by" on the first line with the dash and the effect is funny. Move "in the window" up with the house and the harp loses emphasis; move the harp down with the window and the two lines syncopate. The angles as Gallagher has fashioned them provide the voice with the appropriate tension: they understate the rhythm, and the emotion. Indeed, they function ironically against what might be expected. More than that, the relative variation of line length (a symmetry of doubt) helps increase the pace of the poem down the page, helps, in a word, to authenticate the action—an action that seems to begin in the middle of the story and go backward, into *history*, through and into time, but that really moves through space, as if—in spite of tense—all the parts of the poem exist simultaneously. In the speaker's mind, in the time lapse, they do. The emotion has been brought to bear on this single moment, worked out in its single voice.

Tone is more exposed in free verse, since the rhetoric of open forms is supposed to call less attention to itself. The voice is more available and therefore more vulnerable. Although there may not be enough hard evidence about American poetry since the 1960s, tone seems to have displaced the image as a "technique of discovery." As young poets especially have become more personal, more intimate with their material and less and less committed to experience in capital letters, so have the terms become more particularized, more relative. This shift in emphasis calls for a free verse more flexible than ever, one that is able, most of all, to accommodate a wider, more detailed, even contradictory range of emotional experience—yes, accommodate and control. Tess Gallagher's "Tulips" orders its action as much around what is left out as what is left in. She reaches in all directions at once, still in doubt. The emotional evidence, though, by the time we get to that "picture/holding us all," adds up. To have reversed the order of the action, to have begun with the actual wedding picture, would of course have been sentimental—a surrender of control, and imbalance to the equilibrium of elements. "Those tulips again." One can hardly personify let alone rescue the cliché of those flowers (in a wedding photo to boot) without a careful delineation and organization of materials—without putting things right, in a sequence that best authenticates the emotion. That is what real rhetoric in free verse is about: the best words in their best order in their best order of action, a going down as well as across the page.

The special accretive, vertical power of the free verse poem is very much the issue in David St. John's poem for his son.

> The way a tired Chippewa woman
> Who's lost a child gathers up black feathers,
> Black quills & leaves
> That she wraps & swaddles in a little bale, a shag
> Cocoon she carries with her & speaks to always
> As if it were the child,
> Until she knows the soul has grown fat & clever,
> That the child can find its own way at last;
> Well, I go everywhere
> Picking the dust out of the dust, scraping the breezes
> Up off the floor, & gather them into a doll
> Of you, to touch at the nape of the neck, to slip
> Under my shirt like a rag—the way
> Another man's wallet rides above his heart. As you
> Cry out, as if calling to a father you conjure
> In the paling light, the voice rises, instead, in me.
> Nothing stops it, the crying. Not the clove of moon,
> Not the woman raking my back with her words. Our letters
> Close. Sometimes, you ask
> About the world; sometimes, I answer back. Nights
> Return you to me for a while, as sleep returns sleep
> To a landscape ravaged
> & familiar. The dark watermark of your absence, a hush.

This is no elegy, but it is elegiac; it does dramatize loss, "the dark watermark" of an absence. It is no accident that the last word is also the poem's title—in the text, another metaphor for loss; as a title, the name of the whole. *Hush* does not simply understate the terms of the emotional argument, it is the term of the argument itself. Hush is the voice in which the poem is written, the attitude of the speaker toward the material: an attitude that must be prepared for, organized toward, an attitude that is finally a form of irony in that the hush is effective only in proportion to the emotional extreme it implies. St. John's poem is not sentimental, yet it depends on the full cup to spilling-over. "Nothing stops it, the crying": St. John's problem and potential for power is to surround such a statement with sufficient context to save it. The tone of the poem's voice is what is achieved as it builds toward its last word—not what may be imposed by the assumption of its title.

How is "Hush" built? St. John, first-book poet that he is, has been called both surrealist and sentimentalist. In the early 1960s such a combination of self-consciousness and sincerity led Donald Hall to conclude, in his fine and now famous introduction to *Contemporary American Poetry*, that there was indeed something new going on, post-Eliot, post-New Criticism. Ronald Moran and George Lensing, in an essay in *The Southern Review* of that period, called it the "emotive imagination," this sense that American poetry had turned an important spiritual corner. And so it had. Nothing said or written since has had the aesthetic impact of, say, Robert Bly's commentaries and James Wright's poetry of those years. (A poet like the early W. S. Merwin closes the period.) The sixties opened up not only the idea of the image, but the source of that imagination as well—a source, for those willing to subscribe, located somewhere in the life of the unconscious. What Hall and others were observing, Bly and others were promoting. Bly's favorite term for the correspondence between the deep image and the surface was *association*. It is a good word, a useful word, though it is a metaphor for a metaphor. The issues of Bly's poetics and politics are beside the point here, and anyone reading this essay should be familiar with his program, developed over two and a half decades of editing and writing for *Fifties/Sixties/Seventies*. (It is no coincidence that both he and Pound began their respective assaults with reevaluations of the image.) The corrective balance the seventies have provided for the influences of the sixties is to remind us that the image alone has no voice. (Indeed, as one example, except for his *Silence in the Snowy Fields*, Robert Bly is largely tone-deaf. So much of his work reads and sounds as if the poet were merely the mediator between the unconscious and a hostile world. If there is a voice, it is the voice of the oracle, ear to the ground.) The image is only as effective as its dramatic context, the language, the rhetoric it is carried by. The associations take place on the page: that is to say, they are announced: they are, by implicit or explicit means, made to connect there. The several images of a poem may have no literal center of gravity, but they should have a coherency, a unity of voice, of tone of voice, behind them. That voice is their chief authority, both in terms of control and authenticity. It establishes the emotional and imaginative individuality of the speaker of the poem, even if he or she is a dream-speaker. Image should be the vital evidence of the emotion, as tone is the vital voice of that emotion.

How is David St. John's poem built? By a kind of analogy, of course; by a series, a sequence of images. The success of the poem is dependent on the order and timing of the sequence as much as on the quality of the images themselves. At least that is one level of success. Perhaps more to the point of free verse as an *expressive* form is the rhythm of the presentation. One thing to always bear in mind about free verse, as suggested earlier, is that the line breaks are more eye than ear oriented. The unit of the sentence, as in good, scannable prose, is the ear of the free verse poem. So that more than half of "Hush"—the first half—is a single protracted sentence, varied in line length for emphasis. The lines do not enjamb so much as they anticipate, moving as easily as possible to keep the voice quiet, in control. That first long sentence is really a stanza, closed. It ends as it began, with a clear rhetorical signal about what is coming: *the way*. And is interrupted, conversationally, with a *well*. Those small words, functioning as they do to establish the presence of the speaker in relationship to the image, provide aural context—and transition. Poems of high emotional content seem to call for cause-and-effect connection as opposed to juxtaposition. They need to happen in the sequence of a story being told. Once the deflections—"a shag/cocoon," "a doll/of you," "Another man's wallet"—have been set up, St. John can then get to the actual matter at hand, the absent son, the absent father. The poet plays with the device of the simile beyond its convenience. We know that "as if calling to a father" is no *as if*—that absence is the condition of things here. The phrase "the way" is another form of as if; by its very circumvention it takes us to the center of the problem. The irony in the use of analogous clues and the unexpected, and totally unrelated, nature of those clues (the Chippewa woman, another man's wallet) helps St. John to "stay off his subject," as Richard Hugo once put it. Building his story, he is building his tone. Building it so that the "climax"—the point at which the hush is most called into question—comes long before the end. "In the paling light, the voice rises, instead, in me." The seven lines that continue and conclude the poem accelerate in rhythm through repetition and parallelism. They serve to intensify without exaggerating the emotion. In their several sentences they move at a speed in considerable contrast to the wandering of the first, long sentence.

"As if it were the child," St. John says of the Indian woman talking to her "little bale." The dead child, we are to assume. The success of St. John's tone is that he has written, convincingly, an elegy for the living. On assignment, that is very sentimental stuff. But step by step, he has understated and rescued the situation. Both father and child, separately, are memory. The old attack on free verse would speak of it as spilled prose, something a poet had to do in lieu of skill. Prose or prose-poem, spilled or joined together, such categorizations no longer distinguish the issue. Free verse is of course the form of our time—though to paraphrase Pound, it must be as well written as prosody. It is a different, more expressive music. As distinctions of genre blur, the 1970s may reveal that poetry in general and prose in particular have more than a lot in common. Free verse, at least, as the illustrations of Gallagher and St. John, and even Hacker and Smith, show, has for a long time not had to prove its virtue in a sinful world. What it has had to prove is that it can grow to accommodate the ethic as well as the aesthetic of the individual poet—that by the nature of its speech it may represent more determined moral authority. Perhaps we should not be talking about prose relative to poetry, but fiction relative to free verse. What we want is a whole poem, not the perfected pieces of the poet's workshop: a poem that surrounds its "subject," that completes its emotional arc—a poem that tells us enough of the story that why it was written is implicated in what it says.

"Hush" is a whole poem, a poem that enlarges, not simply one that grows. Its "fiction" exists in the protagonist–antagonist relationship between the speaking father and the indirect speech of the son. If it does not engage the complete story as in the plotted prose of say five to ten thousand words, it does embrace a whole emotion, it does offer what Pound calls "an absolute rhythm—a poetry which corresponds exactly to the emotion being expressed." This sense of fullness, of something being worked out and worked through, relative to the length of passage, relative to the timing of the particulars, is what the voice in free verse is all about.

First-book poets are invariably inconsistent. St. John's *Hush*, like Tess Gallagher's *Instructions*, is no exception. The best work of both poets keeps company with their least. St. John's weakness is precisely opposed to his strength: in his first section, for instance, there is a run of five poems, from "Ruins" to "Oranges," that depends more on white space than substance. They read like practice, warm-up exercises to the larger, brilliantly filled-out pieces that follow.

> My words disappear,
> like gravel
> tossed in a lake—
> sinking
> through the pages of water.

The metaphorical conversion here is easy to the point of cliché, and it concludes a short poem that is already the tag-end of experience we must guess at. Its profoundity is fey—as fey as its source is unaccounted for. "The amber window, dark again." "I lean in the doorway,/and slide my fingers along/the rosewood neck." "I go out on the porch/and watch a firefly weave/through the pines—lost Saint,/stone lantern, looking/for the way." The poems in this group are obviously early poems, without the depth of texture and situation required to believe in their theologies. They have simply not earned their gesture. Thankfully five or so poems are not the representative number in a book sustained by some of the best writing around. Yet such young work does illustrate the indulgence free—or, one supposes, any other—verse is heir to. The late 1960s, notably in the ghost writing of followers of W. S. Merwin, was big on sparing us the details. In Gallagher's off moments we are not spared enough. Too few poems in her collection avoid the expressive impulse to extend the image or the emotion.

> Away from this I am wife
> and another breathing.
> My forehead as field

or cliff, the rain
a tin rushing outside
the window, so close,
your closed eyes, the bed
descending in a shaft of wideness
meant for me. Yet not to be sure
who it was you called, breaking
from words you came alone to,
but that: it was not me.

This is the second stanza of a fourth part in a sequence of eleven. They are all "Songs of a Runaway Bride." "A tin rushing" is nice, but the rest of the writing falls into a slack imitation of the rush itself. Even out of context the stanza should focus more meaningfully and specifically on what is happening. Instead we are given the manufacture of a dream without its primary location in an actual or real world. After the image outside the window the perception moves into and onto its own gratuitous energy, with the result that "closed eyes," "the bed descending in a shaft of wideness," and "breaking from words" meet at no point of unity. The clumsy syntax solved in the last line only emphasizes that we are reading a kind of creative writing, not the poetry Gallagher is capable of. At another, more direct moment, in a poem addressed to her mother, the poet declares: "Life/caught you up in its clumsy arms/and danced you out of your Oklahoma/youth into the milltown/of my birth." This country-music triteness is, again, hardly the norm in Gallagher's work. But it is a habit of mind, similar to the passion to resolve complicated emotional states as simple accretive metaphor.

St. John and Gallagher are good young poets, among the best. As a pair they are certainly less compulsive than poets as vigorous and glib as Marilyn Hacker and Dave Smith. Yet as examples they too suggest an attitude apparently widely accepted: that conviction, whether one is committed to the word or the world, is enough. Technique, to quote old Pound again, is the test of a man's (and a woman's) sincerity. By our lights, the "technique" of controlling tone is such a test. The page should be a sanctity, and what is worked out there should bear the mark of life thought through, deeply felt, even if for only that moment, turned and returned to. A form as dependent as free verse is on the sense and sensibility of particular experience demands the patience to wait out the dimensions and shape of what is to be confronted.

# 4

The guidebook says that for many critics *story* is the sequence in which the events occur as parts of a happening and *plot* is the sequence in which the author arranges, narrates, or dramatizes them. Poets are plotters. What they plot may look like pieces, notably in poetry without the cohesive distinctions of formal pattern. Indeed, one of the principles of twentieth-century free verse has been its reliance on an implied order, a "submerged structure," the arrangement of the archipelago. Fragmentation of matter presupposes fragmentation of method—and so on. The whole panoply of modern art, from Cubism to Theater of the Absurd, is based on the aesthetic designed to attack apparent plot, as, more specifically, the Deep Imagism of the 1960s was intended as an alternative to the rhetoric of cause-and-effect. Free verse, however, has normally provided explicit "narrators" who have tended to plot in sequences that would enhance the unity of voice without compromising the idea of "organic" order. And because the mind of the free verse poem is revealed in the process of plot, confirmed in the act of making its way, the voice is theoretically more exposed: the narrator is revealed by his story, his tone of voice by the arrangement of that story. The reliability of the narrator is directly dependent on our sense of the inevitability of his plot.

Poetry in the 1970s is asking for a more sophisticated reading of the means by which reliability is achieved. If, for the sake of argument, we can begin to think of free verse as a form of fiction rather than a consequence of "poetry," then we might be able to shift the emphasis from the rhythm of the interval to the rhythm of the sequel, from the mere presence of a speaker to the prescience of a teller, from the piecemeal evidence of the image to a full disclosure of the emotion. We might even be able to go so far as to define tone as the point of view in a poem—making our narrator, to borrow from James, the central consciousness. The advantage of this shift in perception would be to make free verse freer—which is simply to describe what is happening. It is obvious, for example, that the prose-poem has taken on renewed life in the last ten years, that poets as different as James Wright and W. S. Merwin have moved, in the course of their careers, from formal to free to prose verse, that even poets still respecting the line-breaks are inviting more and more of the "dailyness of the imagination" into their work. The logic here, though, need not lead us into temptation. *Freer* should refer to a verse at once more responsive and responsible to the debate of experience, a debate implying not only the discrete and discontinuous but the contradictory, a debate in demand of an attitude complete in its understanding of—for want of a word—what Keats called negative capability, a phrase that has long since passed into the language. "I mean *Negative Capability*, that is, when a man is capable of being in uncertainties, mysteries, doubts, without any irritable reaching after fact and reason." If fixed form would tend to resolve too much of the reliability of narrative witness, ease too readily the ironical tension of discourse in a state of doubt, the fictionalizing of free verse would open it to the fuller realization of its resources. Much of the most interesting poetry of the seventies, from *The Book of Nightmares* to *Self-Portrait in a Convex Mirror*, has needed a larger forum than the simple lyric in order to include a larger complement of "uncertainties, mysteries, doubts" and required at the same time an intelligence capable of keeping the debate going. "Any irritable reaching after fact and reason," perhaps after fixity itself, would sacrifice the energy and depth of that debate. It is as if the lyric had come to a fuller understanding of its dramatic, narrative potential—a free verse forum providing world enough and time to both show and tell, to *plot* the memory or the dream, to work out rather than work over the emotion, to let the language of the experience speak to the total condition of that experience.

As Eliot discovered in "Prufrock" and later, more profoundly, in *The Waste Land*, plot should be a psychological rather than a strictly empirical revelation. It should reveal the "character" of the narrator just as it confers pattern to his performance; it should enlarge the psychic space as it suggests movement through time. (The narrator's prescience, not his presumed omniscience, is what we will believe.) One need not expect a forum as large as *The Waste Land* nor as long as Robert Lowell's ongoing autobiography— the parallel of the contemporary short story to the contemporary lyric is as dependable as the parallel of *Ulysses* to Eliot's great poem. The sense of size is of course relative to requirements of content. And the sense of size generated by plot, whether the illusion is of concentration or continuum, is the result of a competition of forces—visual, emotional, structural, and rhetorical. While all such forces operate simultaneously, they must operate together, building not only a fiction but an attitude, the substance of a point of view. In the "post-Eliot" phase, and especially in the generation of the seventies, the intersection of the flexibility of the free verse rhythm with the strategy of storytelling has produced a kind of prose lyric: a form corrupt enough to speak flat out in sentences yet pure enough to sustain the intensity, if not the integrity, of the line; a form wide enough to include a range of reference yet narrow enough to select; a form coherent with and accountable to its sources yet sensitive enough to register variation in the terrain; a form expressive enough to elaborate the most inward experience yet aware enough to attract our public attention.

Yet the phrase *prose lyric* describes the function more than the feel of the form. It describes, for instance, the latest stage in the long-standing career of poet Robert Penn Warren as much as it covers the beginning of the career of a poet such as Dave Smith. It does not, however, describe a shift in aesthetic stance. If nothing else, poetry today is redefining its relationship with its raw materials. The exchange is more intimate than ever, more ironical than ever, more specific than ever, more direct than ever, more relative (i.e., relativist) than ever, so that even a monument like Lowell has, since 1970, domesticized both his line and historical consciousness considerably. The commonplace, the small moment, has assumed the value of what was once modernly reserved as "symbolic." Things now seem to stand mostly for themselves. The resonance of the object and the emotion has become local rather than instantly universal—detailed rather than detachable. The fictionalization of free verse, with its emphasis on the process as opposed to the production, with its increased emphasis on including not only the complication of the emotional evidence but to whatever extent possible the evolution of that evidence—as per, for example, recent poems as ostensibly different as Mark Strand's "The Untelling" and Louis Simpson's "Searching for the Ox"—has introduced a new fluency to the first level at which experience takes on metaphor and meaning. The order of the action can be only half of it; where the raw material comes from and how it is treated make the difference. As the narrator plots his poem, his effectiveness will depend on how well he represents his mixed emotions, the ambiguities of what passes for the ordinary. Poetry, free or half-free, as it opens itself even more to the terms of the personal and the particular, finds more room to maneuver in the strategies of fiction and within the irregularities of prose.

Sources and substance. They are not so much providential as accidental. And the accident has most to do with the person or persona of the poet himself, what he or she brings to the material and what "point of view" is sustained. More than any other measure, tone is the essential means, and end, of the free verse poem. It is its one and abiding convention, the sum of its peculiar, singular parts. So it is less an attitude provided than an attitude achieved, the voice of the emotion earned. It goes without saying that we will believe what we are being told insofar as what we are being told is true, as we willingly suspend, as in a dream, our disbelief. The poet cannot afford the appearance of letting, say, the language stand between him and his vital sources. His proof lies in the very tone of his voice, in the prosody of actual speech, when at some point in the poem that speech takes over and the voice becomes the hero of the story.

*Heroic Simile*

When the swordsman fell in Kurosawa's *Seven Samurai*
in the gray rain,
in Cinemascope and the Tokagawa dynasty,
he fell straight as a pine, he fell
as Ajax fell in Homer
in chanted dactyls and the tree was so huge
the woodsman returned for two days
to that lucky place before he was done with the sawing
and on the third day he brought his uncle.

They stacked logs in the resinous air,
hacking the small limbs off,
tying those bundles separately.
The slabs near the root
were quartered and still they were awkwardly large;
the logs from midtree they halved:
ten bundles and four great piles of fragrant wood,
moons and quarter moons and half moons
ridged by the saw's tooth.

The woodsman and the old man his uncle
are standing in midforest
on a floor of pine silt and spring mud.
They have stopped working
because they are tired and because
I have imagined no pack animal
or primitive wagon. They are too canny
to call in neighbors and come home
with a few logs after three days' work.
They are waiting for me to do something
or for the overseer of the Great Lord
to come and arrest them.

How patient they are!
The old man smokes a pipe and spits.
The young man is thinking he would be rich
if he were already rich and had a mule.
Ten days of hauling
and on the seventh day they'll probably
be caught, go home empty-handed
or worse. I don't know
whether they're Japanese or Mycenaean
and there's nothing I can do.
The path from here to that village
is not translated. A hero, dying,
gives off stillness to the air.
A man and a woman walk from the movies
to the house in the silence of separate fidelities.
There are limits to imagination.

This poem by Robert Hass is from a book-in-progress. As in so much of his best writing it places the problem of the work of art immediately beside the work of life—an imagined event in direct correspondence with a real one. And as typical, whatever ambiguity, ambivalence, or doubt there is lies in the basic situation, clearly, promptly stated. Hass rarely extrapolates from his source; rather he explores what is most palpably provided. Nearly all of his poetry is about limits, the sometimes excruciating but irresistible finitude of things. That is why he can so often afford the sometimes rhetorical and relentless pursuit of the objective and such first lines as "In the life we live together every paradise is lost": his hold on his material feels absolute, even as his spokesman questions such authority. No exception, "Heroic Simile" ends with an apparent admission—there are limits to the imagination—though within the ironic context of the poem and *under* a suprastructure of elaborate connections, the last line looks more out from than back in to what it is supporting. The dramatic situation is clear, once the position of the speaker, the narrator, is established: "I have imagined no pack animal/or primitive wagon." The reality of art, for whatever it is worth, depends here on the ability of *like*. Through the first two stanzas the events move as if observed but without certain disclosure of the point of view. The swordsman in the "heroic" film falls like the hero in heroic Homer, one in terms of Cinemascope, the other, Ajax, in the prosody of chanted dactyls. The rhythm of the images of the movie is to be compared to the rhythm of the sounds of the poetry: contexts of technique. But before the swordsman falls like Ajax, he falls "straight as a pine," and that little sidestep develops into the whole story-within-a-story of the rest of the poem. The method is indirection and it helps to understate and lighten the heroic or hyperbolic potential of the comparison. More than that, the method is discontinuous within the continuum of the line "in chanted dactyls and the tree was so huge," as if the balance of dactyls and the tree were parallel. (The third line offers a similar "parallel.") They may not be parallel, but they are, ironically, equal. In this forest, the pine goes down in falling meter. And on the third day, the peasant woodsman, sawing up the simile of the swordsman, brings in his uncle to help him stack the "logs in the resinous air." As the first half of the poem concludes, the tree has been further transformed and reduced into "ten bundles and four great piles of fragrant wood,/moons and quarter moons and half moons." The hero, as in a folk tale, was too awkwardly large.

The second half of the poem opens with the speaker-narrator announcing his present-tense presence and develops with the revelation of his role as the actual protagonist. The logic of such a strategy is simple enough: to admit the "I" too early would have blunted the story-interest of the plot and, more importantly, compromised his authority over his "material." An identified, individuated voice at the outset would have surely placed the emphasis on self-consciousness rather than on the simile, on who is making the comparisons rather than on the central fact of the connections them-selves. In a word, the point of view would have been overstated through an early exposure that in turn would have emphasized the emotion of the poem over its perception—before that emotion had been earned. To begin with the "I" front and center, would mean sentimentalizating the story, as the narrator would have no chance to prove—only to approve—his position. The moment the voice is identified, however, the narrator becomes an actor in his own fiction. The relative balance and symmetrical look of the first two stanzas—prepared as they are in a sequence of parallels and repetition—becomes attenuated by the acknowledgement, in stanza 3, of an imagina-tion all too aware of its functional limitations. We move from the overvoice of the folktale ("The logs from midtree they halved") to the local voice of the artist-hero: at which point the verse turns a little freer, a little more relaxed, more declarative, and certainly more anxious. It is no accident that as we clarify point of view we complicate the action, and that as we compli-cate the action the narrator is revealed to be the protagonist. Plot is a pro-cess of disclosure, of the piecemeal yielding of information. Once the simile structure is set its source must be identified. Not even the Great Lord can make metaphor. The narrator-protagonist, though, has created an imagi-native problem for which he has been unable to anticipate an answer. The woodsman and his uncle have stopped working because they are tired (story reason) and because "I have imagined no pack animal/ or primitive wagon" (storytelling reason). So there they are "standing in midforest," suspended in present tense between what can be imagined and what is real. They are too canny, he assures us, as if to further his fiction, to call in neighbors and go home with only a few logs after three days' labor. "They are waiting for me to do something" or to be arrested. *Because, because* is the spoken and unspoken refrain in the speaker's voice. Within the aesthetic space of the poem *like* is the connection; but within fictions, both internal and external, cause-and-effect defines relations. How patient they are!—the old man smoking and spitting, the young man, naturally, speculating, worrying. The narrator is under some pressure himself—"I don't know/whether they're Japanese or Mycenaean." Making similes can be seductive, to the point of empathy. As a protagonist, he admits he is no better off than his charac-ters. "There's nothing I can do./The path from here to that village/is not translated."

Had Hass ended the poem with his unvisited village, truncated though the sense of follow-through might be, he would have achieved a certain ironic capability—yet in a tone of voice that would have undercut the implied seriousness of his protestations. Instead, thankfully, he commits himself to the rhetoric of an ultimate concern. Why is the narrator unable to translate any further—indeed, any farther—Tokagawa or Mycenaean? *Because* he is not omnipotent: he is subject to the same laws of life as Kurosawa's protagonist, Homer's protagonist, and his own. "A hero, dying,/gives off stillness to the air," like the felling of a great tree. Hass is no more heroic than his woodsman, but within limits they each have work to do. Cutting up wood, we suppose, can be as imaginative as making a poem if the wood is halved and quartered and bundled and piled into phases of the moon. Looking, listening back, we can see that the whole poem has been pronounced within a clarifying stillness. The moment of reminder of the hero's dying is the peak of Hass's story. Its penultimate couplet—movies/fidelities—however, is the statement that unifies and transcends the limitations of the narration. Chekhov has said that every story has a single center of gravity, a *he* and a *she*. Hass started his story at the movies, he ends it on the way back home. The stillness of the initiating action is to be compared, to be like the silence of the conclusive moment, except that in fact the one has caused the effect of the other. The plot and whatever profundity of the poem stand on the ceremony of contemplation, the couple in "the silence of separate fidelities." The phrase itself is a metaphor of denial, an affirmation of the inevitable and self-contained integrity of things, be they objects or subjects. We can compare, even make beautiful, what seems an unlikely or unserious connection, say between a samurai and a pine—a suicide simile when one considers that a sword too can be reduced to a saw. But the comparison depends as much on differences as similarities—and in the relative world of the real perhaps mostly on the differences. Walking home from the movies is the one "real" act in this poem. It is part of a limited, cause-and-effect world of separate fidelities. In declaring himself in the third person ("a man and a woman") the narrator has kept his aesthetic distance, and difference, without sacrificing his emotional investment. These next-to-last two lines may speak straight out, as to expose, yet they are also dramatic; in their disclosure they are as much a part of the total fiction as the woodsman. "Silence of separate fidelities" is, after all, *the* metaphor of the poem, an entity in which things may indeed be like other things. Yet images exist only in space unless they correspond to one another in that paradigm of sequence we call fiction. If the Hass narrator has failed as a "poet" he has succeeded movingly as a storyteller. At the last, he has said to us directly, in so much prose, that there are limits to the imagination because there are limits to what we can say.

# 5

A significant part of Stephen Dedalus's intellectual heroism is his three-tiered theory of literary art, proposing an evolution from the lyrical (the simplest, most personal) to the narrative (longer, less personal) to the dramatic (as objective as possible). To the extent his hero is successful, Joyce did in truth stage his storytelling, to the point that his great work, *Ulysses*, Mr. Bloom's Day, is *on the page* a great movie—a cinematic as well as dramatic masterpiece. Yet as drama it is an art corrupted, as it must be, by its overall dependence on narrative context and "scenes" of lyric intensity. Poetry, as we have been saying, is dramatic insofar as it presents and lyric insofar as it represents. And insofar as it *coheres* it tells a story. Joyce paring his fingernails aside, no form is strictly this or that; the page cannot afford such purity. The very fiction, not to mention freedom, of free verse consists in the corruption of the form, and its most distinguishing characteristic, rhythm, whether moving across or down the page, is the result of how well or ill that corruption—that lyric, dramatic, and narrative voice—takes. The necessary combination of modes, the necessary corruption, is suggested in the single poem, but stated, completed in the book of poems.

So many books of poetry appear each season, most barely adequate, some exemplary, and a few truly exceptional. The genuinely good book, the one that returns and returns its value, offers more than a miscellany of fine poems. It provides us, we usually say in such circumstances, with a whole conception, a design, a vision, an organic unity, and so on. And it does. But vision, for instance, is the post-perceptual phase; like unity and design and conception, it is the overview, the afterword. The actual oneness of the thing, though, is a mystery, and trying to break it down is like trying to separate a lyric moment from a dramatic one. What pulls us into the good book, the whole book, what keeps our attention, from poem to poem, part to part, is the accumulating strength and complexity and interest and full character of the speaking voice, a voice that must not only articulate but act out the vision of the work. Regardless of the emotional or intellectual debate, the moral authority of any art begins with our sense of being in the presence of oneness. Who speaks becomes more important than what is said, at that initiation. The speaker, like the narrator in fiction, arbitrates unity. Three books, so obvious in their differences yet similar in their emotional needs, three books from among many, stand out as whole and new: Marvin Bell's *Stars Which See, Stars Which Do Not See,* William Heyen's *The Swastika Poems,* and C. K. Williams's *With Ignorance.*

Marvin Bell may have the most refined ear of his free verse contemporaries. He is that rare poet who can hear speech as it was meant to be written. His page is invariably a formal indictment, with even the white space structured, understood, relieved. The first stanza from "The Mystery of Emily Dickinson" is practically in couplets.

> Sometimes the weather goes on for days
> but you were different. You were divine.
> While the others wrote more and longer,
> you wrote much more and much shorter.
> I held your white dress once: 12 buttons.
> In the cupola, the wasps struck glass
> as hard to escape as you hit your sound
> again and again asking Welcome. No one.

Visually the stanza complements the propriety and model of its subject: the rhythm may not be hymnal, but it is hushed, intimate, sure of itself—of when to speak and when to listen. Bell is a Dickinson poet. Has "You were divine" ever been delivered more humanely? He is well established as an intelligence of wit and no little elegance. Poet as elaborator, a Jewish metaphysician. But the new poems, and certainly this small example, look well past the language and the elaboration of emotion to an actual, coherent, present source, to a rhythm as easy and as difficult as conversation. For one thing, Bell is addressing his antagonist directly, "I held your white dress once:

12 buttons." He is speaking, not composing, even as the lines move along in their more or less metrical way, typically between a tetrameter and pentameter in length, yet always at the service of the speech. Sometimes they intensify, as in the *s*-sounding couplet of buttons/glass; sometimes they relax, with the *r*'s in the lines ending longer/shorter. The stanza concludes, as in much of Dickinson, with the real action off-stage. We never hear her knocking, her accent, asking, of all things, welcome. We hear, by analogy, about it, as in an echo, *one* rhymed with *sound*. Had Bell actually stayed couplet-pure, with his lines measured as much for syntax as for speech, this Emily Dickinson poem might have been converted into art before it had a chance to be a poem. Later on, once the speaker transfers the scene from New England back to "home," the story enlarges to include our "sleepy householder at his routine," among the larger details of neighbors and neighborhood, and affection turning toward passion.

> This morning, not much after dawn,
> in level country, not New England's,
> through leftovers of summer rain I
> went out rag-tag to the curb . . .
> bending to trash, when a young girl
> in a white dress your size passed,
>
> so softly!, carrying her shoes.

As the voice of the poem is forced outside, into its own territory, away from the confines of the cupola, the idiom loosens up; the actor who is also speaking must sort between event and the emotional evidence. "I should have called to her," he says, "but a neighbor/wore that to look you see against happiness." His love letter to Dickinson ends with the ultimate compliment, imitation. "I won't say anything would have happened/unless there was time, and eternity's plenty."

"The Mystery of Emily Dickinson," ghost dress or not, is no mystery. It is as domestic a poem as Bell has ever written, in a book of homebodies. The wandering Jew has settled down, "half past the Midwest, going West," to contemplate, among other ontological questions, the size of the self, the limits of the self. "I wanted to see the self, so I looked at the mulberry./It had no trouble accepting its limits." Anyone who has followed the career of the speaker of these utterly declarative lines knows that Bell, from book 1, has been the most self-conscious of poets, maintaining an aesthetic and ironical distance that has amounted to doppelganging. Yet in *Stars Which See*, the person—his voice, his softer rhythms, his talk over the telephone—has replaced the tensions of the persona. The self is no longer the dual subject, the parallel circumstance of, say, an escape into you, no longer an idea with which to complicate the shadows of the poem. The self is now the object, much like a tree, be it a mulberry, a wild cherry, an elm we lost, or just a leaf in July, an object to study, to come to conclusions about—

> It had no trouble accepting its limits,
> yet defining and redefining a small area
> so that any shape was possible, any movement.
> It stayed put, but was part of all the air.
> I wanted to learn to be there and not there
> like the continually changing, slightly moving
> mulberry, wild cherry and particularly the willow.
> Like the willow, I tried to weep without tears.
> Like the cherry tree, I tried to be sturdy and productive.
> Like the mulberry, I tried to keep moving.
> I couldn't cry right, couldn't stay or go.
> I kept losing parts of myself like a soft maple.
> I fell ill like an elm. That was the end
> of looking in nature to find a natural self.

So this poem ends—as it literally does, in four more lines of exhortation—in mock denial, in plainness. No natural self, not in the metaphor of the tree anyway. Perhaps the image "that gives the self the notion of the self" is as unassuming as a fern pot ("I love watching the water/ooze through the crack in the fern pot,/it's a small thing//that slows time/and steadies/and gives me ideas of becoming . . .") or as archetypical as the poem ("Unlike so many others,/I had no wings, just shoulders./I was, like the snow bunting,/of stout build but moderate size./Better make that 'exceedingly' moderate size."). The poet plays with and against the issue throughout the first quarter of his book, finishing the first section with a title poem that, although it mentions neither self nor subject (first-person pronoun) is the most serious, contemplative, beautiful, and self-absorbed of all.

> They sat by the water. The fine women
> had large breasts, tightly checked.
> At each point, at every moment,
> they seemed happy by the water.
> The women wore hats like umbrellas
> or carried umbrellas shaped like hats.
> The men wore no hats and the water,
> which wore no hats, had that well-known
> mirror finish which tempts sailors.
> Although the men and women seemed at rest
> they were looking toward the river
> and some way out into it but not beyond.
> The scene was one of hearts and flowers
> though this may be unfair. Nevertheless,
> it was probable that the Seine had hurt them,
> that they were "taken back" by its beauty
> to where a slight breeze broke the mirror
> and then its promise, but never the water.

Bell's book moves from this title poem through three more stages—from having established who is speaking (point of view) to delineating who is being spoken to in general ("To No One in Particular") and in particular ("To His Solitary Reader") to who is listening ("To Dorothy"). Exposition, complication, resolution. In each of the book's parts the speaking voice tests itself in a kind of small talk, a quietly affirming, confident rhetoric that "whether you sing or scream" begins "inside yourself." At all stages, the reader is aware of his position as the silent partner in a dialogue (different from being the captive audience of a declamation) in which a man, paradoxically, proposes himself in the third person. "Sometimes, you think you know what people/think of you, and it's not much." Still, the pattern of Bell's book is patently not in step with some overt struggle; instead it represents, in rhythms as natural as Williams ("the old Williams"), a story of restlessness and rest ("For us, this was the place to be stopping."), revision, and memorization into the present tense. The ethos of childhood on Long Island has never been more brought to bear on an adulthood in the middlewest of Iowa. In past books, Bell tended to allude to his history; here it is a vital part of the issue, the informing angel of the book's overall tone. It is only appropriate, then, that the poet should end the four sections of his collection with two poems dedicated to his wife and sons. He began the book alone, talking about trees, in a brown study about consciousness. He continued by conducting a conversation with the past, his muse, fiddling with this or that stratagem. Finally, "for you and I have made it this far," he arrives at the house in town, the perfect hometown. A very American story, and this is the most American, our-town of Bell's work. *Stars Which See, Stars Which Do Not See* is about the wisdom of arrival, indeed about wisdom itself, about growth, about coming to terms with the most personal of limits, about transcending the single self for the will and witness of the family, even as that family is as much the place you have come from as the place you have come to.

That, in linear, is the direction of Bell's book. But the title poem, the one without an announced speaker, coming as it does in the first section, implies the apparent antithesis of a journey. It is still life, Seurat. It suggests that wisdom is a word yet to be made flesh. But forget the painting for a moment. Reread the poem. The voice, understated to tensile strength, pokes through consistently to qualify and comment, though more as an overvoice than as a dramatic or narrative interlocutor. We are at that moment in the book when a transition from who to whom is about to be made. The third person of the self, this objective of the subjective case, seems to speak as an entity. The scene—"of hearts and flowers"—may be too beautiful, but it is also claustrophobic, closed up in thought, the sunlight hypnotic on the water. The mind is in love, yet subverted to ambiguity, as the eye submits to pointillist generalization. Hats are like umbrellas, umbrellas like hats—a fair exchange. And the water, the Seine of the scene (the wit is also tautological), hatless and still as if suspended, has "that well-known/mirror finish which tempts sailors." The men and women look toward the river "and some way out into it but not beyond." The voice of the poem speculates that the beauty of all this Sunday afternoon is almost too much, especially when a slight breeze, or the memory of a breeze, breaks "the mirror/and then its promise, but never the water." Hearts and flowers to one side, the poem is exquisite but not perfect. Thankfully, its voice—modulating, withholding—remains the subjective influence. From the post-impressionism of the title on, the poem reads like an extended correlative, a tone poem of the self contemplating, visualizing, voicing paralysis—a moment, not unlike the moment for the men and women looking out over the water mirror, of complete narcissism. What makes Bell's book, beyond the poem, possible and finally powerful is that he steps into the mirror, that water that tempts sailors, and comes out into the future. Nevertheless, as he comments in the book's last poem, "now it seems to me the heart/must enlarge to hold the losses/we have ahead of us."

"Memory is what we are," says Bell. William Heyen, in his *Swastika Poems*, is less interested in the aesthetic, Proustian problem, the personality of memory, than in the larger, shared fact and texture of memory, that matrix in which the personal and public remembering intersect. Heyen's expository epigraph is from Susan Sontag's *Against Interpretation*: "The supreme tragic event in modern times is the murder of the six million European Jews," she writes, and concludes that "ultimately the only response is to continue to hold the event in mind, to remember it. . . . This moral function of remembering is something that cuts across the different worlds of knowledge, action and art." Any response to the burden of such an event, whether in action or art, any public response, implies a presumption of knowledge and guilt and experience, not to say extrapolation, beyond our common lives. For a young American poet, first generation German and/or Jew, who was only five years old the day Roosevelt died, the presumption could come on as disgusting. So it is certainly no accident that Heyen spends the full first third of his book laying groundwork, building credentials, establishing the materials and meanings that will sustain the moral imperative and the emotional charge and discharge of his tone of voice. He is obviously a man with bad dreams.

"Men in History," part 1, begins with a snapshot of the poet's German immigrant father, hick tie and thick kraut hair, 1928, on the boat to America—and *"rivers, trees, land, money."* We learn quickly, in successive poems, that the father has left behind more than the fatherland; he has turned his back on two Nazi brothers, Wilhelm and Hermann, foot-soldier and airman, whom Heyen addresses in elegies of expiation. (Heyen is named after Wilhelm.)

Though named for Wilhelm, your poet-brother,
I often curse the two of you and spend my hours
writing verses that wonder how your fiery,
German romanticism started,
and where, at last, if it did, it died.

That German romanticism, and expressionism, is at the source of Heyen's emotion. Along with and parallel to the family pieces, Heyen's own men in history, the poet places a letter to one Hansjorg Greiner, another dead Nazi (October 20, 1944, at War Camp Arsk, the Urals), Stalingrader, and allegorical stand-in for the German army. The Greiner figure, though, is here less to juxtapose the brothers than to generalize the Heyens' direct connection to their relatives and one-time countrymen in Germany ("we say your name//to ourselves in the slow syllables of prayer"). Once past the personal biography, the first handful of poems, the facts blur into a fantasy, or phantasmagoria, of Fuehrer-hatred, Fuehrer fascination.

Born in Brooklyn of German parents, I
have lived with him for thirty years.
I remember lines scratched on our doors,
the crooked swastikas my father cursed
and painted over.

He came to our city,
and the people were shouting and crying.
They hailed the Fuehrer
as the deliverer.
I was in the crowd, caught
in delirium, a moving box,
pushed forward.

Placed against the fantasy, immediately, is the imagination of pain, the Jewish problem.

They walk into the house.
Concrete floor and no furniture.
Maybe two hundred nozzles stick out.

> The two windows and the door lined with rubber.
> It's a shower, all right, but gas comes out,
> and twists their bodies into awful shapes.
> Gas does not put them quietly to sleep.
> Their flesh is torn with their own or others' teeth . . .
> Their bodies were bluish red.

The selection ends in nightmare, a "Darkness" in which the poet admits "this love I have,/this lust to press/these words," and admits himself into the processes of defilement and death, and admits the reader too into his litany of the very kind of atrocity his rhetoric has railed against. The Fuehrer becomes father-figure.

> He
> tells me lower,
> and the black breastbone aches with it,
> the last black liquid
> cupped in the eyesockets smells of it,
> odor of cyanide's bitter almond,
> the viscera smeared to the backbone
> shines with it . . .

Part 2, "Men in History," is the real risk in Heyen's book, speaking as he does, in nouns of direct address, to the leader and those led. To create a way out of his story he has had to prepare a way in—because the story had to be told. It is a question of authenticating the action within his poems as it is the voice without. The family poems, the first five or six, are solidi-fied, fixed surely on the page. They communicate that palpable sense of source and direction that only autobiography can provide. The moment Heyen moves into the fiction of his fiction, the Jewish question, a quality of masochism takes over, the demands of self-inflicted injury, demands that we must share. What was lyrical and dramatic in the rhythms of a growing empathy, a German family as victim too, becomes, in the nightmare poems, a ritual of the grotesque. The moral imperative, in brutal imaginative steps, becomes the moral absolute. If we had only the initial section to judge from, Heyen's critics might be justified. But Heyen's story is a whole one, a work-ing out and to and through. No sooner has the smell of almond and dead smoke left the air than we are placed in prose, some twenty-five or so years later, in Belsen. The shift to prose, in clear relief to the Aryan free verse that precedes it, is brilliant, brilliant as an emotional strategy, brilliant in the total rhythm of the book, because it stabilizes a sensibility pushed to an extreme. This mid-section is entitled "Erika," after the bell-heather, "the heide, a health plant, wild and strong." Heyen elevates the metaphor by showing us where, in the dead camp, camp of the dead, the heather is, "stiff blooming" over the Bergen-Belsen graves, now in December a "green, dark green" but in early fall, "a reddish blue," a bruise, a blush. He has come to this place as an adult in order to make his life coherent with his childhood ("All those years/there was one word I never heard,/one name never mentioned."). Such *returns* amount to the moral functioning of remembering. Walking Belsen's grounds as a tourist, Heyen reruns all those hideous war camp movies through his head—"the mummified bodies, the Lugers held against the temples of old men, the huge eyes, the common graves from which arms and legs sprout like mushrooms." Near the end of his commentary, and tour, he is able to acknowledge, first-hand, first-person, the dimension of man-made, manufactured death. He can hardly, himself a man now and a German child, believe it. The Erika, he says, is the blossom of memory, a real flowering in real time, "blowing green or blooming violet-red over the dead." Completing his passage, he hears out the caretaker of the place reciting some of the things he still finds that turn up at Belsen: "a pin, or the twisted frames of someone's glasses, or a key, or a wedding band." If anything authenticates Heyen's imperative tone and purpose, this prose, this standing outside the emotion long enough to see in perspective, does.

The third and final section, "The Numinous," opens the line and the feel of the line to an earned understanding of irony, resisting a seduction perhaps set up by the Erika, a flower of eloquence, to now exaggerate the emotion. "Reader, all words are a dream./You have wandered into mine./Now as workers rummage among the corpses,/we will leave for our affairs." The brutalities have hardly lessened in magnitude, but the attitude assumed has replaced the earlier potential for didacticism with the power of persuasion, the power of the poet to transform his swastikas into "frost stars . . . their strict/crooked arms pointing/this way and that, scare-/crows, skeletons, limbs/akimbo." Because they are at last beyond the burden of exposition and preparation, these final poems are better able to project the solutions of imagination—"Noon, I walk among the thousands dead, hear//crows cry *rawr, rawr* through the dark air./I watch them drift to nowhere down the wind . . ."—and to listen to experience before talking back. It is as if Heyen had to pass through a certain self-contempt, a stridency in the voice, in order to integrate a personality, a wholly American presence. For example, there is nothing like the beauty and music of "Simple Truths" at the beginning of the book. It is the penultimate poem (discounting a German song, "Ewigen Melodien"); it embodies the journey made as much as the vision achieved of what Heyen set out to do.

> When a man has grown a body,
> a body to carry with him
> through nature for as long as he can,
> when his body is taken from him
> by other men and women who happened to be,
> this time, in uniform,
> then it is clear he has experienced
> an act of barbarism . . .

Numinous, the metaphor for the whole section, implies the holy, the magical, even the totemic, the dream-word. Swastika may be Heyen's *numen*, his word. His numinous word-made-flesh, however, is the body, the electric Aryan body. "Simple Truths" forces the reader to go back to the intensity, the insistence of some of the early poems for a second look. They may be nearly blasphemous, but they are en route, in process toward a vision of the carnal, the corrupted body incarnate. By reenacting, as both participant and narrator, the gothic yet banal science fiction of the death camps, by dramatizing while declaring the simple truths of the body broken down to bread and then to flour, of breath reduced to spirit, by extending through some eighty odd lines the single, free verse sentence, the remembered fiction of *when* and *from* and *if*—

> and when we remember,
> when we touch the skin of our own bodies,
> when we open our eyes into dream
> or within the morning shine of sunlight

and remember what was taken
from these men, from these women,
from these children gassed and starved
and beaten and thrown against walls
and made to walk the valley
of knives and icepicks and otherwise
exterminated in ways appearing to us almost
beyond even the maniacal human imagination . . .

and when we read a book of these things,
when we hear the names of the camps,
when we see the films of the bulldozed dead
or the film of one boy struck on the head
with a club in the hands
of a German doctor who will wait
some days for the boy's skull to knit, and will enter
the time in his ledger, and then
take up the club to strike the boy again
and wait some weeks for the boy's skull to knit,
and enter the time in his ledger again,
and strike the boy again,
and so on, until the boy, who,
at the end of the film of his life
can hardly stagger forward toward the doctor,
does die, and the doctor
enters exactly the time of the boy's death in his ledger . . .

—by all of this, "the swastika shapes of trees struck by lightning," the "automatic electric Aryan swerve," the repetition and return, language and the "bloodstream and the brain-current" the language stands for, by all of this and the perspective of thirty years after swastikas on the windows in America, Heyen remembers and makes his memory ours.

The named obsession is one thing, the unnameable another. The fourteen poems of C. K. Williams's *With Ignorance*, alternating between a sort of street-talk storytelling and incandescent lyricism, seem to end where they begin, at the peripheries of speech and naming, with ignorance. The difference, of course, is that his book moves from a negative to a positive pole, from "a mouth full of nails" to "a silence rising through light." It is inevitable that a poet preoccupied with the inarticulate and inarticulated should fill the page with lines as long as prose, in pursuit of a right-hand margin. "It must have been like always carrying something there that weighed too much." Indeed. Richard Howard once referred to prose as the medium out to eliminate itself, to use itself up in the irrecoverable rhythms of speech. He called it "the dialect of negation." Williams's lines eventually enjamb or turn back to recover breath, good sense, or hope. And yet they read as if determined to turn into silence, or light. The poems themselves in this his third volume, posing story against song against story in a cause-and-effect pattern, accumulate much as the individual lines do, *toward* something more than *to* something. Rhythmically, it is a book about momentum as much as meaning. Even so, Williams is fond of interrupting himself with gestures like "This is going to get a little nutty now" or "There's another legend" or "I was dreaming about the universe." Occasionally he interrupts himself at the start of the poem—"This is a story." Still, the rhythm of the book as a whole is no horizon line. The moments of the emphatic lyric, such as "Spit" or "The Race of the Flood" or "Near the Haunted Castle," offer the stories a place to get to and leave, as if the emotional life being freighted in the narrative moments had too much left over and some accounting had to be made.

"The first language was loss, the second sorrow," Williams says on his last page. Almost every line, every image up to and including that page rehearses that knowledge, a knowledge exercised again and again against ignorance. But ignorance here suggests something deeper than unknowing; it speaks from a position of primacy, from "the gut cave, the speech cave," from "the hide, the caul, the first mind." That is why the voice throughout the book is so consistent, so complete. It comes from an absolute source, an emotion so exposed as to call into question the very idea of artifice. No wonder, then, the technique of Williams's total fiction is to hesitate or spill over, interrupt or repeat, pledge doubt or reassurance. *With Ignorance* is predicated on one of the most dangerous clichés in literature, that to recreate the condition one must imitate its origin. The artist, not the man, rescues that cliché. The artist in Williams recreates the *condition of ignorance*, "not to know how silently we kneel in the mouth of death," in its full voice, the voice of letting go, letting out, letting alone, the pure voice of the prose lyricist.

> There's a park near here
> where everyone who's out of work in our neighborhood comes to
>         line up in the morning.
> The converted school buses shuttling hands to the cannery fields
>         in Jersey were just rattling away when I got there
> and the small-time contractors, hiring out cheap walls, cheap
>         ditches, cheap everything,
> were loading laborers onto the sacks of plaster and concrete
>         in the backs of their pickups.
>
> A few housewives drove by looking for someone to babysit
>         or clean cellars for them,
> then the gates of the local bar unlaced and whoever was left
>         drifted in out of the wall of heat
> already rolling in with the first fists of smoke from
>         the city incinerators.

Here is a poetry that proves that meter and metaphor are not necessarily symbiotic, that the music must be in the source before it can be in the sound of the line. The feeling of and a feeling for things, the empathy, is in the very length of the line, the inevitability of the line, beyond the ability of the music—"then the gates of the local bar unlaced and whoever was left drifted in out of the wall of heat"—and beyond, almost, the endurance of the page. It is not simply that Williams's lines are long, but that they contain so much, carry so much, say and say.

*With Ignorance* is about a man in trouble, but thank God it is real trouble. "Are we commended to each other to alleviate our terror of solitude and annihilation and that's all?" This is the conclusion of the poem, "The Shade," already quoted from.

> I say it again: my wife, my child . . . my home, my work my
>         sorrow.
> If this were the last morning of the world, if time had
>         finally moved inside us and erupted
> and we were Agamemnon again, Helen again, back on that
>         faint, beginning planet
> where even the daily survivals were giants, filled with light,
>         I think I'd still be here,

afraid or not enough afraid, silently howling the names of
    death over the grass and asphalt.
The morning goes on, the sun burning, the earth burning,
    and between them, part of me lifts and starts back,
past the wash of dead music from the bar, the drinker
    reeling on the curb, the cars coughing alive,
and part, buried in itself, stays, forever, blinking into
    the glare, freezing.

Unlike Bell and Heyen, Williams is not returning to anything. Ever the urban dweller, his poems normally begin at street level and end up on the side of the mountain. Ever the actualist, he picks up the detritus lying in front of him, peopling it with friends, locals, his wife, his son and daughter, the drunk on his front step, and then he takes all this literal data and places it in a configuration, in a series of configurations, in a sequence of near-allegories in which everything is at stake and everything can be lost. What is remarkable about Williams's tone of voice, the commitment of his line, the relentlessness of his music, is the extreme to which it all takes us without leaving us there. One comes away from his text feeling filled up, tested, yet emptied too, "like having yourself in a story. Sometimes real life is almost the same,/as though you were being recited; you can almost tell what a thought is before it arrives." Yes, recited, the thought anticipated, the configuration in outline almost formed from word one. The arc of the emotion is nearly the same from poem to poem not simply because of the obsessive nature of the search, but because of the singular and continuing appeal to archetypes—and one purpose of the length of the line and poem is to ensure that transformation from street level is made. The force field of Williams's page is tremendous because the rhythms and images are so inexorably located in the first mind of their maker and are articulated from that first voice he calls silence. His poems are dream-speech, he their dream-speaker.

I was dreaming about the universe. The whole universe
    was happening in one day, like a blossom . . .

Perhaps the best model for the breadth of lyricism, the converting of the ordinary into the extraordinary, the presumption of innocence in the face of ugly evidence, the placing of metaphor and myth against all that is dumb and blind and deadly—perhaps Williams's best model is after all in prose, in the complicated lyricism of James Agee. Let us now praise famous men certainly: with a compassion that will not condescend and with a passion that will not give up. Williams is proletariat, and his romance is with a fulfillment we can imagine but cannot achieve—a romance dating back to Wordsworth. We live in an era in which elegies are love poems, love poems are elegies. We celebrate grief as if we had invented it, and perhaps we have. Poetry in our time has been more and more thrown back on its primary sources, its first cause, its first music. At one emotional level feeling itself is the issue, not what we feel. In the work of a poet like Williams (and a prose writer like Agee) one senses he has entered the essential body of poetry, before the names have been quite made up.

> Old father, wouldn't it be a good ending if you and
>     I could just walk away together?
> Or that you were the king who reveals himself, who folds
>     back the barbed, secret wings
> and we're all so in love now, one spirit, one flesh, one
>     generation, that the truces don't matter?
> Or maybe a better ending would be that there is no ending.
> Maybe the Master of Endings is wandering down through
>     his herds to find it
> and the cave cow who tells the truth and the death cow who
>     holds sea in her eyes are still there
> but all he hears are the same old irresistible slaughter-
>     pen bawlings.
> So maybe there is no end to the story and maybe there's
>     no story.
> Maybe the last calf just ambles up to the trough through
>     the clearing
> and nudges aside the things that swarm on the water
>     and her mouth dips in among them and drinks.
> Then she lifts, and it pours, everything, gushes, and
>     we're lost in both waters.

Williams is right, there is, finally, no story. Only the weight each line is asked to carry.

1977

# II
## IMAGE AND EMBLEM

# 1

Wordsworth and Coleridge make an odd couple, though the very existence of *Lyrical Ballads* suggests the difficulty of aesthetic dichotomies. In the Preface, Wordsworth proposes to "imitate and adopt the very language of men," a language of the rustic life. Thirty years later, in *Biographia Literaria*, Coleridge finally declares against such nonsense. "Anterior to cultivation the *lingua communis* of every country . . . exists everywhere in parts and nowhere as a whole. . . . The language so highly extolled by Mr. Wordsworth varies in every country, nay, in every village, according to the accidental character of the clergyman, the existence or non-existence of schools. . . ." Coleridge is of course being impressively literal-minded: his old friend is speaking as a poet, not a linguist. Wordsworth wants to replace the neoclassical idiom of the eighteenth century with the resonance of the colloquial. Rather than be put in the position of addressing a culture, as a poet he wants to find a way of remaining a man speaking to other men. The author of *The Prelude* has different reasons from the author of *The Rime*, because the language of experience, it seems, is to be distinguished from the language of the imagined event, as the language of prose is to be demarcated from the language of "poetry." Wordsworth would exalt common experience through the sympathy of the word; Coleridge would celebrate the imagination through the alchemy of the word. Wordsworth would look out on the landscape in order to interpret himself to the world; Coleridge would look out on a landscape in order to invent himself back into one.

Aesthetic distinctions therefore are relative, and often irrelevant. But they should never be arbitrary. The first part of this essay attempted to sort out, through young and very recent examples, one reading of free verse—a verse preoccupied with its own voice and rhetoric, the voice of the emotion, a voice tested by its ability to create and control tone. We noted that the terms and means of fiction, as well as the larger rhythms and language of prose, help establish a forum for such poetry—a free verse or prose lyric. Yet Dave Smith and Tess Gallagher and C. K. Williams do not necessarily represent the major American mode of the 1970s. The poetry of the prose lyric hardly constitutes a movement. And while the Hardys and Housmans and Frosts have their following, the history of the uses of the image, of the alchemy of the word, of the placing of the object, rather than its subject, at the center of the work has foregrounded almost every other poetic consideration. Contemporary poetry is still in phase with its reaction to that history, a story as international as it is old. Many younger poets find themselves in transition between a free verse voice and a more formal one, a voice that has idolatrized as well as idealized the image. Many others find themselves in an ambiguity, between what the art can afford and what it cannot afford to do. The language of the emotion, as Coleridge in the last year of his life was at pains to clarify, is expressly different from the language of the image. William Matthews, who excels at both a colloquial diction and the simile, opens a new manuscript of poems with a "subject" even Housman could claim, spring snow.

> Here comes the powdered milk I drank
> as a child, and the money it saved.
> Here come the papers I delivered,
> the spotted dog in heat that followed me home
>
> and the dogs that followed her.
> Here comes a load of white laundry
> from basketball practice, and sheets
> with their watermarks of semen.
>
> And here comes snow, a language
> in which no word is ever repeated,
> love is impossible, and remorse. . . .
> Yet childhood doesn't end,
>
> but accumulates, each memory
> knit to the next, and the fields
> become one field. If to die is to lose
> all detail, then death is not

so distinguished, but a profusion
of detail, a last gossip, character
passed wholly into fate and fate
in flecks, like dust, like flour, like snow.

The question for a lot of younger poets is at what point does plot become pattern and cause-and-effect become juxtaposition? At what point does the informing emotion translate into presiding image? At what point do spatial relationships supersede temporal connections? That point is close at hand in a poem like "Spring Snow." For Matthews has chosen to perfect the emotion rather than perform it, to sublimate his sources rather than expose them, to convert rather than directly convey his trouble. Moreover, the music of the piece is dominated more by the visual than by the voice-print—snow falls through every line, collects in each stanza. Naturally, befitting the temperature, the feel of the poem is cool, in playful but serious study, as the announcer-speaker directs and calls attention to this or that detail of the vernacular of his memory. *Here comes, here comes,* he says, yet we never really sense that the material is raw, is being compounded of his original problem; instead it reads like the result of a prior commitment—recollected in and remaindered to tranquility. In fact, the I of the poem, child and man, exists in subordination to the larger subject of the snow, grammatically and effectively. One of the ways the five stanzas will develop is to heal the difference between subject and object, since the snow, and its variations (including childhood), will become both. No surprise, then, that the "free verse" rhythms are most relaxed in the first two stanzas before snow, as such, is ever mentioned. The information is all Americana—from powdered milk to newspapers to spotted dog to the white laundry to the sheets. To rescue these memories from Norman Rockwell, Matthews punctuates them with qualification. The powdered milk saves money, the spotted dog is in heat, the sheets are watermarked with semen. Matthews is a master at redeeming the domestic cliché. And while the reader's attention is being directed at the details, the poet is patiently working the underground: snow is their coordinator, their coincidence, their coming together, all in "a language/in which no word is ever repeated,/love is impossible, and remorse . . ." Between the *And* and the *Yet* of this middle stanza the poem begins to close in on itself, to concentrate its thought and rhythms, so that by its last ellipsis nearly every line will have been divided and sub-divided. The reason for the increase in intensity is not long sought. This is a metaphysical poem, with snow as its conceit. Its method is inductive—we move from the particular world of powdered milk to the general world of idea, snow as a language, in just three moves. "Yet childhood doesn't end." Past the fulcrum stanza, the poem is all idea, the extended metaphor of childhood's snow, which in eight lines takes us through man's fate. It is as if we were being instructed, having been eased earlier, and ever so lovingly, into the possibilities of snow. This is a piece of sharp intelligence and wit, willing to play the big idea off the trite domestic and able to succeed because it never loses its cool. It moves at a pace with thought. The *real feel* takes too much time.

So the voice of the poem, at least the I, is more guide than hero, a kind of helping pronoun-verb. The intimacy is with the image, and the dynamic lies in its "accumulative" powers. The spring snow unifies not only by summarizing its subordinates but, more importantly, by effecting their simultaneity. Snow is a dialectical image, maintaining distinctions while at the same time resolving their differences. Snow is the real hero of the poem, and childhood its informing emotion—and childhood does not end, but accumulates, each memory knit to the next, as the fields become one field, a far field. And death is not so distinguished if to die is to lose all detail, to *let loose* all detail in a profusion of gossip and character. Our fate is flour, says the poet, like powdered milk. The poem extends itself in circles around the common center of that presiding metaphor. So the voice gets lost in all the detail? The voice *is* the detail, the dialectic of the details. The voice is visual, an excellent example of what Eliot called the auditory imagination. The typical free verse voice, depending as it does on a first-person protagonist, on or off-stage, looks to linear measures of its needs and requirements. But a poem organized around an object is formalized by that object; it depends on the discipline inherent in things themselves, and the space those things occupy. Snow, the color at the center of the wheel, is the absence of color, the perfect absorbing emblem. Snow, the subject of the sentences and the poem, becomes the object. The very rhythm of such metaphysical logic is bound to be carefully considered, since it represents the rhetoric of thought, of thinking through. And the rhetoric of thought, like snow accumulating and disappearing, is a rhetoric of silence, of white space, of an octave almost beyond normal hearing. Matthews is not quite that pure, nor is his snow. It is a spring snow, anyway. Yet this transitional poem of his, repairing as it does an idea out of an image, is sustained by its correspondences—exchanges at a level just above the easy assumptions of emotion. As in Stevens, his voice is in the music of a mind at work. Its tone is an aftereffect, a color quality.

Snow, then, is the stuff of childhood creating the character of fate. And fate, goes the cliché, is character. Such reasoning indicts the past, and though he makes much ado about memory ("each memory/knit to the next"), Matthews is much more taken with what the present will provide and the future confer. The image, as form and idea, is not interested in the rhetoric of the past or even in the mimesis of memory; it wants to be new knowledge, it wants to penetrate the future—it wants, at the least, to be the memory of memory. That is why its preferred medium is space rather than time: the whole point of the figure is to try to transcend the limitations of the linear—that unbending line of direct communication with the past—and move into the focus of the singular, kinetic moment when the truth and the shape of the truth are all true at once. The image is the perpetual-motion machine of continual arrival. *Here comes, here comes.* The image, time-bound as it is in language, is the most plastic form the poem will ever know, yet, paradoxically, because it is in language—snow is, after all, only a word—the image is also the most abstract form. The metaphor may be, for instance, the past married to the future, but its moment is in and out of time. The image is an idea with a body. And its resonance lies more with what we know than with what we remember. (Something like the future tense of memory.) That is why Matthews is apparently so little concerned with *himself.* The self, like a live-in parent, would complicate the speed of imaginative connections by tying them into knots with their primary, perhaps emotional sources. The self would spell out, in its own voice, the elements that make up the image. It would untranslate, decode, attach the language of the image. It would tie it to time, especially as the self *itself* is a metaphor for memory.

If Matthews is in transit from one rhetoric to another, a poet like Larry Levis is caught between. His second book, *The Afterlife*, is an admixture of the opportunities of the image and the emotional demands of the self. This is as accurate of the twelve-part poem that ends the book, "The Rain's

Witness," as it is of "The Map," a small love poem that starts out on the Great Plains and finishes twenty lines later in South America. The collection's title piece, "Rhododendrons," is also such an admixture. It begins right after the weather of a spring snow.

> Winter has moved off
> somewhere, writing its journals
> in ice.
>
> But I am still afraid to move,
> afraid to speak,
> as if I lived in a house
> wallpapered with the cries of birds
> I cannot identify.
>
> Beneath the trees
> a young couple sits talking
> about the afterlife,
> where no one, I think, is
> whittling toys for the stillborn.
> I laugh,
>
> but I don't know.
> Maybe the whole world is absent minded
> or floating. Maybe the new lovers undress
> without wondering how
> the snow grows over the Andes,
> or how a horse cannot remember those
> frozen in the sleigh behind it,
> but keeps running until the lines tangle,
> while the dead sit coolly beneath their pet stars.
>
> As I write this,
> some blown rhododendrons are nodding
> in the first breezes. I want
> to resemble them, and remember nothing,
> the way a photograph of an excavation
> cannot remember the sun.

The wind rises or stops
and it means nothing.

I want to be circular;
a pond or a column of smoke
revolving, slowly, its ashes.

I want to turn back and go up
to myself at age 20,
and press five dollars into his hand
so he can sleep.
While he stands trembling on a street in Fresno,
suddenly one among many in the crowd
that strolls down Fulton Street,
among the stores that are closing,
and is never heard of again.

The imagination here is obviously more extravagant and the emotion more evident than in Matthews. The rhythms are longer, more ragged, freer, as if the poet is having trouble making up his mind, and he is. The poem reads like a high-powered journal entry, full of observation, speculation, and intention, leading a line out in one place, tucking a line in at another. "As I write this," the author finally reminds us. . . . He seems to be searching around for a story to tell, a narrative logic to follow. Thus he offers one example, and another, lets them stand for a moment, then goes on to the next. Since there is no clear plot, there must be a pattern, an architecture, a principle of order to the way the evidence unfolds. Unlike "Spring Snow," the image of the title does not dominate, it lives as part of a greater strategy, a scheme determined less by a sequence of objects than a single, distracted subject, the speaker. This is an I poem, as familiar with his material as any free verse voice, yet at the same time separate because he tells no story. The pattern is simply a function of the speaker's anxieties, arranged in ascending order. He speaks from a position of paralysis, and desires, ultimately, a condition of nonentity, the way smoke revolves its ashes. Winter is "off somewhere, writing its journals/in ice," while the speaker is here, watching "some blown rhododendrons," writing his—a surrealist text in which a house can be "wallpapered with the cries of birds," a young couple can sit "talking/about the afterlife," where maybe "the whole world is absent minded/or floating." Because he must invent in order to write, because his view is limited, perhaps only a window wide, the speaker is forced, like Keats, to be monk to the monastery of his imagination. Listen to how his associations attenuate. He opens his part by announcing that in spite of the fact winter has moved off, he is "still afraid to move,/afraid to speak," a situation he qualifies with a simile qualified with a metaphor amended by a disclaimer: "as if I lived in a house/wallpapered with the cries of birds/I cannot identify." We must assume that writing down his fears is at one with documenting his imagination. Hence the ability of his images to call from deeper emotional sources, to admit to their vision a certain vulnerability. The speaker is willing to declare himself negatively capable—that is, able to imagine doubt, and, eventually, to find in that doubt his desire. It all depends on where he places himself in relation to his raw material. He is, in effect, at his desk, looking through his window on the world, watching a young couple, some flowers, and speculating, projecting, and listening to the wind. The couple is apparently talking about the afterlife, the next day, the life beside this one, the future—in a word, absurdities. As it all comes to the same thing, why not talk past death. So the speaker assumes. But he has to laugh at himself, an odd, forgiving laugh. He doesn't know; he has doubts enough about this life, let alone after. Perhaps someone *is* whittling toys for the stillborn—a brilliantly painful, almost sentimental possibility.

By the fourth stanza his thinking and writing have achieved their most impressive elliptical orbit. Like the world outside, his mind may be absent or floating: because if new lovers "can undress/without wondering how/the snow grows over the Andes," a horse cannot be expected to "remember those/frozen in the sleigh behind it, /but keeps on running until the lines tangle,/while the dead sit coolly beneath their pet stars." *Pet* stars. That last detail moves Levis beyond the ironical range of Chekhov. Only a mind afloat could fix the connection between a death-sleigh and lovers undressing, ignorant of the cold, continents apart. Only a mind absent could perpetuate the absurdity of the cool, forgotten dead in the dead of winter, sleigh lines atangle under domesticated stars. *As I write this, as I write this.* Now, *in medias res*, he wishes us to know that he is still in control. His mind has gravity. With the sighting of the rhododendrons, the speaker turns from the paralysis of winter to the "desires" of spring (not unlike the spring in T. S.

Eliot). *I want,* he says, for the rest of the poem. Were we to make a list of the speaking parts in action—

> I am still afraid
> as if I lived
> I think
> I laugh
> I don't know
> As I write this
> I want
> I want
> I want

—they would chart pretty clearly the path he has followed. Once he acknowledges to us his artifice, the language of the image, he can substantiate as well as state what he wants. And he wants, he tells us, to remember nothing, to be nothing; he wants to assume the shape of absence, the formula of a circle, "a column of smoke/revolving, slowly, its ashes." A circle, however, takes us back, back to a starting place, a place of disappearance, of anonymity, of ending, but a starting place. So many young poets, like Levis, are in an ambiguity over the uses of the past, the uses and abuses of the self. William Matthews, on the other hand, in "Spring Snow," plays it close. He has premeditated his position and found his correlative. His past is not much more than a proposition wagered in the argument of an evolving metaphor. He is more concerned with the idea of memory than the experience. That is why he begins his poem in the past—it amounts to the exposition preparing the complication of his central figure, a formal rather than an emotional need. And that is why Levis ends his poem in the past—it is what he has come to, his point of departure. He has been trying to tell us all along a story, but he cannot locate himself within a linear context. He cannot find time. He is imagining, he realizes, very early in the poem, within an emotional vacuum. He must find a source for his distraction. So he finds where he came from; he remembers. He wills himself, he *imagines* himself—in the least imaginative moment of the poem—back to Fulton Street in Fresno, trembling, one among many in the crowd, among stores that are closing. He wants to disappear into that anonymity and never be heard of again. He wants to disappear into memory as if to transcend it. He wants to forget himself, so he can sleep, he says. No wonder he was afraid to speak, to be heard from. He wants the life after memory, the afterlife, the afterspeech. Because speech after memory is the language of the image. The image would disappear into memory, as in the closing of a circle, so as to transcend it—into a kind of ghost speech, a language of absences, the language of narrative afterlife, or its transcendence.

# 2

Valéry tells the story that "one day someone said to me that lyricism is enthusiasm, and that the odes of the great lyricists were written at a single stroke, at the speed of the voice of delirium, and with the wind of inspiration blowing a gale. . . . I replied that he was quite right; but that this was not a privilege of poetry alone, and that everyone knew that in building a locomotive it is indispensable for the builder to work at eighty miles an hour in order to do his job." Like the late Impressionists, the Symbolists are concerned with the effects of light—the kinetic qualities of light on and from a discontinuous surface of color. Speed, in particular, impresses them: how to prepare a poem that will allow the reader to make rapid, even simultaneous discoveries and connections between its various, often disparate objects, images, and words: how to sustain *that* enthusiasm. The answer, in part, certainly, lies in the dialectic between the continuum of light and the surface discontinuum of color, a harmony based on the tension between the single, and singular, effect of the poem (Poe's idea) and the means by which that effect comes into being. Valéry speaks of things "being transformed into one another"; Joyce, in *Portrait*, defines such transformation, and transport, as an epiphany, a showing-forth of the oneness of the experience. Both are interested in illuminations—in maintaining the integrity of particulars while achieving an immediate apprehension of their unit, their unity, their correspondence. Such talk is, of course, heady and abstract, about three feet off the ground. But for a moment it is necessary. Symbolist theory is based on getting beyond what Mallarmé calls "a commercial approach to reality." To borrow again from the painters, it is based on a

Argument & Song

Cubist perception of reality, of seeing the object in the "round" all at once, and seeing it new, in some new order; something analogous, for writer and reader, to seeing at the speed of light, indeed *hearing* at the speed of light. "We now *hear* undeniable rays of light, like arrows gliding and piercing," says Mallarmé.

So much intellectual and aesthetic history comes together here at the turn of the century and so much of it is in reaction against the sweetheart Victorians that one is tempted to take the *symbolistes* at their word, face value. "Nature has no imagination," to quote Gautier. Whether God is a literalist or not, many second-rate writers did and do use "imagination" as if they were inventors. The best of the so-called Symbolist period, however, are after an absolute poetic state, something like an ongoing Byzantine high. They recognize, along with Mallarmé, that "we dream of words brilliant at once in meaning and sound, or darkening in meaning and so in sound, luminously and elementally self-succeeding. *But,* let us remember that if our dream were fulfilled, *verse would not exist*—verse which, in all its wisdom, atones for the sins of language, comes nobly to their aid." Such poets are looking for that old alchemy of the word, for a music comparable to incantation—"the ideal would be reasonable number of words stretched beneath our mastering glance, arranged in enduring figures, and followed by silence." In saying this Mallarmé has described the idealization of the image, as word made Word, and replaced the sins of speech with the idolatry of signs. The rhetoric of silence is the rhetoric of the image, of the voice transformed, transformalized into visual terms, as if an emotion could be absorbed by and communicated through an emblem. It is up to Mallarmé's follower, Valéry, to follow through: "We must draw a pure, ideal Voice, capable of communicating without weakness, without apparent effort, without offense to the ear, and without breaking the ephemeral sphere of the poetic universe, an idea of some *self* miraculously superior to Myself." So much for vulnerability and bad nerves. If we say that the image alone has no voice we are admitting only that the image cannot exist in isolation. For all its high-flying intentions it is inevitably subject to the laws of gravity—the leaden laws of the body, the limits, as writes Robert Hass, of the imagination, the laws of some rhetoric. In theory, and beyond historical context, poets such as Mallarmé and Valéry are trying to find a way of writing poetry and talking about poetry that will permit them to organize and unify and transcend outside ordinary human experience, speech, and a self all too subject to empirical accident. Ordinary life is a family matter. The extraordinary poem must seem to begin and end in itself; its sources are part of its secret. As we have said, even memory has too many fingerprints. "It is no use appealing to our memory; it gives us much more evidence of our variation than our consistency. . . . In our desires, our regrets, our researches, in our emotions and passions, and even in the efforts that we make to know ourselves, we are the toys of absent things." Absent things sounds platonic: presences, essences inherent in yet separate from the real, diurnal world, just on the other side—perhaps the other side of language, if a language pure enough, that is, close enough to the conditions of either music or silence, can be found to take us there, to signify, to translate.

If Mallarmé could have found a way he would have written poems of one word. As it is, his poems are very much one word at a time, almost at a space, so that the effect, even in literal translation, is one of plasticity, the word as object. Hence, to simplify, each word, like color on canvas, returns more than its original value, it gives back light: it evokes within a pattern of such evocations—vast, says Baudelaire, as clarity. There is little room left for the clubfoot of a speaker, a self-dramatizing self—at least a self acknowledging its source—among such a concentration of things, and the voices of things. Or put another way, the self has been sublimated to sensibility at the point when objects, and the language itself, assume the status of symbol. The idea is to crowd the word with as much *reasonable* as well as emotional opportunity as possible—a synesthesia in which the sound of a word can be part of its color, the rhythm of a line its formal space. The point at which the whole poem becomes the object, the symbol, the engine, the correspondence of correspondences, the transportation for the spirit and senses, is the moment it becomes an emblem, a fixed epiphany, a sudden manifestation. Only then can Nature become a temple of trees in which "colors, sounds, and perfumes correspond." Trees with eyes.

For younger poets the historic influence of the French Symbolists comes down through a very long and diverse line, ranging in emphasis, and language, and opposition, from Rilke to Lorca to Montale to Neruda to Pound, not to mention, preeminently, Yeats, Stevens, and Eliot, followed by the distillation of the image in the international 1960s. They taught us how to pay attention to the poem as form. Yet the dilution of

Symbolist theology began almost immediately in the work of Valéry's contemporary, Stephan George, and in other important followers such as Jorge Guillen and Gottfried Benn, whether the poet was inspired by muse, angel, or the duende, or, like the Symbolists, by the dream in the Word itself, a harmony of elements just outside human range. And of course it has continued, like an alluvial flow. But follower or imitator, modernist or young poet in the 1970s, the real essential difference between poets preoccupied with free-verse voice and a verse emblem is a difference of the degree to which the poet will admit himself into his poem—and the terms of such a testament. As Guillen once wrote, "Pure poetry? This platonic idea could never take form in a concrete body." Perhaps not. An embodiment, however, may be something else. What the Symbolists left us, and leave us, is the notion of the image as an ideal, an entity self-generated, an art admitting absolutely its artifice. The symbol itself becomes the subject, whose verb equivalent, *symballein*, means to put together, to construct, to build an idea, a body. In its oneness and wholeness, the symbol intends at the moment of its showing-forth, at that epiphanal moment of uniting the total work, to resolve, to surround "the spirit and the senses," to make subject-object indistinguishable—to be that golden bird on that bough, in a permanent state of present tense, singing. The speaking voice, as a free verse instrument, is too flawed, it would seem, to handle both itself and symbol simultaneously. The voice, for one thing, has too many personal problems. Memory, like the force of gravity, for one. The Symbolists and their followers taught an entire generation, sick of "progress" and of war and the emotional logic of both, to imagine beyond memory, to travel to the new place, not so much as an escape as an illumination. The burdens of the sheer weight of experience could be transcended, left to time. Image or symbol or emblem might not have much tonal range, but each would offer the I an aesthetic alternative, an outside opportunity.

The perception that the image is an idea with a body and that that image idealized—given subject–object status—is a symbol and that that symbol, or symbols, enlarged to the stature of a poem as an emblem, such a perception only begins to address the principles of organization, rhythm, and meaning—nor does it address where the symbolist poem is calling from, if calling at all. For instance, who is speaking these three lines from Hart Crane's "Lachrymae Christi"?

> From flanks unfended,
> Twanged red perfidies of spring
> Are trillion on the hill.

If not a persona, then no one. And in this particular poem, by America's great symbolist, there is no declared I, not even a voice, as such. No one "talks" like that—"Twanged red perfidies of spring." The question of who is speaking or where the voice is calling from is important because an answer would help us to come to terms with this difficult poem, a poem too long to quote here. The answer has to lie in the dominant symbol, the Christ-on-the-Cross figure itself, a figure we find at the end of the poem being addressed directly—"O Nazarene . . . /O/Dionysius." The Christ figure is *the* apostrophic object in this poem, the focus that organizes and relates by its evocative presence the other images. No one identifiable is speaking, but there is a beautiful voice in Crane's poem (in spite of "twanged") and it is calling from the very object it is addressing. The subject, the implicit source of "speech" here, is, from the beginning, the object. A metaphor of tears, in effect, is speaking—or, by some kind of sublimation, being spoken through. As Crane comments in his famous letter to his editor, "metaphor is so organically entrenched in pure sensibility that it can't be thoroughly traced." The impression that poets of a symbolist bend of mind are preoccupied with form is nonsense; in terms of prosody they generally follow convention, or play with it. Free verse poets, from W. C. Williams to C. K. Williams, those are the poets preoccupied with form—with form as discovery. The symbolist poet, regardless of disguise, is concerned with architecture, with building within the volume (for both eye and ear) of the space. The poet who speaks directly to us depends on authenticating his emotional life in rhythms linear to that life; he structures time. The symbolist authenticates his imaginative life in rhythms equivalent to that life; he structures space. Indeed the "symbolist," whether he is Hart Crane or W. S. Merwin or Charles Wright, goes a step further: he organizes the silence around the object, he fixes or suspends his poem in time, so that it has a quality of being set on the page—set as rhyme and meter set. Free verse is always reaching out, extending time, distending its space. The symbolist poem is always turning back in on itself, contracting, even if at the speed of light, structured toward stasis, toward that still point where the voice produces echoes.

# 3

The Symbolist commitment to the craft of the poem as something supremely artificial, perfectible, as something wholly apart from rather than a part of the "suffering mind" that creates it, as something not only autotelic but anonymous, underlines its intellectual bias and its understanding of the image as an expression of the highest consciousness. The Symbolists, particularly Mallarmé and Valéry, are not big on inspiration—all that heavy breathing from the bellows. The image is *made*, made from the sense and senses at work on the subject–object matter—an afternoon with a faun, a journey on a drunken boat, a meditative day spent at the marine cemetery ("Smash, my flesh, this meditative vase!"), or perhaps a moment of watching a panther in the Paris zoo (Rilke apparently studied the animal for weeks). The self, in such circumstances, is irrelevant; the self is not perfectible. Worse, the self seems always to have its sentimental bags packed, ready to go anywhere, and ready, at the drop of an emotion, to leave in its wake a trail of tears. The Symbolists, and symbolists, in "perfecting" the poem, perfect that version of the self translated into sensibility, and sensibility, like its objective correlative, is, to repeat, an idea, a mind with a body. Perhaps the chief difference between sensibility and the self is that with the former the body is inside the mind.

The Symbolist model, however, is conservative compared with the Surrealist, which is an extreme version of the poet's relationship with his material, the mind's relationship to the matter. Even sensibility is too soft for Breton: "Surrealism, n. Pure psychic automatism, by which it is intended to express, verbally, in writing . . . the real process of thought. Thought's dictation. . . ." If the Symbolists seek an anonymous art, the Surrealists promise an autonomous art. Mind without the pretensions of the body, mind as the ultimate image-making machine. Almost autonomous, anyway. Again, outside historical considerations, we can safely say that the Surrealists offer the image in the extreme—not the extreme of Dadaism, which is automatic typing, but an extreme of consciousness and independence of image. Apollinaire's famous "Sun throat cut" (Louis Simpson's translation) ending to his poem "Zone" exemplifies how little the speaking voice and the source of that voice have to do with the level at which the language here is operating. The words are signs, though not quite symbols: that is, they are pure images, but they are not idealized images; they come at the end of a beautifully long, scattered poem, in which the I is an eye, a camera recording, with its sound equipment on. "Zone" is a delight to the eye of the reader as well, more so because its music is weighed in favor of its images—an inevitability once the voice becomes a visual experience. For years the Surrealists were put down as fringe poets, crazies in the middle of the street trying to stop traffic for attention. At their best, though, they have exercised a tremendous influence. They described the future for poetry, free verse or otherwise, Imagist or deep image. They demystified the Symbolist ideal of the object. When Apollinaire writes, in Michael Benedikt's translation, that

> This meadow is sickly but pretty in the fall
> Cows pasture there
> Filling themselves with poison
> Saffron color of tree-rings and of lilacs
> Flowers there your eyes are like those flowers
> Near-violet like their rings and like this autumn
> And my life for your eyes slowly fills itself with poison

he is not exactly writing the typical nineteenth-century love poem, but he is acknowledging some correspondences with flowers of evil and "swiftness" in the image (Breton's word), all in *frisson nouveau*; and when he continues, in the second stanza of the same poem, "Saffron," that

> The school-children run up with a racket
> Playing on the harmonica but very neatly jacketed
> They gather saffron flowers which are like their mothers
> Daughters of their daughters and colored like your eyelid
> Which flutters as flowers are fluttered by the mad wind

he is not just corresponding but looking ahead to *association*, to larger "leaps" in the imagination. He has domesticated his object considerably; he has also energized it through the tension of disparate relations, poisoning the pastoral, if you will, and then lifting those relations to the level of the lover's eyes. Fairly dynamic stuff, especially the speed with which one image turns into another and back again, but changed. That is the auditory imagination given the goose. When he writes, in another poem, that "Your right eye fluttered like my heart/Your eyelids fluttered like flowers flutter in wind/And may the doorway of the look of your right eye open once more" and that "My heart is like a flame upside-down," all images laid down before World War I, he is anticipating a depth and resonance of imagery unavailable to his French Symbolist countrymen.

Surreal literally means super-real . . . all the lights on. When Robert Bly, some fifty years after surrealism and imagism (postcard poetry, Bly calls it— "pictorialism"), speaks of the image he suggests it has to do with a dark, interior world in which "the imagination out of its own resources creates a poem as strong as the world which it faces." The contradiction between light and dark descriptions here is only superficial. Sub-real or super-real, inner world or outer, dream or daydream, the image is the most consciously discovered part of any poem, an illumination, a revelation, the highest *form* of intelligence—though its source may be subconscious, subterranean, dark, deep. Bly is looking for something "deeper" than eye-level; he wants the image to have true spiritual equivalency. He wants the source included with the substance so that the image is not left out in the static cold, like an artifact in orbit, but implicates, clearly, where it came from. He is looking for an organic image, a light around a dark body. He is looking for dragon smoke. Very few, if any, younger poets have taken Bly at his word. (Gregory Orr may be the exception.) To be committed to the image-object-emblem matrix is to keep one's sources secret. To be a "symbolist," having passed through the "free verse" of surrealism, is to surrender the narrative, self-centered values of cause-and-effect. Bly himself is fairly circumspect in his use of an I. Only in his prose-poems—some of his finest lyric moments—is he able to admit his full voice and thereby his full source. The rhetoric of sentences seems to force him into a richer report. There his images live in time as well as space. But though the evidence of influence is at best circumstantial, Bly has produced more quarrel than confidence. Which may be his best influence.

If Bly, an American and Minnesotan, and possibly the most interesting, if didactic, poetry theoretician (some would say theologian) to come out of the 1960s, has not exerted all that much influence on younger poets, who has? Those in a symbolist or surrealist line, those who place a certain "aesthetic distance" between themselves and the poem, those who place the image—whether simply architectural or archetypal—at the center of the work, those who formalize the relations within the poem—these poets have been directly influenced by an international group including such "recent" figures as Henri Michaux, Francis Ponge, Jean Follain, Octavio Paz, Vasko Popa, Italo Calvino, Carlos Drummond de Andrade, and such established figures as Bonnefoy, Guillevic, Alberti, Borges, Char. It is a very large snowball. As poets committed to the image or the image-model, as in the paragraph poetry of parable and fable and "prose-poem" and tale, and all of it running on abstract time, they can agree, with Valéry, to "that discourse, so different from ordinary speech, which is verse, which is so curiously ordered, which answers no need *unless it be the need it must create*, which never speaks but of absent things or of things profoundly and secretly felt: strange discourse, as though made by someone *other* than the speaker and addressed to someone *other* than the listener. In short, it is a *language within a language*." It is, in fact, the language of the image treated as absolute knowledge, based on *otherness*, the otherness of the subject-object. The language within a language—a "language" that, not surprisingly, translates and transcends national lines—is the rhetoric of silence, the rhetoric of the image, of the voice sublimated to sensibility. In this new formalism it is as if the poem were a ceremony or ritual performed within the decorum of space, in a kind of no-time, suspended above the clumsiness of moral, diurnal, literal concerns, or if not above them, then *beside* them, placing such concerns in a long and very large perspective. We are the toys of absent things, says Valéry—character, says William Matthews, passed wholly into fate and fate in flecks, like dust, like flour, like snow. We find ourselves in otherness, because as soon as there is only myself, said the poet, there is nobody.

The rhetoric of silence is rather popular; it fills the poetry workshops of America, because like certain kinds of painting and music and dance it looks easy. In the right hands, says a Mark Strand or W. S. Merwin or early John Ashbery, however, it is the dominant and exquisite mode of the 1970s. Its achievement has been to realize, again with Valéry, "that all possible objects of the ordinary world, external or internal, beings, events, feelings, and actions, while keeping their usual appearance, can be suddenly placed in an indefinable but wonderfully fitting relationship with the modes of our general sensibility. That is to say that these well-known things and beings—or rather the ideas that represent them—can somehow change in value.

They attract one another, they are connected in ways quite different from the ordinary; they become (if you will permit the expression) *musicalized, resonant*, and, as it were, harmonically related." Among young poets the music of the auditory image is various but consistent. In Daniel Halpern's third book of poems, *Life Among Others*, the life, and harmony, is mostly still. Here, for instance, an idea turns into an object.

> I hear callers in the trees
> but I stay in one place,
> knowing motion is nothing
> if I can't stand like this,
> hour after hour.
>
> In this immobility a fire inflates,
> and so much turbulence within the static—
> the owls call, still in their trees.
> They can see in the night, they don't need to move.
> I don't move myself—the river moves
>
> somewhere, the clouds without sound
> move and move. They drift and disband.
> The dogs are still, except for their jaws,
> which click in the night.
> They smell the darkness, they don't need to move.
>
> My work is to stand still and see everything.
> My work is to rethink the immobile,
> the owl and dog, and without moving release them,
> release myself, let everything live again,
> recalled into movement and loved, wholly still.

The speaker here, or listener, is a bit in the position of the Chinese jar, except that sound rather than air is the medium; he is also a bit in the situation of that other famous jar, in Tennessee, about to take "dominion everywhere." He is at a still point, anyway, and potentially the central active agent—though not a catalyst, since he too will undergo change—in a transformation. The poem is a restatement, if not a representative, of a great deal of the stasis—the suspension, in close space, of the needs of narrative complication and conclusion—prevalent in younger contemporary poetry. Naturally the poem is entitled "Still." In its décor and decorum it is a formal version of free verse: it is celebrating a ceremony, which is the work of standing still, seeing, re-thinking, and finally releasing the immobile. The "story problem" of the poem is to get the callers from a pole position of isolation to the pole position of being *recalled* into relationship with a witness. Why does the witness bother? Because he too will be released from immobility, released in order to "love." First, of course, before any changes can occur, the speaker must confer a value on the condition he and the owls and the dogs share—"motion is nothing/if I can't stand like this,/hour after hour." That value is expressed not only in the condition (motion as something) but in the context (motion as the terms of things) of stasis—and both condition and context are correlatives of the speaker's mind. Therefore a fire *inflates*, "and so much turbulence within the static"; therefore the river moves "somewhere"; therefore the clouds move and move, soundlessly. The speaker imagines, assumes, they drift and disband. The dialectic would seem to move between having called and being recalled, with the listener as mediator. But stillness seems to be the recommendation here. The river moves—like the blackbird flying—the clouds move. It is the motion of the mind that is at issue, to release, to recall, to "remember" the sounds of the owl and the dog, now singular, to "let everything live again,/ recalled into movement." Very quickly the speaker has himself moved from a position of being on the periphery of the still place to being at its center, its "emotional" center. *Love* is his word for the place he has come to in his mind. Love is the recognition of relationships within being "wholly still," the still point, impressionist, as if the problem were the ontology of point of view.

Halpern's poem is written under glass. It offers the rhetoric of silence with an edge. The l's of call, recall, still, immobile, smell, wholly, for example, clarify, sharpen the silence, the stillness of the set with the tensile precision of a scale. The lines moving along in a firm but quiet declarative, repeating and clustering certain sounds and phrases, making sure subject-verb-complement stays in its place. Mostly, however, it is the pace of things that so remarkably illuminates the formal stance. The poem is about form, the ceremony of stillness, so no sentence is allowed to complicate or extend itself ("which click in the night" is the weakest writing). We learn by attachment and variation of sentence length. We learn along with the speaker what his work is. The form and music of the mind, that is what his work is—how to resolve yet sustain the dialectic of movement (sound) within stillness . . . the assonance of the o's within the still sound of the i's. Halpern's poem ends as it began, but changed. That is its formal declaration. *Still* becomes an object, the speaker a function of that object.

When a speaker sublimates as much to "ceremony" as the voice in "Still," he is purifying the symbolist aesthetic to a very fine point. Halpern's voice in this poem is anonymous; indeed, it depends on a nomenclature of allegorical outline. As the plural (potentially particular) owls and dogs become singular references, the speaker is defined, delineated by his work, his singularity. "Loved" is the one lush moment in this severe poem. Like the possible story it will not tell, cannot reveal, "Still" suspends its emotional life until the last line. "Loved, wholly still" has the effect, after so much stillness, of affirmation, almost exclamation—recalled into movement. In one of her best recollections into movement, a poem entitled "As the Window Darkens," Laura Jensen places her version of a "silent poem" in her version of the dark.

As the window darkens, as the light yearns
over the couch, as the plants drift like swans,
this is a silent poem. It will not flower
in water like a party favor, nor
will it bleed like the universe. It will
be the knot of wood that looks like a rabbit,
a knot of wood tense and growing stiffer.

The window darkens to mirror. It chimes
the reflection and what it should have been.
Have the trees and antennas seen this
blot for years, pumping like a gauge?
No wonder the birds flew away, crying out.

It is not true that the beautiful
are always false and the ugly philosophical.
But the clumsy stand as surely as the deft
at dark windows, knowing they have been deceived.

This is unbearable because we know
we see a door closing and we wait to see
that door close in our dreams, shutting us out.

How many years can come as gently as lamplight
out of the wind, each year with its own place
and the circle it made around a friend?
What the world likes is a bootstrap and locket,
work and sentiment ebbing with the light.

The ocean is a sigh at night, a dark vase
of flowers before a dark window, salt water,
someone pouring it from an abalone shell
when it first was made. It goes on forever,
a fountain, a fortuneteller in the palm of sand.
The ocean is a dish of water carried by a woman
where the worry of our lives lies down.

The voice here is more anonymous than unnamed, the imagination more surreal than symbolist. So the poem has, naturally, a little different and developed emotional climate from a poem like "Still." (It appears in the fourth, and best, section of Jensen's first full volume, *Bad Boats*.) Yet there is no I— in fact, "This is a silent poem." It moves within the structure of the moment, its timing is spatial—its seven-five-seven-five-seven stanzaic pattern breaks down into images placed against, in response to, "reflections." The poem has a magisterial feel, of much being made of little, a macro of the micro world of a room and what is just outside the window of a room. It does not hesitate to state significance, in lines portioned out to complete the thought, to give the thought and the image their full measure of resonance. It has at the same time, however, the Dickinson quality of an undertow of tension, of that white sustenance, despair: "we see a door closing and we wait to see/that door close in our dreams, shutting us out." It wants to play off the universe against a party favor, a bootstrap against a locket, because that is what the world likes, "work and sentiment ebbing with the light." Hyperbole is habitually being tied to understatement ("the ocean is a sigh") or the reserve levels of objects are juxtaposed. One senses quickly that the surreal combinations are less a response of the imagination than of the off-stage emotion, if the two are separable. There is something of deeply personal value at stake in this silent poem. Its closely watched intensity shows through every disguise, as if the first-person were only preoccupied with herself in the third.

"As the Window Darkens"—all within the space of that moment—is a poem obviously trying to see in bad light, even to see itself. As an entity it will not do certain things—flower or bleed—but it will *be* certain things, for one a simile tied and qualified to a metaphor. These beginning anti-transformations and transformations take place *while* "the light yearns/ over the couch" and "the plants drift like swans." The first stanza is very busy with setting the reader straight, though that is saying it too harshly. It is setting itself straight really, and will continue trying to do so for the next three stanzas. Outside, "the window darkens to mirror," with what it should have been. The reflection is awkward, ominous, and frightening. ("No wonder the birds flew away, crying out.") The *it* of the beginning stanza has shifted from being the silent poem to being the window, reflecting, blotting, pumping like a gauge. Not only is the imagination moving toward a complicated interior, the "subject" of the poem, of the sentences, is undecided. Since we are working out no story we need not worry point of view, not in any limited sense anyway. The point of view, of course, is neither that of the poem nor the window; it is the "subjective correlative" of the perceiving mind, a mind finding its "voice" as might a sensitive camera. As least in the first two stanzas the visual voice has dominated. Now in the middle of the poem the poet does decide. Her rhetoric focuses her attention beautifully. The silent poem is the window darkening, and the clumsy—who, like the ugly, are considered special because philosophical—*its* complicit witness. The off-stage speaker, trying to see in the dark, has had, perhaps only for us, an insight. What she has revealed so far is her own ability to deceive: the act of the imagination itself is somehow in crisis, because at this point, at any rate, it seems a function of the dark limited to the dark. The first two stanzas therefore represent the very problem they are attempting to resolve. They are clumsy, odd-fitting combinations of things. And this is unbearable because as such they shut us out. The door closing on our dreams is hardly a denial of the sources of the surreal in favor of the real; quite the other way around. In dreams begin responsibilities, as a source of light. Deception is irresponsible. So the poem seems to end, in stanza 4, with a marvelously evocative question—truly rhetorical—and reality's tough answer. "How many years can come as gently as lamplight/out of the wind, each year with its own place/and the circle it made around a friend?" Light years. It is a question directed at the window darkening, the ineffability of poetry, and the imagination as distorting mirror. What the world likes is melodrama, "work and sentiment ebbing with the light," not lamplight.

The imagination is generally problematic, easily indulged, easily abused, especially with roses at sunset. The generation of the 1970s has often enough voided sentimentality with fancy, deft *or* clumsy at dark windows. The last stanza of Jensen's poem is an illumination in answer to if not a resolution of the "imaginative" issues she has debated in the front four stanzas. She turns from the trite world outside the window and the invented one inside the room in her head to what Coleridge calls the secondary imagination—and transformation. For the first time her images are completely coherent, unified in sensibility; for the first time the tension within images is totally at ease with the music asked to say them. She has created without contriving. "The ocean is a sigh at night" expresses not only a leap but a penetration, pursued into the new knowledge of its future. Breton says that "it is . . . from the fortuitous juxtaposition of the two terms that a particular light is sprung, the light of the image, to which we are infinitely sensitive." The terms here, to the bootstrap, locket world, must look impossible, so as to cancel each other out. But with her last stanza Jensen rewrites her poem, its silence and darkness, its deception. The ocean *is*, not *is like*. The tableau As-the-Window-Darkens has found its answer and its correlative. It has found a voice, in an image that is as elaborate as it is pristine. The argument of the body of the poem is burdened with the discrete and disparate, of odd angles and wrong sizes. Those differences *are*, in fact, the argument of the poem. Each stanza embodies its step, its part of the pattern, tries to illuminate its area of the space. The final stanza is the countermotion to these "worries." It is a surreal metaphor, and because it has a common center it gives the reader a whole music, not simply parts of speech. As we move from a sigh at night to a dark vase of flowers before a dark window to someone pouring salt water from a fresh abalone shell, we should not forget that we are still in the same metaphor, an extended grammar. And still it goes on forever, a fountain, a fortuneteller in the palm of sand. This is a simultaneity enlarging what will suffice. Except for the poem's own internal sense of form, the conversions could likely go on forever. So why stop now? Form? Yes, form in the absolute of solving what it set in motion. This is a silent poem, but tense. The speaker, just off to one side, has all along been forced into an imaginative strategy she cannot integrate. Thus she must repeat and think out loud solutions. Now, by the end, she talks herself into a presiding image, something overwhelming, yet something her imagination, and her emotion, can control. The ocean is her object. And if she can put a fortuneteller *into* a palm of sand, she can do anything, because an ocean is a fountain *and*, at the same time, a dish of water (salt water) carried by a woman, where the worry of our lives lies down. The imagination is speaking, in the fixed time of as-the-window-darkens, in the rhetoric of the emblem As-the-Window-Darkens.

Though the temperaments and temperatures differ, both Halpern and Jensen resolve their poems by returning to the original issue, or image, but changed. In formal patterns of mind and structure—to the extent that there are clear gestures of rhyme and an economy of the measure of a given line within such patterns—and in the terms of the perceiving mind dissociated, as in a first-person regarding itself in the second or third, from the considering body, both poets return to a rest, to a place of resolution. Even if that place is an object, signaled by the poem's title. Jensen's returning to an object apparently alien to the props and set she has effectively established only looks like the kind of leap we have been led to expect by the deep imagists. The ocean, brought immediately into metaphor with the interior, subjective world, is a conclusion to the resonance of the poetry that precedes it. From the beginning of her poem Jensen has been looking for an image of position and authority, an image she can develop without deception, yet an object in consequence of her landscape. On the far side of that window—but not too far—that looks in on furniture and plants and looks out west over a world of trees and antennas and birds flying off, is an ocean, going on forever, with the sun going down. The speaker is standing at that window looking out into a mirror. Halpern's return is more difficult to describe since it appears, by his own words, that he has not moved. The entire "process" is of course "produced," but it is also ontological: it is the mind thinking in senses, trying to order and reconcile what is real and what is imagined. It is dialectic as familiar as Stevens. The moment movement can be understood as stillness and stillness movement, the moment of that complete exchange, is the moment the mind is most alive, sensual, and capable. The problem is how to deal with such a potentiality, such a future, as it is happening. So the poem is a circle, whose center is to be defined by its circumference. The limit of the poem is its minimalization of details and the rare air it moves in. That limit is also part of the original issue of the poem, stillness and how it sounds. The poem is almost surreal in its precisions and the absolute nature of its objects. Finally the speaker of "Still" is able to *see* what he has only heard or assumed, and finally he is able to rethink and recall what is real, which is itself the subject and object of transformation.

Halpern and Jensen epitomize, for young American poetry, the risks of thinking through and thinking over the image. The strengths of both these poets, stretched over the length of a book, can become weaknesses. *Bad Boats*, as a collection and extension of individual pieces, is stunning but often flawed by Jensen's inability to translate, let alone transform, her experience. Without the quick study of immediate, clarifying imaginative resources—the "swiftness of the image"—her poems flatten to simple statement and sometimes sententiousness. The last stanza of "Talking to the Mule," for example, has none of the easy access of the first. The poem begins in the evening with "a snail/passing through life across your lawn,/ his trail official, a government seal." The lawn itself is "delicious, dry and cool,/the color of pepper." The limitation of the lawn negotiates if it does not quite unify the set-up of images here as we proceed, in the middle two stanzas, to actually talk to the mule, who is alien and vulnerable under stars. As alien and vulnerable as the off-stage speaker herself. So there they are, the two of them, almost absurd company, the one at pains to speak, the other dumb—stars above, lawn below. Rather than end with signals, the poem chooses significance.

> Rub your nose along the fence.
> Tip back your head and bray,
> for the night is yours. It is never
> against you. You are not its enemy.

This whistling in the dark is straight instruction, without benefit of irony. At no point has it been proved, let alone provided, that matters could become so threatening. The content of the stanza feels attached, its anxiety assigned; no wonder, then, the poet is reduced to the cliché of "the night is yours." Perhaps had an I been invited into things, Jensen might have been forced to impress us with a more accurate reading of her position, of why she must talk to this mule, and why we must listen. Another talk, "Conversations in the Primate House," opens with the kind of deep image shorthand that writes itself very close to self-parody.

> I am betraying a white horse
> standing beside a Polish store.
> But that horse was my betrayer,
> like the moths it beat on your window screens
> in autumn, deciding your future.

The apparently arbitrary selection of materials, their far-cry potential for relationship and the willful play of idea against object—none of this interaction is convincing. No question that betrayal is the thesis of the poem, but why a white horse *beside* a Polish store (a very different problem from red wheelbarrows beside white chickens), whose arbitration is determined by a persona non grata, a betrayed betrayer? How probable is a white horse–moths simile, tied immediately to the abstraction of "deciding your future"? The possible speed of these images/ideas is delayed and interrupted by unprepared-for complications. Or is the point simply one of the non-objective object, a pegasus being made capable of being like the lower-case life of a moth beating "on your window screens." The poem does in fact end with the betrayed sister opening her wings. Perhaps the deep image is operating at new depths here. Yet even if the imagination in the five stanzas of "Conversation . . ." could be coherently accounted for, the poem as a whole feels forced, its real or aesthetic reason for being never acknowledged. It provides the reader with no clear palpable sense of one body necessarily filling another. It reads like the impersonation of a poem, in a persona voice unable to confirm a vital connection to its original source, the poet herself. As with several pieces in *Bad Boats*, it fails to transcend its own autonomy. The speaker haunts the poem like a ghost, unsure of who the antagonist is—white horse, sister, keeper, or reader. Each of these is in turn addressed, suggesting that Jensen cannot focus her attention, let alone her imagination. Nevertheless, Jensen, like Ashbery, may be ahead of us; she may be writing in a fourth-person, as if she were indeed the toy of absent things.

236

Halpern's *Life Among Others* is not so much a collection as an extended metaphor, broken in rhythm periodically by poems of richer flesh tones such as "Lime Kiln," "For You," and "Long Distance." His book is more about— *about* as in circulate—stillness among others, and otherness. That is its real life, its recall into movement. And though the poem "Still" is one of the book's models, it is also a clue to the seductions of silence, when the purification of narrative ambition passes into suspended animation. The best poems (the sequence of "White" poems, "I Am a Dancer," "Glassworks," "Fish," the title poem, etc.) depend on high contrast, sharp edges, the delineation of contours. "Glassworks," a perfectly pitched example, announces Halpern's formal aesthetic best of all.

> You run out of invention and the glass stem
> that holds the object snaps.
> Nearly complete, the object rolls away
> with the truth of completion still unformed.
> What a sad life that uses the body
> like this, to support what lives above it,
> and make it live below intelligence.

What happens when the poet really does run out of invention, when the stem snaps, when he is forced, like Jensen, to live above the body in a dimension singularly intellectual? What happens when the emotional life has been rarefied rather than "released into movement," when the stillness becomes inertia? One thing that happens is that "the truth of completion" remains unformed. "Begin" is a small poem stunned by "the air that fills speech."

> We are in the room.
> The light, the lizards on the screen
> and the overhead fan are givens.
> Now as we sit the light is going out.
> Have you come to take what I say
> to others? I say little:
> the air that fills speech lies
> in its chamber.

Light the candles—we will sit up tonight.
If you are quiet I will tell you.
I need only begin. Can you hear me?

This is the no-exit of portentousness. Whatever its intended emotional equivalent, whatever its external causes, the poem exaggerates its effects by concentrating on the object *begin* at the expense of a context. It is a poem—even among the lives of others around it—in a vacuum, offering forms of silence to fill a silence. The poet could argue that *beginning* is exactly the point, that air filling speech defines a vacuum. But the point is lost in the existential rhetoric of its own imitative fallacy. The poem occupies too little space, takes too little time; it yields too little texture and creates too little tension to sustain the implications of its claims. The reader is finally reduced to wondering just what the speaker might tell us. A certain "witness of the body" is missing, a certain conflict or juxtaposition. Something that we need to know has been solved in advance of the page, something that we should be hearing is undisclosed. More invention, however, will only entertain us; we need a strong "glass stem" holding the object up in order to be engaged. As it is, the surface of the poem is its depth. The rhetoric of the image and of silence depends on context as much as on coherency. If it will not take up time, then it must at least invigorate its space. The reader must sense that as form—the illustration of content—calls attention to itself it does so within the larger form of implication. Objects must inevitably become symbols, ideas with bodies. The more autotelic the art the more risk that it will admire itself in the mirror of its own making and become so self-absorbed as to lose sight of where it came from. An image allowed its context is an image with as much past as future, whether the poet, a Halpern or a Jensen, will admit it or not.

# 4

So the history of the Modernist movement in poetry is a history of the image. Indeed, if Modernism—that conglomerate term for an age and an evolving, often contradictory aesthetic, ranging from the Symbolists to the New Critics, nearly a hundred years of *ars victrix, ars poetica*—if Modernism expresses a single, consistent concern it is with the image. But it is a history more autobiographical than biographical, a history of performance over theory. Whatever their differences regarding the relative preciousness of the word, the Valérys and the Eliots could agree that the rhetoric of the image is the rhetoric of an abiding reality, that the achieved form is the end-all and be-all rather than the go-between of experience. This emphasis shifted, of course, in the 1960s, as the image got linked with a priori states of being, whether through archetype or deep image. The image according to Robert Bly was a passage rather than a room with a view. In this "post-Modernist phase" Bly still remains the self-appointed American spokesman for the image. And before him, Pound.

In his classic, and iconoclastic, treatise on the "Imagiste faith" and later reiterated in "Vorticism," Pound writes a whole shopping list of do's and dont's and definitions. All of them, however, relate to his insistence on the image as "that which presents an intellectual and emotional complex in an instant of time." He goes on to refer to "the image itself as speech," the image as "the word beyond formulated language." Whether these descriptions are more symbolist than surreal in implication, surreal than symbolist, is beside the point. They are meant to be Imagist, a movement dedicated to the precision of the language of the image. They define an energy as much as an engineering. In his most extensive commentary on the subject, the Vorticist essay, Pound investigates the analogy between the image and painting, static and plastic, with similar intentions to those of Mallarmé comparing poetry to music, and establishes that "the image is the poet's pigment"—a fairly deadly phrase. In a better moment he analyzes the image as "accelerated impressionism," creating effects of "simultaneity." He concludes his prose with the distinction that the "image is not an idea. It is a radiant node or cluster; it is what I can, and must perforce, call a Vortex, from which, and through which, and into which, ideas are constantly rushing." The difference generalized here between the image and idea is close at best. Pound himself blurs the distinction with his example of the Japanese *hokku*, a form he sees as not only pure but primary.

The footsteps of the cat upon the snow:
    (are like) plum-blossoms.

He tells us that the parenthetical matter is added for the edification of the "one image" poem to English readers. The colon, apparently, is not clear enough. He is using this form, he continues, to illustrate what he calls "super-position"—the perception of "one idea set on top of another." The fact that he has used idea and image interchangeably is inevitable considering that the radiance of the node derives largely from the light of an idea. What differentiates the poetic image from picture-taking is its ability to implicate and impact *idea*. Together they impart plasticity to the language. But beyond the idea of image and image as idea is the notion of super-position, a compound painters might perceive as juxtaposition. Whatever it is labeled, the technique of replacing the rhetoric of the simile with silence amounts to far more than a simple adjustment of words. It amounts to a relocation of who is speaking in relation to what is spoken through. The distance between the cat walking on snow and plum-blossoms is healed effectively enough by the colon. *Are like* is the voice of the negotiator of that exchange. Remove the role of negotiator and we have more than image as a *form* of speech. We have the voice of the image, its language spoken. The risk, of course, of the image on its own is the risk of the image in isolation, the image in a vacuum, tone-deaf. It might well formalize and super-impose its space at the expense of significance. A poet like Jean Follain, for example, constantly runs the risk of the reductive in order to achieve the aural ability of the visual, even visionary.

Black Meat

Around stones called precious
which only their own
dust can wear down
the eaters of venison
carve in silence
their black meat
the trees on the horizon
imitate in outline
a giant sentence

No surprise the translator is W. S. Merwin—the internal connections, associations, and carry-over of the poem are precision-tooled. It appears to be a metaphor of a metaphor, the title. Yet, if it is a metaphor, a speaking of the unknown in terms of the known, it is self-reflexive. Its mind is a mirror of its own making. It looks in rather than out—there is nothing to look out to. Its correlative is self-contained. The poem is not about anything, it represents something, an archetype, which only its "own/dust can wear down." It represents a structure, a super-position, of correspondences—two sentences in silence, imitating in outline. It speaks for itself.

When a Follain or a Ponge or a Popa, or even a Ritsos or a Bonnefoy, promotes an austerity of image so severe it reads as if it had been written itself, a dimension beyond the image as word has opened up. The image-object, the thing itself now speaks. The poet becomes a parallel circumstance. The international influence on younger American poets is more indirect than certain, but it is felt for sure through the seminal work of Mark Strand and W. S. Merwin, particularly in *Darker* and *The Lice*. It is not simply that the voice of the emotion has been sublimated or that the outbound energies of free verse have been checked and balanced; it is not simply that the stated relevance of content has been re-routed back into the form or that the relationship between storyteller and story has been turned into a tension between objects. What has happened is that the lyric voice itself, a sound so relative to its source as to be indistinguishable from that source, is being purged into metaphor. "The old dogged ways of writing poems," says Sandra McPherson, "cover with snow." Symbolism, surrealism, imagism, deep or shallow—these sound like archaisms. We are now writing, in earnest, an absolute poetry.

*Wearing White*

The old dogged ways of writing poems
cover with snow. Juncos, bodied like lynx tails,
fly out of the empty prison.

Dipping his hand in blood the taxidermist complains
nothing will stay on this white. He raises
a frozen wasp by a leg, beginning to move.

On maples the sensory tips say: we refuse,
not another experiment. They wonder if they are not
warped by feeling. Frosting the interior

that faces them a pocket watch hangs, stopped
and silver. It listens as the leaves clatter
into glassy cornerings. An idea

of what to do with an idea: I am wearing white—
the height of the heart of a tree in my boreal
cloths. My seamstress sets down

her needle, with a headache. Like windows
painted shut, snow everywhere hardens. My hands
are cold, and they must keep cold, like milk.

This poem is a little more intensified, squeezed together, than most in this, McPherson's third collection, but it is representative of the mental set of the book. *The Year of Our Birth* is filled—or super-positioned—with local information, sourcebook detail, materials at hand, and lots and lots of reading. The reader can travel from gray pennies to ruby-throated humming-birds, from "On a Picture of My Parents Together in the Second Grade" to a "Poem Whose First Stanza is Martin Heidegger on Georg Trakl," from prairie dogs to cellar spiders, from solvents to centerfold—each transit by turning a single page. There has always been something dangerously inno-cent about McPherson's poems, as if the reader were being plied by a wise child. They have appeared to be pieced together, placated from oddments and made to cohere out of almost implacable differences. Sometimes, in fact, this rhetoric of ellipsis has kept us outside admiring the fragments for their brilliance but wondering why the poet could not have supplied a fuller syntax. The new book, however, makes virtues of such vices. Ellipsis is the condition of things here. Nothing is faced or followed through directly, because as the emotional life is to be dealt with it must be deflected or deferred. The best poems, such as the Heidegger/Trakl poem, or "A Co-conut for Katerina" or "The Bittern," circumlocute their painful sources with so much ease that we are actually moved by the *form of their appear-ances.* "Inside the coconut is Katerina's baby"; "Here I am then/in the only life that is clear,/clearer than all that's said about it"; "In the end I see/ nothing/but how I go blindly on loving/a life from which something is missing"—such are the life lines of these three poems and they can hardly suggest the beautifully circuitous routes we are asked to travel around them. McPherson's mode is an extreme of Pound's super-position—a collateral structure in which the parts seem only eventually to relate—while her own point of view is an emotional position somewhere in space but close. "Wearing White," for instance.

No doubt this poet has the eye of an avenging angel. The juncos are "bodied like lynx tails," a frozen wasp is lifted "by a leg, beginning to move," the snow everywhere hardens "like windows painted shut." Her imagination is acute, accurate, but there is also a satanic quality to the sensibility informing it. There is an anger withheld, a frustration of follow-through, that tightens the nerves. Even in the above examples the exits feel closed. Eventually, though, these images and those of the rest of the poem, discrete and diversionary as they are, accrue toward a single image, that of wearing white. Unlike the imaginative lives in "Spring Snow" or "Still" they do not subordinate to dominance, and unlike the images in "Rhododendrons" or "As the Window Darkens" they do not coordinate a catharsis. Each image seems to stubbornly maintain its individual integrity. Hence the juxtaposition of materials, as if in a model of a mind unable or unwilling to resolve what looks like arbitrary distinctions. The old dogged ways of writing poems cover with snow—wearing white becomes as much a technical disclaimer as "an idea//of what to do with an idea." The poem is structured between the image of cold white to start with the "idea" of cold white to end. The problem is to work the one out of the other. What do juncos, small and gray-white and furry, flying "out of the empty prison" and the wasp in the bloody hand of the taxidermist ("nothing will stay on this white") and the sensory tips of the maples, refusing one more experiment, have to do with one another—besides their snow-cover? Well, for one thing, each is diminutive of the other, and for another, obviously more vital reason, each is vulnerable to its immediate circumstance, a circumstance squeezed tighter by understatement. The juncos may be leaving a prison, but it was an empty tree-house anyway. One imagines them flying out into a blank, winter landscape. The wasp is just beginning to move. It will sooner or later "stay on this white." And the sensory tips of the maples: "They wonder if they are not/warped by feeling," because—and this is the center of snowy brilliance in McPherson's poem—"Frosting the interior/that faces them a pocket watch hangs, stopped/and silver." Not content, the poet adds that the watch "listens as the leaves clatter/into glassy cornerings." Junco, wasp, and sensory tip are all touched by snow; they may or may not be a part of the old dogged ways of doing, yet they do exist in the medium of their own subtraction, whiteness. They *are* a part of separate but equal scenes, almost superimposed. Having got this far, the poet proposes what to do with them by annealing them with an idea—an idea of what new to do. Instead of stepping in herself, an act that might thaw things out too much, she acknowledges her counterpart, her persona, her stand-in, as a way out of the old, self-conscious ways of writing poems. She discloses a possibly unifying presence, a lady wearing white, capable of the strictest symbolic speech and insight. But Emily Dickinson in her tower, "the height of the heart of a tree," dressed in her boreal clothes is less an absorbing than a competing figure. Although the seamstress with a headache and the snow like windows painted shut hardening everywhere and the hands like cold milk fulfill and complicate this final scene exquisitely (one senses that the real white work of the poem is sewing and that McPherson is the seamstress), the idea of what to do with an idea completes the poem—it does not consolidate. The poem hangs together through sustaining the tension between "scenes," not by resolving it.

Had McPherson begun her poem as it ends, with cold hands and a persona, the sequence of images would have come off as consequences of that voice and the emphasis would have fallen for the time-bind of narrative, one thing leading to another. McPherson is not interested in submitting a story. As it is, "Wearing White" is taken from the great Book of Things, selected objects that in and of themselves evoke, name, or conceal regardless of context, objects whose imaginative lives seem independent of the poet, objects that are images with the potential of ideas. McPherson's arrangement is in the order of illumination, of white becoming whiter, one image, by proximity, intensifying the next. Yet the imaginative center of the poem is hardly the delayed appearance of Dickinson: it is that stopped and silver pocket watch. Up until then the stanzas have been closed systems, two sentences, three lines each. The moment the maples assume "consciousness" and are "faced" with their own emptiness—time, like an eye, frosting over; time, like an ear, listening "as the leaves clatter/into glassy cornerings"—the stanzas begin to enjamb and the logic of what to do with an idea forecloses. We must imagine this poem as a model of a quick mind at work—a mind certainly constructing the poem, but a mind also making choices, admitting that such choices are being made. The cold color of white may be the medium of exchange; it is clearly the nature of the space occupied. Each part "hangs" in a white interior in an odd-fitting equilibrium with the whole. Even the poem's music is white—precise, completed, at one with the condition of its watch, stopped and silver. The poet might argue that the entire poem is in the voice of her persona and represents the mirror of *her*, Dickinson's, mind. Perhaps. But as that voice does not dominate and is in fact deferred, it speaks from the position of one object among others. The voice of the whole is in the mind of the poet; only that mind, analytical and clear, can be in all the poem's places at once, organizing the space and silence. Only that mind can hear the order in the discordance of objects speaking.

An absolute poetry, an autotelic poetry, like the Urn itself, is finally an abstract poetry—a poetry whose ultimate concern, through its images, objects, its absorbing emblem, is with that ulterior dimension we call *idea*. Time is space to such poetry, lyrical space, both the space within the poem and without. Structure amounts to an enlarged, often elaborate metaphor, accommodating as much distance and difference as possible. Sometimes such poetry makes a music of edges, sometimes a music all even surface. Whatever the shortfall, the means, it sees in idea, it hears in idea. Absolute poetry has more than once been passed off as form as idea. Absolute poetry is what is left over after the indicated poem is through—the ghost form, the music around the poem. And what is the ambition of such form, such music? It lies somewhere in the imagination of the sublime. It is not enough to sublimate the speaking part of the self into a visual vocabulary, to effect "the voice of things." At its best, and almost on its own, that voice must intimate as well as translate. The image may be an idea embodied; it can be an idea ennobled. "Wearing White" is, all together, too geared to its own fragmentary, asymmetrical energy to focus—with that oneness of the idea—its possible emotional impact. Its music is atonal, intentionally off center. It is a poem absolutely in the present, dissonant tense. Coleridge puts it this way: "Beautiful is that in which the many still seen as many become one." McPherson's poem is the beautiful in which the one still seen as one becomes the many. Hers is an absolute poetry of the image. William Matthews concludes his new manuscript, *Rising and Falling*, with a poem that eloquently and movingly fits Coleridge's definition of the beautiful, an absolute poetry of the idea.

*Long*

It's about to be too late.
Every shred of the usual weather
is precious and sexual as it goes,
the way the links of a fugue become
one another's strict abandonments.

As for the future, it will not swerve.
Fire sleeps in the tree. Which tree?
Fire sleeps without dreaming and cannot
say. If we call the future's name
it becomes our name, by echo.

And from the dead, not even
a plea that we leave them
alone, each dead locked
in its dead name. If the dead complained
they would say we summon them poorly,

dull music and thin wine, nor love
enough for the many we make,
much less for the melted dead
in their boxes. Above them
we talk big, since the place is vast

and bland if we tire of looking closely,
washed bland by light from what light
lets us see, our study,
the scripture of matter,
our long narcosis of parting.

This is an exceptional piece of work. Its title is not only the noun but the chief adjective of its grammar—the idea of the poem and the idea around the poem. In its full moment the poem transcends the incorporation of the image, the embodiment of an idea, and ennobles its own invention. *It's about to be too late*—the kind of colloquial departure inherent in "That is no country for old men"—becomes, five stanzas later, our long *narcosis of parting.*—What is an idea, anyway? Often enough it is a paradigm of what is possible, if everything is possible. Often enough it is the antonym for a thing. An idea ought to be the kind of metaphysical experience Eliot assigned to Donne, the sentient brain as a part of the sensual body. It ought to be no more abstract than a word made flesh. For Matthews, an idea is at least an image with knowledge, which is a far different *thing* from an image with personality alone. "Long" is the enactment—"Pipe to the spirit ditties of no tone"—of knowledge. If an idea can be a thing in nature. . . .

Perhaps what is most extraordinary about this poem is how it formulates rhetoric from idea. It does not pretend to impress us with pocket watches, stopped and silver, wallpaper with the cries of birds, or a childhood falling through our lives like snow. There are, flat out, no similes and no symbols, in any legal sense. Nothing in this poem is *like* anything else. Nothing *stands for* anything else. Something *is* something else. "Long" is the final logic of metaphor: its comparative life comes from within, its implicative, its extra life, from without. It is the thing known made form and named within the context of the unknown. There are not even any images, in terms of the discrete. Instead the poem reads as a single, self-sustaining "image"—a fugue whose links "become/one another's strict abandonments"—an image of a statement played against a statement ("Fire sleeps in the tree. Which tree?/Fire sleeps without dreaming and cannot/say."), an image of words repeating and renewing themselves.

> And from the dead, not even
> a plea that we leave them
> alone, each dead locked
> in its dead name. If the dead complained
> they would say we summon them poorly . . .

This is free verse well in love with itself, free verse formalized and formulated so as to call attention to the discretion of its moves. The internal

rhyming, the assonance, consonance, the soft touch on the alliteration—
these are all clear enough. But underlining the overt technique is the pace
of the sentences, as in this stanza we are led into the air before turning back
for three lines, then led out to *complained* and *poorly*. "Long" is seamless. As
other examples have shown, discrete images tend to separate the poem from
its implicit center of gravity, and the greater their distinction the more the
poem is forced out to its peripheries. This can create tremendous tension
and power. It can also waste opportunities. The symbolist ideal, extreme
in the opposite direction, would center the poem everywhere, simultaneously, so that each word and each line would be an echo of what preceded.
There ought to be a metaphysical compromise, oneness without sameness,
unity of music without locking in the metaphor. Matthews's poem offers
little that is directly visual because it is modeled on the metaphysical assumption of a language of idea: not an idea of what to do with an idea, but
an idea of how to be an idea. "Long" is the condition of an idea, its music.
It cannot afford the distinction of images when its imaginative life depends
on the resolution of such distinctions. That is why it feels, as an entity, at
once abstract and palpable, exquisite and earned. It is a poem perfected
by its working knowledge of itself.

It is as if knowledge, the witness of knowing, were speaking the poem,
speaking from and to the "narcosis of parting." The speech of this knowledge, as it paraphrases experience, is neither carnal nor spiritual, but aesthetic, insofar as aesthetic still refers to the beautiful. An idea such as "our
long narcosis of parting," is beautiful, transcendental. It informs every line,
carries every sentence of this poem. "It's about to be too late," the poem
begins. The future will not only not swerve, it will not answer when called.
Its one potential is to repeat what we ask of it, the way fire is the only answer to fire. We know what the future is anyway. As for the past, the dead,
the dead are neutral, anonymous, gainsaid. And if they did say they would
say we summon them poorly, dull music, thin wine. Down there, in the real
future, fire talks, as by the light of our own and the sun's small fires we talk
big in a big place, save when we study. Unlike fire, we cannot sleep without
dreaming, saying, studying in silence, over and over, our scripture, our long
addiction to parting. The poem's title and first line suggest the dialectic of
the poem, the last line the synthesis. It is the latter knowledge, inevitable
and everywhere through the piece, that gives the voice its omniscient-like

presence, that sense of the idea passing into and surpassing the form. The emotion of that knowledge, like everything else here, lives *in potentia*, though it is essentially the same at the beginning as at the end. It is *our* knowledge that changes, grows. Whatever the voice of the image achieves, it can never achieve, in its distinction, what the voice of the imagination itself comes to. The imagination is a source, not a resource, coming from a place where emotion and intellect, image and idea, are words for something synonymous. The imagination, as the Symbolists were telling us, is perfect knowledge. So there is no room for a first-person in a poem that has preempted his particular needs, and the "we" as provided here is editorial rather than actual. This is a poem within a poem, that is the resonance of its form, that is the perfection of its knowledge, as if the medium of the space it moves in has a music, and it has. "Long" sounds omniscient because it reads like a lyric held within the longer, deeper breath of an ode—a lyric that speaks from the condition of the truth it is addressing.

This larger, encompassing form, this ambient lyric, this idea, and even ideal, of form, is what keeps the poem with ambitions of an absolute from collapsing in on itself. As the image has a kind of afterlife, so its fullest voice—the "imagination" of the image—produces a kind of aftereffect, the future's name becoming our name. But we are talking about more than the connotative power of metaphor, about more than the power of any individual image. We are talking about the visual and vocal potential of the whole poem embraced in its total moment, and movement. If, as we have said, the imagination is speaking in Matthews's poem—the idea of omniscience, of certain knowledge—that imagination serves the purpose of establishing both the limits of and a countermotion to the poem's ambition of perfecting *itself*. Within itself, "Long" is a work of low-value intensity. Compatibility, in fact, is what makes it move so smoothly at the surface. Outside itself, though, between what it is and what it knows, between the stated and figurative forms of *long*, between the poem of twenty-five low-keyed, ironic, self-preoccupied lines and the ghost poem of a wider, greater, classical, contemplative utterance, is a tension of high value. The idea of the ode, the mind and music of the ode, with its ability to complicate an inner life and its need to engage the philosophical, with its ability to celebrate and its need to stabilize, is the lyric at its most transcendental—the lyric, in this case, taking the part of an overvoice, an environment, a perspective on longing.

## 5

When Larry Levis writes of "Rhododendrons" that he wants to resemble them, nodding in the first spring breezes, "and remember nothing,/the way a photograph of an excavation/cannot remember the sun," he is in danger of isolating and therefore insulating his image from the drift and dramatic situation of the whole of his poem. The logic and will of the discrete image, surreal or *au naturel*, once it is pursued for its own aesthetic sake, is to become an island, maybe a gorgeous island, just off the mainland. When Sandra McPherson writes, in a poem whose title is its first line, that "The gun is such a horse/people are thrown around by it/it eats carrots and sugarcane/it has an iron shoe for defense and games," she is in danger of turning the absolute image into the arbitrary. Whether the image is low level or not, the question becomes less one of can the poet turn a gun into such a horse—and she does, for eighteen more lines—than why she would bother. The image on its own, if we fail to exert enough personal authority, is suicidal—its will is to disappear into the future, into space. The force of gravity for any poem is the result of the source of that gravity, as the first principle for any poem is the place the voice is calling from. With the free-verse voice the problem is not so much accessibility to the source as control of its emotional life; with the more formal, because more objectified and intellectual, voice of an absolute poetry the problem is not so much control of its imaginative life as accessibility to the source. The free-verse voice calls attention to its tone; the formal voice of the image calls attention to its aura—and its aural context, since we are to be seeing and hearing simultaneously. As the ultimate appeal of emotion is to the self, the ultimate appeal of the image—as a medium for emotion—is to an idea. The idea appealed to in William Matthews's poem "Long," for instance, is the idea (the "tone") of the ode as an expression of ceremony, the invented ritual of "our long narcosis of parting." It is as if Matthews had found his voice in surrendering *his* voice to the form, the ambiance of the ode, a voice only rehearsed in the literal lyric. The voice in free verse seems always ready to start *inside*, the voice of the imagination, no matter how intimate with the material, seems always to start *outside* the form—the one in position, the other, to use Pound's word again, in super-position. Too often, as in the examples of Levis and McPherson, the particular image or image-based poem is unable or unwilling to generate this appeal to antecedence, to the source outside, even as that appeal is to be made to the assumed or implied ambient form of the poem itself.

Historically, *emblems* have been regarded as didactic devices aimed at moral instruction—the device being the image-symbol, as in an engraving, and the moral some attached verse motto. Metaphorically, however, emblems ought to be regarded as unifying figures and figures of speech, or figures evoking unity. Emblems could then be seen as ideas formulated as images—forms as coherent content—capable of sustaining an atmosphere, the aura of a voice. In 1977, three books were published of genuine presence, books that through image or impersonation create a series and in one case a sequence of emblems of whole power and imagination: Norman Dubie's *The Illustrations*, Charles Simic's *Charon's Cosmology*, and Charles Wright's *China Trace*. The first books of emblems became sourcebooks, little libraries of ethical information and image. They were often categorized according to special emphasis. Some were noted as books of fables, some as proverbs, some as epigrams. The fact of category is important here because we are speaking of modes of aesthetic behavior. Dubie's book, for example, is a book of tableaux, impersonations, lyric drama, fictions, illustrations, all fabulous. Simic's is a book of folk wisdom and humor, allegories, inventions, lore, prophecies, superstitions, all proverbial. Wright's is a book of signs, symbols, allusions, assumptions, transformations, parts and pieces, equations, all gnomic, hermetically sealed.

As a book of emblems *The Illustrations* is a series of events dramatizing and extenuating their circumstances. The poems are either acted out through the artifice of a persona, ranging from Virginia Woolf to Czar Nicholas to "The Negress" to Mandelstam to Ovid; or they are dedicated to friends and relatives as elliptical letters of concern, *illustrations* of artful but moral points; or they are *after* art, painting in particular, whether it is Brueghel, Klee, the walls at Lascaux, or "Jacob Boehme's Triptych of Winter Hours: 1620." The subjects and objects of Dubie's poems look like illustrations, illuminating the names and dates assigned as part of a Proustian milieu. The subject, on the other hand, looks like Art, complete with its "ice water, blue spikes of lupine, and morphine," that is, the absoluteness of art as understood in Paris in the 1920s. Actually *The Illustrations* is a run of elegies, and the connecting emotion is the imagination of grief. Its emblems are all events, contrived and reconstructed, situations treated as single, complete objects, objets d'art, that beyond the exercise of a speaker themselves speak. Norman Dubie is their Proust, their ghost writer. The book is a collection built between "The Boy Brueghel," the second poem, and "The Moths," third from last. (This poet is adept at postponing entrances and exits.) The book's inspiration, its deepest breath, is the consequence of and a response to the initiation into the knowledge and idea of death. In the latter poem, "The Moths," Dubie juxtaposes a lengthy reenactment of sixteenth-century pilgrims landing and dying near his boyhood home of Bath, Maine—"The peninsula seen from the hills near Bath/ Was a sullen black orchis, its back almost broken"—with an even longer recital—"in a future/that repeats the past"—of his own arrival at an understanding, twenty years after the fact, of the death of his mother. The poem is a personal and public history, as close as we are likely to get to this poet.

> When the father dies you follow him to the grave
> And then walk away without him. I followed my father
> To the edge but then walked back with him
> Talking about something unimportant. We learn
>
> From pilgrims raising their great beige mainsail . . .

"Living here in the desert," the poet tells us, with perspective, "I can now describe the peninsula." The mother is Dubie's, perhaps everybody's original figure of grief. He constructs his six-page poem so as to make her the final figure in a strategy of sad figures, a last referent. As in every other instance in his book, Dubie turns from the free-verse possibilities of declaration to the elaborate illustration of his voice. A situation, an enlarging tableau, is being worked out in "The Moths." The poet ends the first half of his poem with moths being compared to "blotches" on the cheeks of the dead or "like some soft fossil of a shell/You might discover out walking in the woods." He concludes that his mother "pale with her red hair rests,/At midnight, looking out of the kitchen window where/All summer the fat moths were knocking their/Brains out against the lamp in the henhouse." Dubie dramatizes his imagination by delaying his emotion. That is in the nature of emblems. But Dubie is a master at extenuating circumstances. His elliptical elegy for his mother becomes all too ultimately a celebration of grief. "Now the moths are replaced with large/Flakes of snow, and there's no difference, moths/Or snow, for their lives are so short/That while they live they are already historical."

The Brueghel poem, "February: The Boy Brueghel," is an exacting emblem if a more elaborate design. It is so much of a piece it must be read almost as a single stroke.

> The birches stand in their beggar's row:
> Each poor tree
> Has had its wrists nearly
> Torn from the clear sleeves of bone,
> These icy trees
> Are hanging by their thumbs
> Under a sun
> That will begin to heal them soon,
> Each will climb out
> Of its own blue, oval mouth;
> The river groans,
> Two birds call out from the woods
>
> And a fox crosses through snow
> Down a hill; then, he runs,
> He has overcome something white
> Beside a white bush, he shakes
> It twice, and he turns
> For the woods, the blood on the snow
> Looks like the red fox,
> At a distance, running down the hill:
> A white rabbit in his mouth killed
> By the fox in snow
> Is killed over and over as just
> Two colors, now, on a winter hill:
>
> Two colors! Red and white. A barber's bowl!
> Two colors like the peppers
> In the windows
> Of the town below the hill. Smoke comes
> From the chimneys. Everything is still.

Ice in the river begins to move,
And a boy in a red shirt who woke
A moment ago
Watches from his window
The street where an ox
Who's broken out of his hut
Stands in the fresh snow
Staring cross-eyed at the boy
Who smiles and looks out
Across the roof to the hill;
And the sun is reaching down
Into the woods

Where the smoky red fox still
Eats his kill. Two colors.
Just two colors!
A sunrise. The snow.

The poet breaks in periodically ("A barber's bowl!/ . . . Just two colors")
to exclaim approval and let us know someone is out there; but these are
not interruptions, they are insights brought immediately into focus. The
poem is a shaggy sestina within the ghost of a greater skill, the sestina form
itself—"a scheme of cruciate retrogradation," as one guidebook calls it.
However odd the fit, it is a beautiful poem, an evolving emblem, a summary of pursuit and discovery, sunrise and snow, in which the image becomes the word as music and the object—the poem itself—is continually,
through the busy syntax of the simile, being changed and absorbed in a
child's eye view. "Everything is still"—and if there is to be a rhyme, a leg-
ible mark down the length of the page, it is to rhyme with the hill and the
kill. The action effects simultaneity in just those two colors. It also effects
Brueghel's famous ability to invite into the real landscape the surreal, as
when those trees, hanging by their thumbs, climb out of their own blue,
oval mouths. Everything is still within the kinesis, the perpetual motion of
things turning into one another, the image of what they are becoming what
they look like, but all out of the sweet sight of the boy. Who is seeing it,
then? Of course. The poem would naturally be impossible with Dubie *in* it.
Out of it he can play with all the omniscience he needs. Yet the poem does

fail as in a child's drawing, an allegory of objects, beautiful and cruel, or as in an illustration in a children's book about a boy in a red shirt who wakes to find near his window an ox broken out of its (his) hut and staring cross-eyed back at him. More than one poet has been cross-eyed. There is a moment close to the end of "The Moths" when the speaker remembers that "once I woke in the morning/To the slobbering head of a cow moose through the window./And my father during the week is at school in Bangor." And my mother is dead, he goes on in effect to say. In each one of his "Illustrations" Dubie is formalizing by transforming another version of grief, lifting it to the level of an event suddenly out of his hands. Projection is a condition of his, his most necessary aesthetic habit. When we look at the list of his assignments, Virginia Woolf, Osip Mandelstam, Paul Klee, his mother, we recognize what he calls "the regalia inside," the intaglio of an emotional life so complicated by the imagination that we are asked neither to weep nor simply watch but to wonder at how far outside the body of his grief the poet is allowed to stand. The more fabulous the emblem perhaps the greater the distance. After all, the boy Brueghel, looking out past the ox, across the roof to the hill where the sun is reaching down into the woods with the fox still eating, is smiling.

*Charon's Cosmology* is a book of "parables and paradoxes," but mostly passages from one shore of the river Styx to the other, and back again, essentially "confused/As to which side is which." Simic is well known for playing both sides against the middle, a combination of gallows humor and *duende* unique in our poetry. His cosmology this time is the star-chart of the Underworld; as he invents Hades, he invents a full series of rituals, characterizations, witnesses, archetypes, as well as the invention of himself as agent and prophet. In "Landscape with Crutches" everything is done "with a hell of an effort," from the daylight needing a crutch to "the smoke as it goes up," from the trees "about to stumble" to "the wind on its ghost-crutch," from the "bread on its artificial limbs" to "my mother, mind you, using/Two knives for crutches as she squats to pee." In "Eyes Fastened with Pins" no one knows what a long day death puts in, waiting for its laundry to be ironed, waiting for supper, watching its table set, having worked for the live-long day going about its lonely, often difficult rounds, wrong address, locked doors, and the rain beginning to fall and "Death with not even a newspaper/To cover his head, not even/A dime to call the one pining away."

In "Poem," the father "writes all day, all night:/Writes while he sleeps, writes in his coffin" and—three stanzas later—

> When the bottle empties,
> His great dark hand
> Bigger than the earth
> Feels for the moon's spigot.

Simic's peculiar surrealist technique is to ply the huge truth with the image of the homily, to surprise the conventional wisdom with the barbarity of the cliché. He loves sorting out what we might have expected and replacing it with what we would rather not believe. So the fat rat, in "Progress Report," the "one with baggy pants," is about to get cut up by the pretty girl with sweat on her brow, but that's okay, he's spellbound, while his friends in the maze "study the stars, defecate,/Do the tango,/make valentines,/Salute the general, wear mourning bands." Sometimes, however, the replacements and transpositions turn toward something darker and more personal than rats with mourning bands, and more grotesque, something of a kind of Slavic expressionism. In "Travelling Slaughterhouse," he thanks Dürer, "I like that horse of yours./I spent my childhood hidden in his guts." By the last lines "we are a travelling slaughterhouse . . . /he lets me eat his heart out." In "The Summons," the robes of the judges are magnificent—"When they enter among the assembled/The one with a head of a lamb will be mine,/With a throat of a lamb//Recently slit." And in the title poem, the ferryman, who is likely confused as to which side of the Styx is which, is forgiven.

> I'd say it doesn't matter
> No one complains he's got
> Their pockets to go through
> In one a crust of bread in another a sausage

Behind the folk wit and wisdom, behind the tragic domestic, behind the ghetto detail, behind the junk-trunk of endless little objects, is the archetypal world itself, an architecture of forms and first images and figures in outline, with a music of bone flute and skin drum. Behind the tragic-comic mask stands the information and intelligence of what the texts call mythic consciousness. Simic correlates his sense of it as "the evening's capacity/ For lofty detachment/ From the extraordinary event." The extraordinary is ordinary to Simic, and the ordinary something extra. He is not so detached as he is aloof from most everything but pain. His "Description":

That which brings it
about. The agent.

The old sweet temptation
to find an equivalent

for the ineffable.
This street. Grey day

breaking. So many things
to evoke, name.

Standing here, partaking
of that necessity.

\*

Among all the images
that come to mind,

where to begin?
Contortions, infinite shapes

pain assumes. Some old woman
for instance,

a lame child
passing me by

with incredible exertions
for each step.

\*

A street that always
somehow resembles me.

Grey day and I
the source of light.

A corner where
a part of myself

keeps an appointment
with another part of myself.

This small world.
This dumb show.

*

The two of them,
all haunched up, limping,

hand in hand,
afraid to cross the street

on some millennial errand
to a prison, some infirmary

where they'll take bread
out of their mouths,

where a doctor
won't use any anaesthetic.

All around and throughout this poem stands the agent who "brings it about."
This is Simic's *ars poetica*, the internal history and structure of an imagination translating its needs. Because the poet needs to find an "equivalent//
for the ineffable," the untranslated, and untranslatable, world of the afterlife. But here on this street, grey day breaking, there are so many things to
evoke, to name. The important values, we know, are relational, therefore
"partaking" of the necessity for naming may be enough. Which leads us to
where we sort out the infinite shape and contortions that pain assumes. For

example, two stereotypes—an old woman and a lame child "passing me by/ /with incredible exertions." Pain is relative. So the street always somehow resembles me, that source of light against the grey day, as in that small world, dumb-show corner of myself, where I keep all appointments, the old woman and the lame child become fixed, all haunched up, limping, hand in hand, afraid to cross the street.—And Simic leaves them there in himself, afraid. Their errand, millennial and mad, is to pain itself, to a prison, *inside*, some infirmary where they'll take bread out of their mouths and the doctor, as in a death-camp, will not use an anaesthetic. This is the demiworld of a Beckett and a Gottfried Benn, with the dimensions of the celestial. Pain, ineffable pain, described if not defined, is the informing emotion, but it is an emotion emblemized, suspended in the consciousness of an agent determined not to judge. Simic is a genius at equating the ineffable, entertaining us with it, and then turning it back on us. In poem after poem in this new book, we feel the presence of his ghost moving things from one side of the river to the other, working silently and carefully behind the form, within the form, until there can be no difference between context and consciousness. The aura and aural dimension around Simic's proverbs are of the voice of a passenger on a river in a place of disaffection, being rowed back and forth under a star-chart that does not change.

*China Trace*—a concentration of the oriental and the occidental, noun to noun, the one word qualified by the opposition of the other—is the emblem for a book of emblems. It is the quintessential abstraction, the idea of the word made manifest as the Word. Flesh, for Charles Wright, is under continual review and revision: "Nothingness, tilt your cup./I am the wafer just placed on your tongue,/The transubstantiation of bone and regret/To air and a photograph" or "I write poems to untie myself, to do penance and disappear/Through the upper right-hand corner of things, to say grace." In each of the sequences of short, Montale-like, hermetic poems here, the body as a host, as a form, is continually being transformed back into the object of the poem and, by that means, back into a state of grace—the body corporeal made "the breath of the dream." Above all, says Coleridge, the symbol is known "by the translucence of the eternal through and in the temporal." The eternal, for Wright, *is* temporal, the art of repetition and renewal of particular, natural, luminous processes—particular because of what those processes seem, natural because of what those processes are, luminous because of what those processes can mean. Nature is a temple. Hence the path this poet must follow—his trace, his trail—is through a landscape made visible, made audible, made real because it must be imagined. No poet of his generation is as moved by absolute metaphor as this one. And China is Wright's metaphor for the imagination, his own imagination, its provinces, its terrain, its vernacular—a mandarin Southern rhetoric.

The overall order of this book of order is bicameral, with identical epigraphs, from Calvino, fronting each half. "'On the day when I know all the emblems,' Kublai Khan asked Marco, 'shall I be able to possess my empire, at last?' And the Venetian answered: 'Sire, do not believe it. On that day you will be an emblem among emblems.'" It is clear from the clear accents, the formal measure and resonance of the line, the assured intelligence of the phrase, the inevitable symmetry of the close form, that Wright wants to possess what is passing from him, and short of that, move with it, changed, and short of that, "Divested of everything," wants to be

> A downfall of light in the pine woods, motes in the rush,
> Gold leaf through the undergrowth, and come back
> As another name, water
> Pooled in the black leaves and holding me there, to be
> Released as a glint, as a flash, as a spark . . .

The order within the book is less apparent, and is supposed to be less than apparent. The same objects appear again and again, as totems or signs. Fire is a favorite, and wind and water and names of flowers and flowering plants and moths and tongues and spiders and clothes and stars and the sky and Captain Dog and hearts and the dead heart of the moon and birds like the gull "locked like a ghost in the blue attic of heaven." In a word, nouns, things under a levy of symbolic speech. Faces are popular enough to serve as a frame for the book, those faces "Falling into darkness . . . /like beads from a broken rosary . . ." in the initial poem, "Childhood," to that face of the sun gone down on the Pacific, "Released in his suits of lights,/lifted and laid clear," in the final poem, "Him." No question this poet has his own coveted order in mind; no question the reader could calculate an order of his own. The point is that the poems grow as a group, in the unfolding emblem of a search, pause for a rest at "Invisible Landscape"—an obvious and centrally located image—and start out once more. They acquire as they accumulate, all fifty of them, as they stand related by selection and juxtaposition. A trace may be a search, but it is also a way. "Snow," like all of Wright's objects, is a common denominator.

> If we, as we are, are dust, and dust, as it will, rises,
> Then we will rise, and recongregate
> In the wind, in the cloud, and be their issue,
>
> Things in a fall in a world of fall, and slip
> Through the spiked branches and snapped joints of the evergreens,
> White ants, white ants and the little ribs.

As in so many of the titles here, this poem is a perfection of the process of formation and reformation the incarnate will undergo—a rising and falling in a world of fall. (Dust and snow: the elements we began this essay with.) What if we reverse the pattern, and out of falling rise?

> White ants, white ants and the little ribs
> Through the spiked branches and snapped joints of the evergreen,
> Things in a fall in a world of fall, and slip
>
> In the wind, in the cloud, and be their issue,
> Then we will rise, and recongregate
> If we, as we are, are dust, and dust, as it will, rises.

The grammar of the experience may be a little retread, but the trick is simply to illustrate the internal logic of the natural world Wright is emulating and being changed by. "Snow" is a symbolist–surrealist paperweight of a poem, illuminated from within, impervious without. To make it work we must be able to turn it over. The way up is the way down, and had the poet reversed the order of his whole book we would be reading no sorrow but the sun rising into the transparency of his childhood and Wright's goodbyes to all that is past in his life and toward "The names/Falling into the darkness."

The trail, whatever its route, is traced in the light of the form—eight lines, nine lines, ten lines, a dozen, all hard, high-gloss surfaces. "This triviality," says Joyce, made Stephen Dedalus "think of collecting many such moments together in a book of epiphanies. By an epiphany he meant a sudden spiritual manifestation." Wright's book of epiphanies, his book of emblems, his book of lines, manifests a fundamental tension between the "triviality" of the local object and its will for "transubstantiation," between the body and will of the poet ("my slow rise through the dark toward the sweet wrists of the rose"). The word, the spirit, inside the word is the result of that tension, and that word is spoken *sotto voce* each time the speaker looks "up at the black bulge of the sky and its belt of the stars," each time he watches "the snow bees sent mad by the sun." The landscape out there, with its "houses of ample weight," its yards "large and windraked," that landscape of solitude and "the emptiness everywhere," that landscape of sorrow hanging "like a heart in the star-flowered boundary tree," of a childhood "shrunken and drained dry, turning transparent," that landscape, that China, traced and retraced, is the landscape within. Wright's imagination may look bravura, but its sounds, its figures in speech, are secrets he has come only this far to tell us. "The unborn children are rowing out to the far edge of the sky."

> I'd like to be with them still, pulling my weight,
> Blisters like small white hearts in the waxed palms of my hands.
> I'd like to remember my old name, and keep the watch,
> Waiting for something immense and unspeakable to uncover its face.

The ambition of any emblem is to speak of things beyond their occasion and keep the watch of things immense and unspeakable. And the idea of ideas is that there be such a thing as meaning outside the corporation of the body, a meaning beyond corporeal memory. Wright's emblems give voice to the possibility that poetry need not memorize what it can transform.

1978

# III

## NARRATIVE VALUES, LYRIC IMPERATIVES

# 1

There's an ode to memory in Robert Pinsky's latest book, *Jersey Rain*, that harkens back to the best of his strongest lyric writing, particularly the poems in *History of My Heart* (1984) and *The Want Bone* (1990) and in more recent work such as "Avenue" and "Impossible to Tell." It's called "The Green Piano," and it takes the first six of the triadic stanzas—half the poem—just to set up.

> Aeolian. Gratis. Great thunderer, half-ton infant of miracles
> Torn free of charge from the universe by my mother's will.
> You must have amazed that half-respectable street
>
> Of triple-decker families and rooming-house housepainters
> The day that the bole-ankled oversized hams of your legs
> Bobbed in procession up the crazy-paved front walk
>
> Embraced by the arms of Mr. Poppik the seltzer man
> And Corydon his black-skinned helper, tendering your thighs
> Thick as a man up our steps. We are not reptiles:
>
> Even the male body bears nipples, as if to remind us
> We are designed for dependence and nutriment, past
> Into future. O Europe, they budged your case, its ponderous
>
> Guts of iron and brass, ten kinds of hardwood and felt
> Up those heel-pocked risers and treads splintering tinder.
> Angelic nurse of clamor, yearner, tinkler, dominator—
>
> O Elephant, you were for me! When the tuner Mr. Otto Van Brunt
> Pronounced you excellent despite the cracked sounding board, we
> Obeyed him and swabbed your ivories with hydrogen peroxide.

A good many of Pinsky's virtues are out front here: his scrutinizing hi-lo diction ("bole-ankled oversized hams" . . . "ponderous/Guts of iron and brass" against "Angelic nurse of clamor"); his love of domesticating detail ("half-respectable street/Of triple-decker families and rooming-house housepainters"); his mock-elevated tone that graduates without undercutting the seriousness of the humor ("Great thunderer . . . O Europe . . . O Elephant"); his penchant for extending the exposition—in a word, his agility at bringing the reader immediately into a place in time and into the strict character of the moment without sacrificing his distance. The most difficult mastery in lyric poetry, especially free verse, whose effects tend to be internal, is authority, an authorship, in this case, of simultaneity, in which the point of view of the speaker is the child and adult at once. In "The Green Piano," the boy is observed and the poet the observer, yet in the voice of the emotion the actor and narrator are the same—indeed, their implied separation in time intensifies the memory, as if longing itself, whether we wish to go back or project into the future, could change anything. Memory makes time fluid, it forgives the past once it comes to terms with the past. But it cannot change it. It can, however, in the right hands, transform it through specific connections and by enlarging the small specifications of its world.

The piano itself undergoes any number of conversions, all speaking to its nurturing humanity, its generous size, its emotional displacement— "yearner, tinkler, dominator"—while the majority of the poet's hyperboles and apostrophes go in the direction of the instrument's mothering, homing instincts, including, by association, the seltzer man and his "black-skinned helper" who deliver it ("Even the male body bears nipples"). The piano is mammalian, in keeping with the poem's true understory, involving—as if it were a detail—the effective loss of the speaker's mother. The piano takes on the role of mother.

> Ivory and umber, so you stood half done, a throbbing mistreated noble,
> Genuine—my mother's swollen livestock of love: lost one, unmastered:
> You were the beast she led to the shrine of my genius, mistaken.
>
> Endlessly I bonged according to my own chord system *Humoresque*,
> *The Talk of the Town, What I'd Say.* Then one day they painted you pink.
> Pink is how my sister remembers you the Saturday afternoon

When our mother fell on her head, dusty pink as I turn on the bench
In my sister's memory to see them carrying our mother up the last
Steps and into the living room, inaugurating the reign of our
    confusion . . .

Both mother and piano will be in need now of perpetual repair. What ought to be noticed is the turn in the narrative, the way the apostrophes to the piano "grow" from exaggeration (childhood) to the direct remembered witness of the grown son for whom the piano (transformed from sickly "pea-soup" green to being in the pink) will become the "mahogany breast, who nursed me through those//Years of the Concussion."

Pinsky's rabbinical remove from his material, his intimate distance, if you will, allows for the tonal juxtaposition that creates at once the humor and the fine emotional faultlines. This is a poem of tenderness, even for-giveness: in celebrating the used piano, through all its transformations, color schemes ("Pink one, forever-green one, white-and-gold one"—rhymes with Baldwin), and pathetic fallacies, the speaker comes to ac-cept the incapacities of the mother, both her illusions (her "swollen livestock of love") and her years of confusion ("They sued the builder of the house she fell in, with a settlement/They bought a house at last"); he comes to accept, as Pinsky does in so much of his best writing, the mul-tiples and layers of the world he grew up in, a world he understands in the vocabulary of narrative values—the names, the places, the nouns of the real nailed in real time. Yet Pinsky's brilliant eye and scrupulous dic-tion, his examining and patient voice always lift the matter at hand from the autobiographic and analytic to something like the oracular. His lyri-cism is never pretty, it's too specific for that, but it is intense, exhaus-tive, serious, and saved, if not redeemed, by its found humor. "Our mother fell on her head . . . inaugurating the reign"—the Jersey rain—"of our confusion." To remember with passion and write with separation, a com-bination never easy, is to understand that the important stories cannot be willed but must be met and greeted. The welcoming American poetic voice accepts contradiction, as Whitman says, and as Dickinson, in the lightning strikes of her poems, demonstrates.

Sharon Olds, through a half dozen strong collections, has internalized the archetypal parent to the point that, unlike Pinsky's evocations, time

and place are indeterminate, almost entirely unspecified, as if the staging
of the action were yesterday or any day in memory. The narratives of her
mother and father are ongoing, and the poems they help bring into being
feel like interruptions or illustrations from an indelible lifelong dream. You
could pick among many fine poems and find, again and again, the right
example. Such as "Wonder as Wander," from her seventh volume, *The
Unswept Room* (2002).

*Wonder as Wander*

At dusk, on those evenings she does not go out,
my mother potters around her house.
Her daily helpers are gone, there is no one
there, no one to tell what to do,
she wanders, sometimes she talks to herself,
fondly scolding, sometimes she suddenly
throws out her arms and screams—high notes
lying here and there on the carpets
like bodies touched by a downed wire,
she journeys, she quests, she marco-polos through
the gilded gleamy loot-rooms, who is she.
I feel, now, that I do not know her,
and for all my staring, I have not seen her,
like the song she sang, when we were small,
*I wonder as I wander, out under the sky,*
*how Jesus the Saviour was born for, to die*
*for poor lonely people, like you, and like I—*
on the long evenings alone, when she delays
and delays her supper, walking the familiar
halls past the mirrors and night windows,
I wonder if my mother is tasting a life
beyond this life—not heaven, her late
beloved is absent, her father absent,
and her staff is absent, maybe this is earth
alone, as she had not experienced it,
as if she is one of the poor lonely people,
as if she is born to die. I hold fast
to the thought of her, wandering in her house,

a luna moth in a chambered cage.
Fifty years ago, I'd squat in her
garden, with her Red Queens, and try
to sense the flyaways of the fairies as they kept
the pollen flowing on its local paths,
and our breaths on their course of puffs—they kept
our eyes wide with seeing what we
could see, and not seeing what we could not see.

For many readers Olds is a kind of throwback to the confessional poets of the 1960s, those readers perhaps still longing for poetry therapy to replace the current poetry theory. Olds, however, is no victim; in recognition scene after recognition scene, poem after poem, she is either participant in or complicit with the sinning. What lifts her material is the fact that she and her parents—or daughter or lover—are parts of a larger drama, ancient in its implications, present in its symbolic acting out. In this particular elegiac memoir of a piece, the mother is at that slow still moment at the edge, held in simultaneous time in the mind of the speaker. Past and present, as burdens, become one, just as the mother's future ("as if she is one of the poor lonely people") may become the daughter's. *Seeing* is the chief trope in the poem: indeed, memory, for Olds, has always been a form of watching or being watched. The plot problem—"I do not know her . . . I have not seen her"—feels familiar. The distinction in the material arrives with the insight that the speaker not only shares this mortal moment with her mother but has shared it, fatally, from the beginning. "Fatalism" has been one of the powers in the spiritual life of all of Olds's poems; here it plays out as a chronic gift for loneliness, isolation, kept anger.

The pain in the poem is palpable and brings up certain artful, or artless, issues and questions that, for me, bother the narrative in interesting ways. For one thing, the poem is only three lines shorter than Pinsky's, but because of its monolithic shape and because it's only four sentences long (thus accelerating the pace) it seems to read faster, or at least it would if Olds hadn't abruptly changed the flow and hadn't interjected two odd images. For another thing—well, there is no other thing, there is only the way the recessive lyric element rubs against the grain of the vertical structure. The first use of the dash is simple enough, since it works to link the appositional "high notes." The second and third dashes are problematic in that they appear in the same extended sentence and suggest a parenthesis when in fact they function in-dependently: they interrupt and separate rather than link. The third dash, indeed, seems to set the sentence in predicate motion all over again with a string of six *is*'s, as if to mirror the mixed mind of the speaker. Whatever, this passage is alive with stress; it moves, haltingly, with energy. The two an-nounced images (the high notes "like bodies touched by a downed wire" and the mother as "a luna moth in a chambered cage") threaten to take us out of the consciousness the syntax is building—images invariably stop time, and narrative, above all, is about time, at one speed or another. The luna moth, in particular, reads at first like an embellishment, until the garden scene that follows, where the moth transforms into a child's version of "the fairies," the pollen, and "our breaths," all shareable and mortal, showing "our eyes" what we could and could not see fifty years ago.

Wondering becomes wandering in this poem, Olds inseparable from her mother, Olds the wonderer, the mother the wanderer—all of it within tight halls and rooms or within the closeting of the poem itself. The magical Red Queens and the memory they evoke intensify the envisioning of the mother in the present, the present tense, and help underwrite the speaker's implicit anxiety over what becomes of us, which is usually that we become our parents, one or the other. The mad-hatter, marco-poloing behavior of the mother may appear to be the destiny of the old, "the poor lonely people,/as if . . . born to die," but by ending her poem in the deep, magical past, in a garden as op-posed to the cage, the speaker is forced to come to terms with the future, a future that can be understood only once it has been lived, once it is too late. The fated nature of things, the fating of children by their parents, is a haunt-ing theme in Olds. What saves it from the doldrums of confessionalism is that its actors perform as archetypes not stereotypes, and that the chief protago-nist, Olds herself, is also, movingly, under indictment and, equally, forgiven.

# 2

Narrative is one of those loose-fitting generic literary terms that gets applied like mayonnaise, like metaphor and tone. In the post-World War II generation, it has become a term handmade for literary theorists and speculators, narratologists and narrativists, and other neo-narrative onlookers. Even narrative poetry, linked to neo-formalism, has had a turn. Postmodernist Paul de Man has written that narrative as a figure is "the paradigm of all texts," whose "unreadability" engenders further texts, suggesting a deconstruction of a line—whatever its shape—without beginning or end: for the maker an endless formal possibility, for the reader an endless reading. Whatever the implications of this deconstructive insight, and however true, it's been passé for some time; which is to say that it has become an assumption since the symbolists that the text is artificial, even when it pretends to be organic. For the poet, form draws the line, shapes the figure, and limits the circumference. For the lyric poem, narrative functions as form, as an internal, achieved construct, working from the inside out, from the living guts, which is why the sequential, suggestive shapes of lyric poems so often resemble shapes in nature, which also create an artifice: the meander, the branch, the elliptical circle, the hexagon within the snowflake or the xylem of a tree, and the spiral or the gyre.

The relationship of the needs of narrative meeting the needs of lyricism—or at least the line break and the stanza—is old hat, depending on how you frame the question. For the modernist it takes on subject status beginning with the Romantics, particularly the Preface to *Lyrical Ballads*. In making so much of the language of men and the rhythms of prose as the idioms of a relativist reality as opposed to the absolutist and moralistic mindsets of eighteenth-century diction, Wordsworth describes a separation between two kinds of language. "I have wished to keep the Reader in the company of flesh and blood," he says, "in a selection of language really used by men." (I think he means Dorothy, too.) It's not too long before this essentially Miltonic-blank-verse versus Popeian-verse-couplets argument sublimates into the now familiar and ongoing debate between formalism and free verse: you hear it in Whitman's ars poeticas, Dickinson's letters, Eliot's English commentaries, Pound's ABC's, Williams's *Paterson*, Moore's use of syllabics, Crane's explications, Olson's *Maximus*, Lowell's conversion, Ginsberg's *Howl*, and Plath's "Words dry and riderless." You hear it now, in the last twenty years, in the quarrel between poetry and theory, coherency and indeterminacy, self and construct, autobiography and history, personalism and politics, lingua franca and linguistics . . . a quarrel between who or what is speaking the poem and in whose or what language: the discourse of our dailiness or a discourse of a discourse.

These meter-making and -unmaking arguments have, historically, obscured not only the way in which good poems are at once formal and free, personal and political, of a piece and difficult, but the way in which the lyric poem continues to depend on narrative's "fare forwarding," that constructed sense of followability, line-turn, connection, disconnection, and one damn thing after another. Verse and prose distinctions mask the multiplicity of languages we have come to accept in a poem, in a single work as well as a single career. These forced distinctions also blur the demands of rhythm, cadence, and spoken emotional texture in a line, in favor of an idea or agenda. Eliot's *Waste Land* and Berryman's *Dream Songs* are obvious examples of dramatic and dynamic multiplicity, but the former leads to the great harmony and unified resonance of *Four Quartets* and the latter comes out of the riven complexity of the mono-voiced *Homage to Mistress Bradstreet*. Plath and Ashbery, as "language poets," both evolve and combine rhetorics over a lifetime, crafting and recrafting. Some years ago, in an overview of recent American poetry entitled "Contemporary Modes," the critic, Sven Birkerts, spoke of "a bewildering plurality of poetic styles" and thus tried to bring clarity to the unclear by dividing the scene into "two kinds of poets: those for whom the world is prior to the word, and who use language to depict reality; and those for whom the world is only accessible through language, who use words to create reality." Poet Alan Shapiro, in 1996, split the categories this way: "While the world of American poetry is too heterogeneous to be usefully described in terms of one dichotomy, the recent debate if not recent practice of American poetry does seem to divide itself roughly into two opposing camps: one based in the lyricism of subjective life, the other in the skepticism of the intellect." Then he goes on to add, in a curiously infected diction, that "in the former camp . . . we find mostly free verse poems underwritten by an unexamined faith in old-fashioned notions of individual authenticity and self expression. In the latter camp, embodied most rigorously in the poets associated with the Language school, we find all fictions of unmediated selfhood thoroughly exploded, and subjectivity in general sacrificed on the experimental altar of the indeterminate sign."

Birkerts and Shapiro are correct in drawing lines down the center of contemporary American poetry, if for no other reason than the fact that there is so much of it and just to begin to sort and judge requires a certain arbitration. Curious, though, that Shapiro, whose poems fall well within the scope of his first category, falls prey to the language of his second category when he writes in the abstractions of "unmediated selfhood" and "the altar of the indeterminate sign." Perhaps the drawn differences aren't so different. Does Hart Crane's sometimes beautiful unreadability make him a poet for whom the world is accessible only through words? Does Elizabeth Bishop's beautiful readability make her a poet mired in self-expression? What really is the difference between the world and the word, once you've got past the chicken-or-the-egg part of it? A sentence is a narrative, the word a world, the way a man or a woman is made of words. You can screw up a sentence any way you want—make it, unmake it, invest it, divest it, add, subtract, reorder it, reduce it to a word, it is still alive in time, with time. It still proceeds from the breath—of the world, into the world. I would submit that there is no such thing as an "indeterminate sign"; there is only a less determinate sign. And I agree with De Quincey, that time is a "greater mystery" than space, that connections hold more power than divisions, and that words are not singularities and stillnesses but move together with the arrow of time.

3

When Robert Pinsky insinuates his mother into his poem, through her affection for the piano and her ambition for her son, he permits her presence to define the emotion; he asks her, in effect, to become the real antagonist and source of imaginative tension. The mother, after her fall, is carried "up the last/Steps and into the living room," just like the piano. And in the years of confusion that follow, it's the piano that will assume the mothering role. This is the kind of dramaturgical information narrative brings to the occasion of and reason for our poems—emotive as well as imaginative, spiritual as well as material. Narrative provides not only the characters but the character of the event. For Sharon Olds it's the memory of fifty years ago brought painfully, and immediately, into the present, lyric moment. "I do not know her . . . I have not seen her"—the mother will die with the daughter's knowledge that our most fundamental relationships can also be our most alien, and that this fracture will continue. The speaker will pass this knowledge on, in a larger narrative. Paraphrasing "content," however, is dangerous in that it tends to reduce the language of the experience to a sort of rue, even roux, when the poem as an entity has spoken well enough for itself—not only in the best words in their best order but with an intensity that brings art to life. Charles Bernstein is correct in saying that "there are no thoughts except through language, we are everywhere seeing through it, limited to it but not by it. Its conditions always interpose themselves: a particular set of words to choose from (a vocabulary), a way of processing those words (syntax, grammar): the natural conditions of language." Nor are there feelings in a poem without language, just as narrative—the impulse to sequence and consequence—underwrites the natural condition of a sentence, which is vocabulary turned into syntax and grammar. The lyric shape of this natural condition is poetry, the art of the need of language to connect.

The secret subject, or subtext, of narrative is time; the subtext of time is mortality, mutability; the subtext of mortality is emotion. Loss is our parent, poetry a parental form. "Twenty-four Logics in Memory of Lee Hickman" is a late poem by Michael Palmer from his *Selected Poems 1972–1995*, overtitled *The Lion Bridge*. Palmer is commonly associated with experimental writing in general and Language poetry in particular; he seems to me to be the closest poet we have to a classical French symbolist. "The call to language in a poem," he has written, "does not begin or end with its discursive flow and does not give way to qualified priorities. Not to make of poetry a 'purer' occasion, simply to give credit to its terms and the range of possibilities it attends. Poetry seems a *making* within discrete temporal conditions ... and is profoundly meditational and relative and exists as a form of address singularly difficult to prescribe or define." This strikes me as very much an update of the theoretical thinking of Mallarmé and Valéry and Eluard. Palmer's work is certainly interested in "the range of possibilities" and is "profoundly meditational," but what interests me in his formulation is his reference to "discrete temporal conditions," a typical oxymoron from a poet who wishes to separate just at the moment he connects. Palmer's poetry flows beautifully, but discretely.

The bend in the river followed us for days
and above us the sun
doubled and redoubled its claims

Now we are in a house
with forty-four walls
and nothing but doors

Outside the trees, chokecherries, mulberries and oaks
are cracking like limbs
We can do nothing but listen

or so someone claims,
the Ice Man perhaps, all enclosed in ice
though the light has been shortening our days

and coloring nights the yellow of hay,
scarlet of trillium, blue of block ice
Words appear, the texture of ice,

with messages etched on their shells:
*Minna 1892, Big Max and Little Sarah,*
*This hour ago*

*everyone watched as the statues fell*
Enough of such phrases and we'll have a book
Enough of such books

and we'll have mountains of ice
enough to balance our days with nights
enough at last to close our eyes

"Words, after speech, reach/Into the silence," writes Eliot, and Palmer is nothing if not a poet of the language of and reaching into silence. This is obvious in his most austere writing ("The voice, because of its austerity, will often cause dust to rise."), such as "Recursus" and the brilliant "I Do Not" ("I do not know English."). Yet even in his most severe symbolist voice he speaks from circumstance, from time and place, from specifics, within an overt, or covert, gesture toward action, motive, identity. In a different context, Eliot also says that "Poetry is not a turning loose of emotion, but an escape from emotion; it is not the expression of personality, but an escape from personality. But, of course, only those who have personality and emotions know what it means to want to escape these things." In Palmer's poetry, universally, you feel the pull of the terrific tension between the source of "these things" and the resource of their transformation. What arrives at the page is a kind of distilling, utterly clarifying provenance of the word. The "logic" of "Twenty-four Logics" is meant to emphasize the integrity of the line over the sequence of the eight stanzas, in order, perhaps, to maintain equally the tension and to create a kind of float over the flow. As a poem of observation, it's not that far from the out-of-doors of Gary Snyder, what with the bend in the river, and the chokecherries, mulberries, and oaks, the coloring of night, the color of hay, scarlet trillium, and blue blocks of ice—a good reading of a mountain scene. The difference, of course, is that Palmer is a poet of committed interiority: the outside is immediately indentured to the inside—within the self and, in this case, within the forty-four walls and "nothing but doors" of a house.

"Twenty-four Logics" starts off, fait accompli, in the past tense, but quickly sets up in the present, active voice, and ends its progression in a future, speculative tense ("we'll have"), creating at least a patina of narrative. It moves through time, recording time, in other ways as well: "the light has been shortening our days"; "Words appear . . . //with messages etched on their shells:/*Minna 1892* . . . ; "*This hour ago//everyone watched as the statues fell.*" Ice is the presiding metaphor, in both its destructive and enabling modes, and it, too, suggests a passage through landscape in time. An anaphoric "enough" is about all Palmer will give the reader of the announced emotion, the elegiac claim of the material and the valuing of memory. That's a feature of Palmer that is especially appealing—his lyric reading of the mortality of the word, the price of its purity and beauty and hard-won artifice. There's a passage in Palmer's most recent book, *The Promise of Glass*, that illustrates pretty effectively the distance he keeps in the connection between his narrative source and its lyric transformation. It's a beautiful but brief sequence called "Five Easy Poems," dedicated to the contemporary French poet Anne-Marie Albiach: and no one in contemporary American poetry builds fictions of silence against appearances of fact with more subtlety and style than Palmer. Thus to start his elegant quiet suite of dedicated poems, he leads with a "Note" of rather outré exposition that is really a prose-poem.

In the summer of 1982, I went to the Hotel de l'Odéon in Paris in the hope of meeting the poet Anne-Marie Albiach. She was for the moment in residence there, but without a phone, and Claude Royet-Journoud had suggested I simply drop by and try my luck. I had first read her book *État* in the nineteen-seventies, and it had seemed a perfect work, a work perfectly realized and perfectly necessary. It had filled a space in the poetic imagination of the time that had until then been awaiting it, unoccupied.

At the Hôtel de l'Odéon, the poet Anne-Marie Albiach was not in, so I left a copy of my *Notes for Echo Lake* for her with the desk clerk and departed. After my initial disappointment, I gradually began to comprehend that this had been a most excellent first meeting with the poet Anne-Marie Albiach. Neither had failed to meet the expectations of the other. The poet Anne-Marie Albiach had been spared the *embuscade* of *gaucheries* and malaproprian ejaculations with which it is my habit to greet the French. Our conversation, in short, had never deviated from the highest plane. And, as is the case with absence generally, a trace of the erotic had lingered in the atmosphere, at least from my point of view.

This non-encounter (or what the post-structuralist might term this "in-place-of-an-encounter") served further to spur a series of reflections on the *odéon*, that is the odium, that public space for theater and the performance of poetry from which, these days, poets not infrequently find themselves excluded. Such reflections have continued to the present.

Now these "Five Easy Poems," dedicated with love to Anne-Marie Albiach on her sixtieth birthday.

Remember "91 Revere Street," the autobiographic section from Lowell's *Life Studies*? In microcosm, Palmer's "Note" serves a similar function as Lowell's prose in relation to the follow-up poems—in Lowell's case, the poems in the section titled "Life Studies"; in Palmer's, his five easy poems. It's as if, in both instances, the prose rehearses themes and images distilled in the poems. Palmer's "Five Easy Poems" are among his most elegantly rendered—"a perfect knowledge of the fragment/and the discourse of liquid surfaces"—; and if the poem for Lee Hickman is an elegy, this suite represents a love poem. It's the narrative relation between the prose and the easy poems that's interesting.

"Poetry is prose bewitched, a music made of visual thoughts, the sound of an idea," writes Mina Loy, in 1925, the year of André Breton's surrealist manifesto. Whatever Palmer's relation to surrealism, his "prose" here is bewitched with music and the sound of an idea. First, the lyric leitmotif of the phrase "the poet Anne-Marie Albiach," with its rhythmic naming "trace of the erotic." Then the charmed word-play: the title "Note," for instance, found in the title of Palmer's gift, *Notes for Echo Lake*; the use of the French "*embuscade* of *gaucheries*" (an ambush of awkwardnesses) met immediately by the exact example in "malapropian ejaculations"—gauche and left-handed at the same time; and the self-irony in the reference to "the post-structuralist," who would translate "non-encounter" into "'in-place-of-an-encounter,'" which is precisely what Palmer has done. Next the intentional self-conscious distraction of toying with the word *odéon* (Hôtel de l'Odéon) or odeum (public theatrical space), from both of which he experiences a certain "exclusion," or non-encounter. And finally, "Such reflections have continued to the present," and will continue by the implied open form of the easiness of his poems. The tag-line, "dedicated with love," adds to the whole tone a quality of missed opportunity replaced with another kind—art—"I gradually began to comprehend that this had been a most excellent first meeting. . . . Neither had failed to meet the expectations of the other."

# 4

The epistemology of a non-encounter encounter goes a long way, emotionally, in the direction of loss, whatever its recommending rhetoric. Palmer, for me, is not so exquisite a poet that the register of loss disappears into the absences of his text. "Pauses and addictions, colors/of the moment//voices, glances and nervous hands"—these lines from the first of the "Five Easy Poems" speak to the tensions that underwrite much of his work. Palmer's need for an underscoring narrative, a source in time and place, is graphically illustrated by his prefatory "expository" "Note" to a winning of poems that are enlarged enormously by its presence; and in a similar sense his poem titles generally help clarify the mystery of what he's up to, whether it's "Autobiography" or "The Promises of Glass." Noir visuals might be one way to see his poems, since, as cinema, they evoke "a film of smoke and mist," usually with a scarf of red. But what to make of alternate readings of Palmer's resonant poetry, such as Steve McCaffery's comment that "Michael Palmer writes a splendid poetry of displacement, of shifts and nomadic drifts of text through zones of page. The operative semantic is copulative, a linking (purely syntagmatically) of isolated units still preserving their molecular independency. He writes a double assault: on page per se and on the vector of reference. There is no place in his work because there largely is no referent incanted. . . ."

And so forth. And quite the contrary, there's a great deal of place in Palmer's work, often elliptically referenced and usually placed in time, commonly "noted" through the people who populate his poetry. Whatever McCafferey is saying here he's saying it with consistency, yet my impression is that whatever he's saying he's elevating his discourse well beyond Palmer and into a riff of linguistic theory. Syntagmatic, after all, is about word-sequence in a sentence, pure or impure, dependent or isolated. Palmer's syntax within the sentence absolutely holds; it's his sentence to sentence, stanza to stanza "syntax" that achieves "molecular independency." Palmer, in the hands of the theorists, becomes an alien, allied with other aliens, disassociated from the poetry culture of his past, which includes not only the French but poets like Paul Celan and Yannis Ritsos; he becomes separated from the multiple narrative of American poetry before Language poetry identified itself. Indeed, Palmer is interesting to the extent that he is associated with the tradition of the experimental imagination and to those values that connect the word to the world, perception to emotion, and language to motive—values that are part of the blood and brain of poetry, basic to the breath of its art. Language, for every good poet, is always the crisis, and the conclusion.

Comes to mind the passions-of-mind poetry of Jorie Graham, who appears to be of an opposite rhetorical energy from Palmer altogether. Yet for all the layering and packing of her lyric moment, for all the plurality and pressure she brings to her existential sentences (sentences often meant to be forces, of their kind, of nature), she is, at heart, also a poet of silence—that is, "Everything depends on the point where nothing can be said." This assertion is from Graham's latest collection, *Never*, and is amplified, in one version or another, throughout the book, as it is echoed throughout her work.

It's easy to be distracted by the sometimes unfollowable in her poetry, the way her heretical speaker can be distracted by the totality and swift surround of things that circle or imbue "each glistening minute, through which infinity threads itself." And that's another thing: the language of the infinite, the eternal, smack up against the diction of the immediate, the infinitesimal. High and low at once, justified so intensely at the surface as to make complexity out of clarity, aggrandizement out of fragment. Of course, "smack up against" is pushing the verbal violence in absurdly the wrong direction—it's against such busyness that Graham writes her poems. Stillness is what she's after, "a ghost posed on my lips."

Graham is often cited—as if she had received a citation for a "moving violation"—for treating poetry as philosophy, as a glitterati of ideas. But philosophy in what sense? Philosophical is exactly what Coleridge wanted Wordsworth to be; hence "The Poem to Mr. Coleridge," which became *The Prelude*. Lyric Keats equated importance in poetry with philosophy, though in winter, he suggested, let the fish philosophize away the ice. One reader's philosophic engagement can be another's ontological struggle. Graham *is* a thinker in her poems; she is certainly a talker, but a talker in search of the ineffable. If by philosophy one implies a program, then no; if by philosophy one asserts a process, an aggressive working-out and an escalation, a saturation and thorough staining of the moment with visionary potential, then yes. If by philosophy one assumes a debate outside the body of experience or a dialectic imprisoned in enchantment in the mind, then no. If by philosophy one interrogates the imagination, then yes. Graham, for me, is first a poet of passion, and the elaborate syntactical maps she makes, the massive typographical journeys she embarks on, the dense and mysterious territories she attempts to conquer—these and the processing of the discovered language in which she assembles and narrates her play-by-play are all about the energy and aesthetic ambition that become, over and over again, unbearable.

*Never* is the ninth in a series of books that, looking back, have arrived in toto with tremendous commitment to their experiment. All in all, there is singular size to the writing, largest in the sum, while the internal project—some self-occluding inquisition—remains elusive, fractional. The disassembling, the deconstruction of the arrested moment, naturally elevates our sense of duration, as it does in the brilliant verbal surfaces of Keats and Hopkins and Crane, where the language feels poured into too small a vessel. In Graham this impression is one of escalation of the moment in order to see more and include more: a sort of magnification through metaphysics. Her particular genius is to find a means for showing forth her explosive epiphanies. The parentheses, the brackets, the spacings, the unlikenesses and dreams of a unified field, the counter-narratives of the page-long sentences, the self-astonishment of the perception, all her tests and terms, apparatus and awareness are geared against appearances, surfaces, and slippings-away, as if they were transparencies. Some readers may find Graham to be only about surfaces; others may prefer the punctuating paraphernalia. But the interruptions, underslides, and overruns are intended to subvert the narrative and convict the lyricism. As intensity is the urgency in her work, form is the malleable substance. Graham wants in, not out. If her poems seem to devour the page that's because the space is willing to accommodate, the silence able to accept "thinking one thing while feeling another," what Eliot spoke of as a "dissociation of sensibility."

For Graham, dissociation is motivation, it's one of the anxieties that generates her sentences forward at the speed of, effectively, simultaneity, of the many becoming one. The qualities, in fact, that create Graham—her fluidity, her animation, her speculative qualification, her acquisitional drive—are qualities that make her hard to contain in a quote. The "Prayer" (there are three such throughout the book) that opens *Never* is a fair yet brief example of the way her mind works among the "quantities . . . ongoingness . . . and an underneath" that govern what is seen and taken in. Graham, by the way, is a remarkable observer of the natural world, in the metaphysical school of Dickinson, Roethke, Clampitt, Ammons, and Carson.

Over a dark railing, I watch the minnows, thousands, swirl
themselves, each a minuscule muscle, but also, without the
way to *create* current, making of their unison (turning, re-
                                       infolding,
entering and exiting their own unison in unison) making of themselves a
visual current, one that cannot freight or sway by
minutest fractions the water's downdrafts and upswirls, the
dockside cycles of finally-arriving boat-wakes, there where

they hit deeper resistance, water that seems to burst into
itself (it has those layers), a real current though mostly
invisible sending into the visible (minnows) arrowing
                              motion that forces change—
this is freedom. This is the force of faith. Nobody gets
what they want. Never again are you the same. The longing
is to be pure. What you get is to be changed. More and more by
each glistening minute, through which infinity threads itself,
also oblivion, of course, the aftershocks of something
at sea. Here, hands full of sand, letting it sift through
in the wind, I look in and say take this, this is
what I have saved, take this, hurry. And if I listen
now? Listen, I was not saying anything. It was only
something I did. I could not choose words. I am free to go.
I cannot of course come back. Not to this. Never.
It is a ghost posed on my lips. Here: never.

More and more, over time, Graham has recognized a need to ground the present tense of her participial imagination, her "paradigms of consciousness," in an acknowledged world—if nothing else as a kind of doorway to the word. Such grounding not only sets up the tacit narrative between the speaker and what has brought her to the moment of contemplation but propels the initiating action toward its insights. At the beginning of this poem the transforming window of the water allows the speaker to see in detail and the whole at once, the minnow-thousands ("each a minuscule muscle") as well as "their unison . . . making of themselves a visual current." Half of this page poem is built of this "arrowing/motion that forces change," in which the event is both real and rhetorical. "I watch the minnows," the speaker says, "over a dock railing": and in the window/mirror she sees what is there and then what she projects, a classic contemplative posture. What she projects is the mixed realization that freedom is faith and that change means "Never again are you the same." If the longing is to be pure you must not get what you want, a stoicism and Puritanism too often ignored in Graham's poems, since desire in her writing is based upon denial. The second, short half of the poem is a debate or interrogation of what "never" means, which means that "I am free to go" and also that "I cannot of course come back." "Prayer," emotionally, is a love poem about surrendering the past for the sake of the "freedom" of the future, a conclusion that thematizes Graham beyond the ambivalence of the word. But what is the "ghost posed on my lips"? Graham answers with two pronouns—"It" and "this."—What is the ghost except the immanency of, the presence of, the breath of a life once flesh, now the old life. The prayer is for the new life.

"Prayer" is conservative compared to much of Graham's large-minded lyric theater. It is part imploration, part ars poetica, part goodbye. The note on the poem states that it "was written as a turn-of-the-millennium poem for the *New York Times* Op-Ed page," but it's intensely personal and pointedly functional as a starting place in a new book. The poems that follow immerse the new life, the new narrative. In her best work Graham invariably finds herself in a natural or domestic world sometimes blessed but mostly cursed (expectant?) with change—erosion, evolution, "ecocide": these are as much a part of her program as her mutable spiritual themes and their collusive forms. Her forms themselves partake of the rush, relativity, and immediacy of her sense of things: lines that surprise expectation, sentences that break off or run ahead, passages that move by implicit hyphenation in what might be referred to as the rhetoric of the net: first accelerate, then acquire, then arrest and gather in. Then arrival, ellipsis. But one hand—with sleight of hand or otherwise—always holds the net. Which is why, I think, Graham's poems like to begin clearly if in the middle of their narrative event ("Over the dock railing, I watch the minnows"), even when the "event" is in the mind and moving *toward* reference and coherence.

# 5

Or is it the other way around: away from reference and coherence? Between the two poles is the stillness, the at-oneness Graham, in my view, is after. The betweenness nature of her form both resists and responds to narrative values. "Many, if not all, lyric poems have a narrative dimension. Quite a different result is obtained if one approaches Keats's 'Ode to a Nightingale,' say, as a miniature narrative rather than as an organically unified assembly of figures." This from J. Hillis Miller in a piece entitled simply "Narrative." (I would suggest that "an organically unified assembly of figures"—"Thirteen Ways of Looking at a Blackbird," for instance—constitutes a narrative as well.) Paul Ricoeur opens the aperture of the lens even wider: "time becomes human to the extent that it is articulated through a narrative mode, and narrative attains its full meaning when it becomes a condition of temporal existence." If Miller is addressing form, then Ricoeur seems to be talking about content—hence, structure and texture, means and ends, ethos and emotion, as not only inseparable but cause-and-effect. While narrative may be a construct—whether interrupted, deconstructed, diverted, whatever—it is made of organic, necessarily related materials. Discontinuity requires, in the first instance, continuity—though the difference between them is less than we imagine. There are, once again, no straight lines or corners in nature; only ellipses, branches, meanders, circles, and spirals. Form itself is the lyric narrative, cockeyed or connective tissue. In the prosody of the postmodern lyric sentence, the prose aspect is heightened as a continuer, the verse aspect lessened as a retarder. That's why the lineation in Graham's work seems so arbitrary, so often dividing the line right before closure, ending the sentence as the beginning of the next line, indeterminate, as if the mind of the poem had no fixed formal agenda except movement, the future, and the feeling in the poem were finding its way, "folding and branching . . . and overlapping."

Ricoeur adds to his narrative discussion the element of plot, or "emplotment," as he calls it. "Emplotment is the operation that draws a configuration out of simple succession," a simple succession being his reduction of how narrative behaves. No poet of her generation more beautifully enacts emplotments than Louise Gluck, who, in a sequence of nine books over the course of three decades (most recently *The Seven Ages* [2001]) has drawn figures, evoked mystery, and sustained the most convincing introspective narrative. No one has represented the divided self better—the analyst, the observer, the commentator who serves as witness of the one who has come through. No one has better pledged the intimate life. Gluck's appeal to archetype and mythic personae—disciplined in the strictest of lyric languages, severe in the minimalist textures of experience—is commonly cited as the power of the voice in her poems. And although she does have a readily available connection to symbol and myth from a variety of allusive sources—Hellenic, Biblical, organic—and has written directly out of that knowledge (*Meadowlands, The Wild Iris*), she is, for me, the most personal of poets. Indeed, the more myth, the more an outsource is invoked, the clearer her actual psychical presence is. Part of it is the purity of her poetic terms. Part of it is that she makes of memory a fable, a tale, a dark wood that only poetry penetrates. "Fable," in fact, is titled three times in the new book; otherwise the titles all seem to refer to time, to that time when

> There was too much, always, then too little.
> Childhood: sickness.
> By the side of the bed I had a little bell—
> at the other end of the bell, my mother.

The configurations in Gluck's writing attract the adult fairy tale in all of us—the powerful mother, the absent father, the remembered lover, the garden of good and evil. "The Balcony," a high romantic suspension above the small, secondary business of the world, is a poem—and a place—from midway in *The Seven Ages*.

> It was a night like this, at the end of summer.
>
> We had rented, I remember, a room with a balcony.
> How many days and nights? Five, perhaps—no more.
>
> Even when we weren't touching we were making love.
> We stood on our little balcony in the summer night.
> And off somewhere, the sounds of human life.
>
> We were the soon to be anointed monarchs,
> well disposed to our subjects. Just beneath us,
> sounds of a radio playing, an aria we didn't in those years know.
>
> Someone dying of love. Someone from whom time had taken
> the only happiness, who was alone now,
> impoverished, without beauty.
>
> The rapturous notes of an unendurable grief, of isolation and terror,
> the nearly impossible to sustain slow phrases of the ascending figures—
> they drifted out over the dark water
> like an ecstasy.

Such a small mistake. And many years later,
the only thing left of that night, of the hours in that room.

Some attention has to be paid to the aural, annealing strength in Gluck's voice, its sonorous, rapt assumption of authority, the way it lifts the "subject" out of its common clay. It's a storytelling voice, with the speaker as the discrete protagonist; it's a tone of voice given at once to intimacy and awe; hypnotic and, yes, magical, if by magical we mean drama by transformative means.

"The Balcony" is played out in the simple, resonant tense of the past, the autumnal past, "the end of summer." And focused on "a night like this." *This* being the emotional starting point of an unspecified moment in the present spoken from the past into the future, a moment of the memory of a "small mistake" that goes on and on. The song of the on-and-on is Gluck's aria. What works so splendidly here are not only the subtle mixtures, and textures, of time, as the simple past tense ("was") yields to the past perfected ("had rented") to a present whose state of being verb is ellipsed, but the juxtaposition of separate yet collusive realities, as the "royal couple" on the balcony hears from below "The rapturous notes of an unendurable grief, of isolation and terror" from a voice singing on the radio. That "aria we didn't in those years know" they, indeed, know now since the notes in the "slow phrases of the ascending figures . . . /drifted out over the dark water," to be reinvoked in the future, this moment. The secret of Gluck's special tone is that happiness in her poems, "like an ecstasy," is impossible without beauty—a rather Keatsian notion, and as in Keats, just as mortal. Tenderness, happiness, is like the organic life in one of her gardens, subject to all the human seasons, accepted as part of a natural cycle, to be grieved and celebrated equally. Gluck's language is totally disciplined to this tone.

The transparency of her text, in fact, tends to increase the force of her poised emotional content. Like the interiority in James or Flaubert or Dickinson, nothing ever really happens in a Gluck poem, only "internal difference,/Where the Meanings, are." "I could live almost completely in imagination," she says in another of the newer poems. By imagination she means, I think, memory, involuntary memory but with perspective, distance, control. Dreamed but never dreamed up. And though Gluck's imagination is answered with intensity, written out in a fever of unity, book by book, it is experience remembered and received rather than sought for. Her speakers are listeners. In "Formaggio," from *Vita Nova*, the descending figure of the self moves from generalization to exquisite self-realization in breathtaking seconds, from a memory of the safety of Huron Avenue, of fishmonger and formaggio, to "a ribbon/ visible under the hand." Typically of Gluck, "The world/was whole because/it shattered. When it shattered,/then we knew what it was.//It never healed itself." The poem bears this thesis right to the end, where the "deep fissures" and "smaller worlds" of fracture turn into the "many lives" of the speaker, metaphored as "stems/of a spray of flowers." Gluck's skill at moving between worlds, large and small, past and present, oracular and personal, is crucial to her collapsing and focusing of time, her sense of the narrative. Yet the voice never feels rushed or under immediate danger— it has none of the summoned velocity of Plath, for instance—but always patient, lyrically patient, with itself. Its key of omniscience or distance has something to do with how much emotional and narrative ground has had to be covered, recovered, and sized; how many of her lives have come down to just this one. On Huron Avenue, in addition to the fish and cheese and all the other shops, is a flower shop, with wedding and funeral sprays of flowers, of which this one, the one she is holding here at the end of the poem, the one in "the gripped fist . . . /the self in the present," is probably both—wedding and funeral indistinguishable, love and death.

# 6

On October 8, 1817, having recently published a first, poorly received collection called *Poems*, and having close to completed his one and only "epic," *Endymion*, Keats writes his friend Benjamin Bailey that "I have heard Hunt say and may be asked—why endeavour after a long Poem? To which I should answer—Do not the Lovers of Poetry like to have a little Region to wander in where they may pick and choose, and in which the images are so numerous that many are forgotten and found new in a second Reading: which may be food for a Week's stroll in the Summer? Do not they like this better than what they can read through before Mrs. Williams comes down stairs? a Morning work at most. Besides a long Poem is a test of Invention which I take to be the Polar Star of Poetry, as Fancy is the Sails, and Imagination the rudder. Did our great Poets ever write short Pieces?"

There is no doubt that Keats wished to be "among the English poets" and viewed the "long Poem" as his great best chance. After the "test of Invention" that the intermittent *Endymion* is, Keats made two more tries at "epic"— a term now, to all intents and purposes, lost to us; a term now, after Wordsworth, transmogrified into the extended partitioned lyric or simply "long Poem"—one, *Hyperion*, a failure, the second, *The Fall of Hyperion*, a brilliant abortive rewrite. Following Wordsworth, Keats is the poet of modern sensibility who proves that the long modern poem is at best a sustained lyric or at worst a long fragment or sequence of parts and pieces. Wordsworth writes the monumental, many-volumed *Prelude* twice, the second version (1850) also a rewrite of the first (1805); its original intention is to answer Coleridge's assignment to produce a large philosophical poem. It turns into an interminable, episodic, brooding autobiography of "the growth of a poet's mind," rich in example, sometimes laborious in the endlessly talky passages. The foundation poem, however, finally made available in 1970, is a bifurcated work of intensity yet size entitled *Two-Part Prelude*, a literal prelude and otherwise. In valuable ways, it remains the "seed-time" of Wordsworth's total contribution. It certainly contains much of his most valuable blank verse. It, too, is episodic, but the episodes link, meander, and build toward epiphany: their order is internal, organic to their "story," which is at once self-revelatory and ars-poetic. Keats's first *Hyperion* is cotitled "A Fragment," his *Fall of Hyperion* cotitled "A Dream"—both suggest a resignation to ambitious lyricism over epical ambition. Even his odes suggest a suite of poems, linked in time by form and idea; a suite to which Helen Vendler, in her book on the odes (*The Odes of John Keats*, 1983) adds most of the first canto of *The Fall*, bringing the total to some eight hundred and more lines.

This equation of length, size of displacement, and poetic ambition with "the Polar Star of Poetry" is remarkable in the Romantics and challenging to the Modernists—from Eliot and Pound to Williams and Olson. The long poem, says Stevens, is a lot of smaller poems put together. Modernism in poetry means lyricism, whatever lengths you have to go to. Because of its time/duration equivalencies, narrative is the inherent means of acquiring length, weight, even the height of the sublime within the limits of the lyric. *The Waste Land*, the *Pisan Cantos*, the sectioning of *Paterson*, and the *Maximus Poems*—these are lyric poems divided and graduated and augmented. The connections and silences of and between their parts—their juxtapositioning, their paralleling, their plotting—are basic to the shaping of their architectures and fundamental to their specific and aggregate emotional power. "Spots of time" is the concept Wordsworth comes to, in *Two-Part Prelude*, in order to locate those areas of epiphanal experience that not only illuminate but link up to form involuntary narrative as well as proactive memory.

> There are in our existence spots of time
> Which with distinct preeminence retain
> A fructifying virtue, whence, depressed
> By trivial occupations and the round
> Of ordinary intercourse, our minds—
> Especially the imaginative power—
> Are nourished and invisibly repaired . . .

Spots of time are not simply how memory works but how its implicit narrative finds its sources. As inspiration, spots of time help select and define and value our experience; they also help organize our experience into some kind of effective figurative sequence—time spotted, if you will, or stained with those remembered moments of distinction and "preeminence" that through poetry restore or recreate their original power. Narrative order, or "disorder," is inspired by our dream-like memories of a past life that will not let us alone. These spots of time need time to discover their fullest report—hence length, up to a point, enhances the world enough and time our lyric ambition often calls for.

Eliot's *Waste Land* as lyric five-act drama is not that differently organized from the five-part structure of each of his *Four Quartets*. Their rhetorics may be separate but their emotional builds of exposition, complication, climax, resolution, and reconciliation run parallel. Take away his books, treat him like an animal in a cage, force him to think by memory alone, and Pound will write the best of his cantos, their most sustained emotional sequence. The lyric wants muscle but it also wants size; no poem, however small, wants to be small. Dickinson will tie her poems into discrete bundles, like little books or single sustained suites. Whitman will graduate from "Crossing Brooklyn Ferry" to "When Lilacs Last in the Dooryard Bloom'd" to the final drafting of "Song of Myself." Hart Crane will write "Voyages," then *The Bridge*. Williams and Stevens will systole and diastole between page-long lyrics and sequences throughout their careers. Contemporary American poets, in absorbing American influences and effecting a more international style, have spotted time more spatially and subverted narrative to reference or rumor. At least many of the best have, who find narrative value in extending lyric consciousness as far as the tension will take them.

Each of Louise Gluck's books, for example, means to stand on its own as an entity, split into pages as poems but unified as a whole engagement with, usually, a single antagonist or set of antagonists, presided over by a particular metaphor, analogy, or mythic allusion. The seven ages, vita nova, meadowlands, the wild iris. Charles Wright, through more than a dozen books, has rigorously divided and subdivided, acquisitioned and amplified his symbolist, deeply meditative text until it seems that since *Zone Journals*, especially, all of his work is one amended poem. Certainly, within all his writing, one long poem within a longer poem, stanza, part, and section. He has established, throughout his career, the art of the sequence, a veritable edifice of portions and platforms, parts and wholes, grounded but aspiring to some palpable, spiritual sum. The image of the builder, the maker, the artisan is indelible with his mastery of line, pace, and balance. The seasons, the sky, the backyard detail all ignite, in their "weight of glory," the mortal fire of the imagination. Wright's landscape is no less "insoluble," as he says in his latest collection, *A Short History of the Shadow*, than his forms are recurrent, contiguous.

Wright's hermetic impasto, in the post-impressionist, pre-cubic mode of a late Cézanne, and in the sunset tones of Montale, is a spectrum-length away from American Naturalists like C. K. Williams and Dave Smith, each of whom has developed, over time, idioms of mass in narrative, speculative sequences. Williams has fixed on what has been for some time a signature-long but beautifully flexible line, filling the full page with memory poems, philosophical interrogations, unflinching self-analysis, and evocations of a hard-edged, soulful urban pastoral. He has managed, within the parameters of the prose lyric, to make of his penchant for the discursive a real drama of empathy and honesty. You feel, in the hands of one of his poems, the original visceral pressure of the experience. His poems are large, whatever their relative size. Dave Smith also pushes outsized content but in forms that favor density over length. If Williams's energy is essentially centrifugal, Smith's is centripetal, always pulling in toward a dark center of gravity. His lines are percussive, martial, thorough in their report; his enjambments work like arguments against the will of the sentences. No living poet compounds more texture per pound than Smith; no poet better competes with the powers of fiction, the detail in the novel. Smith is a Southerner, a poet of the Field, in the best of that tradition. Which means there is obvious moral weight added to a prosody that is physical. Here are the last three stanzas from a new poem called "Red Dog" (from *The Wick of Memory: New and Selected Poems, 1970–2000*):

You dragged, then lost a bright steel chain: two tags
hung like my dad's world war loudly declared
"Red Dog," your name, our place, and that year's
shots, identities you'd shaken off to wander
the possible world. I'd hear you, coming back,
my son still out looking, afraid you'd got
worse than traveler's bite on your mopy flanks.
His shoes puffed up dirt like spurts of time. You
mostly don't expect to find the lost—and yet,
hopeful, I'd shout, then sleep, then shout. Gone.
You'd wait. You'd creep like sun across the lawn,

then, with him, leap up everywhere, that Spring
of joy breaking roses, crushing mulched shoots
faithfully planted year after year, and roots
whose volunteers you watered dead. Soon we saw
he'd leave, you'd chase God knows what twitch
of spoor, and so we took your balls. You slowed.
Dirt-bedded, you had new smell. Bones fouled floors.
Squirrels reclaimed their nuts. The awful spew
of what spoiled in you, lying by our fire,
comes back to me as the vet says you've worn
out the heart that banged to sleep beside my son.

What does it sound like, I ask. The vet listens.
Once you climbed a six-foot fence, barking, one leap,
a storm of breath we loved. Now you only eat,
120 wheezing pounds, a processor of meat.
Like my dad, you face me, hesitate, then piss
blankets and floor. Deaf, eyes blank, the chain
slipped again, you're lost. You don't miss a boy's
games, nothing swells your interest, even the moon's
rattling tags I've hung above the waiting spades.
The vet claims it's time. We've let you go too far.
Calling at last, I say "Son. It's Red. Come home."

Loss and lost become necessarily confused in this poem, in what might be termed an elegy of anxiety. Lost dog, lost son. There is rough music here, the aural correlative for the muscular, repressed emotion. If the character of voice is one way to extend the single lyric into the richer run of a series of poems intended to act as one sustained meditation, then Smith is another example of how a whole poet returns to central and crucial experience, grounded by a given time, theme, tone, or even landscape, or fixed in repeated forms. "Red Dog" is a singularly thoughtful, forty-four-line brood of a poem; I don't know if it gains from the company of the other "new" poems it's next to. But its voice is certainly amplified and complemented by "In Memory of Hollis Summers," "Floaters," and "On the Job," all poems of farewell, poems of mutual density and displacement. In such a way do narrative values transform the local into the national, the singular into the schematic, the smaller into the larger. In such a way do poets like Graham, Gluck, Smith, and Williams lift the lyric from its moment into a larger space of time. For many years the vastly underrated James McMichael has been creating sequence and long poems that are unique in their mystery, interiority, and novelistic ambition without ever sacrificing the beauty and intensity of their lyricism, poems such as *Four Good Things* (1980) and "Each in a Place Apart" (1994). Larry Levis's posthumous book *Elegy* (1997) is one long twenty-poem encounter with death-powers almost equal to his life-enhancing empathic genius; he wins, hands down, in what is his most compelling single book. And Mary Oliver, whose poems seem to pour from one to the other, as if they were not only inseparable from page to page but at one with the natural world that is their "subject," has published some dozen or so books of poems and prose-poems that could easily be read as a coherent and complete nature journal as witnessed by a contemporary American Transcendentalist.

# 7

Nevertheless, the test of the lyric is its singularity, its ability to stand on its own and generate, within itself and regardless of its compatibility within a series or sequence or sectioning, a discrete power. This is not to suggest a reduced or contracted role for its narrative and emotional reach, but merely to point out that because of their different lengths "Ode to a Nightingale" and "Ode on a Grecian Urn" behave quite differently as single poems, in spite of their formal similarity and thematic connection, and that "To Autumn," as another member of the group, behaves even more differently. "Among School Children," at exactly twice the length of "Sailing to Byzantium," and in exactly the same form (ottava rima) is also different because of size. In both of these cases the difference in length derives from a difference in narrative emphasis, and the longer the poem the more the emphasis. At eighty lines, "Nightingale" moves through time, from dusk to darkness; "Urn," at fifty reiterative lines, moves in a closed circle of time, juxtaposing "visions"; "Autumn" summarizes time in diurnal, seasonal, eternal cycles—in 33 perfect lines. "School Children" sets a scene (the school room), tells a story (Maude Gonne), and has time to meditate on their related meaning (the dancer as the dance). "Sailing," like the shorter Keatsian odes, compresses time and focuses on symbol. Narrative is about uses of time, and is measured through extension and contraction, exposition and suggestion. What is past, passing, or to come is narrative raised to a higher mathematical general standard, while "Hollow of cheek as though it drank the wind/ And took a mess of shadows for its meat"—Maud Gonne's aging face—is the equivalency in real time taking its time. The lyric affects time one way or another. Time, and timing.

Perhaps it is the prose energy inherent in the lyric that opens wider the aperture of the image and that stretches into utterance the phrasing of the music. That energy finds its voice in the narrative of the sentence, and sentences, no matter how interrupted, separated, or segmented. Opening the space, stretching the timing is another means of achieving length and generating power within the single poem. "Necessary Story, why did you begin?" This rhetorical question comes at the end of one of Ann Lauterbach's more in-between-sized poems, "Poem of Landscape," the kind of open-sided frame she is fond of. Lauterbach's signature aesthetic seems committed to interrupting, separating, segmenting her sentences. She completely explodes, elides, even eliminates any sense of the shapely poetic line in favor of a Projectivist plurality of information, imagery, commentary, memory. The compelling sentence pieces she writes in depend on a certain discontinuity, portioning, and edging, a certain "cluster of meanwhiles"; otherwise, the lines spread like sung prose.

In the overall, Lauterbach's poems build cubically, back and front and side-angle at once, with glimpses and partials, memories and immediacies held up in time. This is not to imply that her poems aspire to stasis or a fixed visual point; quite the contrary, they have their own fluid drive, with—like her sentences—interruption, subordination, and dislocation marking the map of the page. They move "in time" by the clock of the emotion, since Lauterbach's "narrative" is the beauty of the feeling she works out of her material. Not that the feelings themselves are beautiful—rather, the art of their rendering. "N/est" is an eight-page poem in deconstructive lyric prose that serves, in essence, as the title poem of her next to last collection, *On a Stair* (1997). It did not make the cut for Lauterbach's *If in Time: Selected Poems, 1975–2000*. It was either too long or too personal. I find it one of the most moving poems of the 1990s. It's organized, naturally, in an extrapolated, separated-out sort of way, apportioned through iterations of associations and reiterations. If *verse* means to return, to repeat, then the order here of the thrust of the implied narrative depends on its verse, its returns to themes and images, one of which is that "I thought the world was held by language as if it were an incipience." This idea of language, of the word before the world, of the world justified by the word, haunts the text of "N/est" because language acts as its valuer, and rescuer.

This turn, this coming about, refuses to let time go,
    but is always using it to

fuel the poem towards the meaning of
the presence of meaning

The presence of meaning, the need and search for it, sustains this poem, both its autobiographia and its ars poetica. The operative word is "towards," a leading-to rather than an arrival, the "presence of" rather than the closure on meaning. Early on (page 2) Lauterbach pretty well sets up the n/est ambivalence of the poem:

I have never explicitly affiliated my not having
        children with

        my father's absences
        I thought I would find him in the heavy
        books of words, dictionary
        which rested on his writing table long after his
        disappearance and which I thought
        was magical, containing all secrets

    or perhaps
    find a way to him on little word boats, paper sails, some
    spirit's breath,
    into a 'conversation,' Paul Celan's term—

The most effective poets, it seems to me, understand that their art depends on their access to their original narratives, those life studies that, involuntarily, inchoately, dream their way back to us. And if our imaginations come from nature, our emotions are ceded by our parents, their absences as well as their presences. Lauterbach rescues the elegies of her life—her father's disappearances, the thrice negating (aborting) of her own parenthood, the deaths and disappearances of the potential fathers, the ongoing generational changes among her parenting friends—through the angular honesty, indirect directness, and, most of all, the suspension-bridge of engineering by which she sorts and rescues her raw materials. Chronology imitated is deadly; chronology received as it evidently occurs to us, shaped by its significance, is alive. Lauterbach's gift is to discover the emotional coherency in the mess of her materials, to bring levels and distances of memory into the presence of meaning.

Although "N/est" ends beautifully grounded—"the rufous sparrows nested in the blue spruce/ listening/ a tiny fledgling came out on a low branch"—it is a poem that floats, or suspends, above the era of its sources. And although its use of time is fluid, as seen through snapshots and quicktakes, quotation and allusion, the power comes from placement, the speed with which one event, one memory, one detail, one reference follows another. White space separating time creates the tension, as if all the memories and references were equal *in* time, while the movement, through time, through the "narrative" of the poem, is focused by the feeling; in fact, *is* the feeling. Everyone dies in the poem, or else has families; everyone disappears, or else has domesticity. It is a poem filled with names of friends and named experience: weddings and birthings and growings-up. Mostly, however, the poem resists happiness in favor of trauma: the death of the poet's father ("I was seven"), the deaths of her three possible children ("I have been pregnant three times// two abortions while in college, one in Milwaukee/without anesthetic"), the deaths or disappearances of men in her life ("the word *name* has *man* or *men* in it") and her hysterectomy:

> then I went into the hospital
> for the operation but the last minute it was decided that
> they would do a D&C, an
> official abortion, rather than risk the hysterectomy
> because when you are pregnant
> your blood is 'frothy' so I was sent home to wait
> wept ceaselessly
>
> an image of a cork on a sea
>
> I saw it on a gray screen
> tiny incoherent scribble
> *don't you want this baby* the nurse asked/she did not understand

Cold quotes don't answer the accumulative lyric and narrative build of this poem, its graphic and gravitational pull. "These steps I took/I do not regret//to be a poet"—under the pain and acceptance of losses there is the moral choice the poet accepts, "a constant iteration of choice/one word instead of another/they call to each other sometimes/constructing a place// in which to live a life." The nest a palm of dry mud on the ground.

# 8

The long, the extended, the series poem is impossible to duplicate and impossible, too often, to quote. Its powerful interior narrative, therefore, gets lost in the paraphrase. The fragility and complexity of "N/est" are page-turners, non-excerptable. The same could be said for Charles Simic's now well-known sequence of prose-poems *The World Doesn't End*, published at the beginning of the 1990s. It is his least middle-European book, meaning his most American, meaning its language, its idiom, and its form are the most open-ended from a poet especially fond of the free-verse quatrain. Whatever else a prose-poem does it scans a different sense of line from verse and invites, at its surface, greater continuity of connection. It also encourages leaps and separations.

> A poem about sitting on a New York rooftop on a chill autumn evening, drinking red wine, surrounded by tall buildings, the little kids running dangerously to the edge, the beautiful girl everyone's secretly in love with sitting by herself. She will die young but we don't know that yet. She has a hole in her black stocking, big toe showing, toe painted red. . . . And the skyscrapers . . . in the failing light . . . like new Chaldeans, pythonesses, Cassandras . . . because of their many blind windows.

The connections here are broken by ellipsis, by comparisons usually referred to, in Simic's case, as surreal. Whether surreal or not, "new Chaldeans, pythonesses, Cassandras" are ironic personifications—old-fashioned pathetic fallacies—unable or unwilling to see the pathos of the young girl with the red toenail and a death secret because of "their many blind windows." Something about the prose-poem permits Simic to "eschew" his common allegorical configuration in favor of a simpler, more direct evocative encounter. This poem also slides easily in and out of context; it's a moment, a little narrative, "a poem about. . . ." It is one among seventy. But why is Simic's a prose-poem and James Tate's "The Eternal Ones of the Dream," from his most recent collection, *Memoir of the Hawk* (2002) (wretched title), not?

> I was walking down this dirt road out
> in the country. It was a sunny day in early
> fall. I looked up and saw this donkey pulling
> a cart coming toward me. There was no driver
> nor anyone leading the donkey so far as I could
> see. The donkey was just moping along. When
> we met the donkey stopped and I scratched its
> snout in greeting and it seemed grateful. It
> seemed like a very lonely donkey, but what
> donkey wouldn't feel alone on the road like that?
> And then it occurred to me to see what, if anything,
> was in the cart. There was only a black box,
> or a coffin, about two feet long and a foot wide.
> I started to lift the lid, but then I didn't,
> I couldn't. I realized that this donkey was on
> some woeful mission, who knows where, to the ends
> of the earth, so I gave him an apple, scratched
> his nose a last time and waved him on, little
> man that I was.

Tate's wonderfully absurdist but moving take on the world—almost always in the reduced, the rendered-down terms of fable, mock allegory, character parody, self-satire—is resolutely in evidence here. It's a "lonely donkey," a "moping" donkey that the speaker meets in the middle of nowhere, and no wonder, since it's also a funeral donkey, bearing "a coffin, about two feet long and a foot wide." The speakers in Tate's poems are invariably dumbed-up in innocence; no different in this "Dream." The coffin seems exactly the size of the "little/man that I was." Innocence usually has a price in a Tate poem. But why is this poem formed in free verse as opposed to Simic's more "lyrical" prose-poem? The line breaks, again and again, defeat expectation. Tate's poem is clearly more purely narrative;

Simic's an image-scene resolved "in a leap of imagination." Is there an issue beyond the linear set-up of a poem that distinguishes lyric prose from the "narrated" lyric, in which the speaker really is a narrator and not a "neutral" observer? Why are Robert Bly's most lyrical poems—if we think back awhile—his prose-poems? He is one of the most interesting prose-poets we have produced. Even *Silence in the Snowy Fields* is less dependent on its sense of line than on some internal music, like the use of the interval, the manipulation of silence. John Ashbery has written no finer lyric than "For John Clare," a prose-poem of three grace-note paragraphs. As so often the case in Ashbery, there is almost no single forward-motion in the poem, rather a shelving of motions. Narrative of tone is what holds it together, the music very much *in* the voice.

One capacity the prose-poem has, immediately, is volume: expository space, width of information, cubic complexity.

Frontispiece

Walden Pond's crowded this Saturday afternoon, cars backed up to the main highway. There's an air show overhead. The Blue Angels zoom and zigzag prankish patterns across the flyway. With a sharp U-turn, we're heading to where the Redcoats first fell in Concord. I can already see rows of stone the militia hid behind, like teeth grinning up from the ground.

A blond boy poses with a minuteman in a triangular hat. His father aims the camera. Can the three Vietnamese visitors see how our black hair makes the boy cower from something he reads in the father's face? The minuteman is dressed in garb the color of low hills. Before he retells the battle here, he says he received two Silver Stars in Danang. The Vietnamese take turns wearing the minuteman's hat and aiming his musket. A thread of smoke ties trees to sky, and when The Blue Angels break the sound barrier we duck and cover our heads with our hands.

At the souvenir shop, I buy *The Negro in the American Revolution* and give it to Thieu. His eyes dart from the book's frontispiece to my face: Jordan Freeman's killing Major William Montgomery at the Battle of Groton Heights. Huu Thinh studies the image also, and says that the American poets he likes best are Langston Hughes and Whitman.

297

Le Minh walks out into a tussle of tall grass surrounding a wooden bridge, and we follow her striped sun hat. Her high heels sink into the sandy soil that's held together by so many tiny white roots. Burrs cling to her nylons. Now it isn't hard to imagine her filling bomb craters along the Ho Chi Minh Trail or reading Jack London in some Laotian jungle. She's ahead of us. On a path that winds back like apparitions imprinted on the living, as if we need to quick-march through grass to prove we outfoxed time.

She climbs into the car, and begins to pick cockles off her stockings. We speed up like shadows overtaking men, smiling and huffing as if we've been making love an hour.

This prose-poem by Yusef Komunyakaa, one in a series in the middle of his 1998 collection *Thieves of Paradise*, is reprinted in a recent new and selected volume, *Pleasure Dome* (2001). For the past three decades Komunyakaa has been no less prolific than Simic (six collections since his book of prose-poems) and Tate (twelve collections since his first) and no less consistent. He is particularly known for his poems from his experience in Vietnam (*Dien Cai Dau*, 1988), where he was a reporter for *Stars and Stripes*, though the majority consciousness in his work is the American South, not South Vietnam. Bogalusa, Louisiana, Blues Louisiana, Black and White Louisiana. His poems have tended toward tight-lined narrative riffs exquisitely timed, richly textured, poems poured in heat. Their implicit ferocity, however, has been tempered by humor, sardonicism, even understatement, yet the transforming anger of his decency and moral imperative informs everything between the lines. Komunyakaa's naturalism is of the country, not the city, so that his idiom is flavored, and he tells a good story. By their nature, his prose-poems are in less of a hurry than his verse, whose supporting music is tucked enjambment, jazz, "neon vernacular." The space, the volume in the prose-poem means, for him, more narrative, reportorial opportunity—more time, more stretch, more loop, more transition, more cover.

"Frontispiece" is a present-tense poem in five cinematic paragraphs, two parts, and several layers. It divides at the middle moment in the gift shop when the speaker hands Thieu *The Negro in the American Revolution*, a gesture that brings into immediate juxtaposition Komunyakaa's essential worlds of his two Souths, Vietnam and America, while being set in the place of the start of one revolution sadly echoed, two centuries later, in another. Revolution and civil war, in fact, become inseparable histories separated only by time; every detail in the poem points in that direction. The cast of characters, both primary and secondary, also partake of this sense of history and its consequences, wittingly or otherwise, insightfully or innocently. The blond boy in the triangular hat, his photographer father, and the tour-guide Minuteman (with his two Silver Stars from Danang) play their parts as necessarily as the speaker and the three Vietnamese (cum tourists) friends play theirs. The set-up is as effortless as it is inevitable: Walden Pond, that American icon of solitude, is now, after a hundred and fifty years, too crowded to linger at; so, with "a sharp U-turn, we're headed to where the Redcoats first fell in Concord . . . and the rows of stone the militia hid behind"; overhead, as if in concert, the Blue Angels break the sound barrier, with a sound like a dropped bomb—"we duck and cover our heads with our hands." If Komunyakaa had ended his prose-poem here, as a sort of short political comment, including the boy's response to "our"—meaning both African-American and Vietnamese—black hair, symbolizing not only their position as outsiders but their place as troublemakers from the past, had he ended his piece here he would have indeed got half a loaf.

History as racism, reductivism, and souvenir. A lesser poet would have left it at that. But one of the powers this prose-poem wants to celebrate is the crossings of cultures and the mixings of time, anachronisms and parallels, the frontispiece in the book and the speaker's face, the Vietnamese who see the connection and the blond boy who is confused by "our black hair." Now halfway through, the narrative complicates its configuration by moving from observation to selection, from reporting to remembering. The transition is Huu Thinh's comment, after having studied the frontispiece, that the American poets he likes best are Hughes and Whitman, two from other "civil" wars. When Le Minh "walks out into a tussle of tall grass" the sequence of events finds its true imaginative, associative subject: "a path/that winds back like apparitions imprinted on the living." It's curious that this elegiac insight develops in the poem's only sentence fragment, forcing the memory of the singular path to assume the referent of plural apparitions, which in the last paragraph become "shadows overtaking men." The pointed—and poignant—play with time and survival and the individuation of the players all rescue the obvious politics in favor of a deeper emotional value—loss, and the living memory of it, a memory still apparitional. The form of the prose-poem gives this "lyric" more narrative open space, surely, but more to the issue it provides time to meander, to build three-dimensional volume, to bend the line, to texture the voice, and to sustain the ambiguity of the moment, as in the closing suggestive comparison, "as if we've been making love an hour."

# 9

It may or may not come as a surprise that when Baudelaire translated Poe—Poe the poet whom Emerson referred to as "the jingle man"—he turned him into prose-poems. Baudelaire was after content—not verse form; gothicism, not lyricism. French, with its accentless accents, seems the natural language of a form whose pitch is a wider range of tone, an admixture of anecdotal evidence, mimetic acceptance, and, most of all, sentences that ride the edge. If, as William Wenthe observes, metrical verse is what the line does to the sentence and free verse is what the sentence does to the line, then prose verse is what the sentence does to sentences, which is to place them within a rhythm of logic completely self-contained, whether the narrative is real or surreal, the emotion open or closed. Not breaking the line makes all the difference, as the language in the prose-poem begins to resemble a landscape as opposed to a work of architecture. And although the visual and vocal surface of a prose-poem may look and sound undifferentiated, inside itself the opportunities for continuity versus contrast, connection versus ellipsis, acceleration versus abruptness are enormous. The larger field of play, the full page, the justified right margin, for one thing, put a wholly different pressure on the material and the nature of its making, on the sentences and how they resist and yield. Everything in a prose-poem, it seems, is built to subvert appearances.

And while exposition may be the enemy of the lyric, in the prose-poem it replenishes, frames up, fills out a world the verse lyric is too often the fragment of. If Komunyakaa had formatted "Frontispiece" as a free-verse lyric, he would probably have had to extend the poem considerably to achieve the multilayers, underconnections, and implicit comparisons—the history, memory, small touches, and so forth. Ironically, the space of the prose-poem permitted him a more direct, succinct reference to war and local, immediate examples of its consequences than the economies of the lyric form might have. The eliding of text in the lyric is a great intensifier, if qualification or fragmentation of narrative consciousness is what you're after. The broken narrative of the dream has been the staple for a lot of "naked" poetry in the last half-century. But because the prose-poem depends on continuing rather than returning, adding rather than subtracting, it can perfect time without interrogation, complete the picture without distortion. The absence and silence of the white space of the page sometimes intimidates the poet, especially in free verse; it has made some poets alternately aggressive or repressive. In the prose-poem the white space is free space.

Stephen Berg has written some of the most intensely focused, personal, naked lyrics we have. He transcends the autobiographic into something quintessential, something close to the quiddity of experience. His "authenticating means" is the transparency of his free-verse lyric form and the naturalist exposure of his content. If Komunyakaa is of the outlying areas of the city, Berg is definitely an inner-city naturalist—grime, grit, the anxiety of the street. His many versions (re: dynamic translations) of international poetry, particularly Akhmatova, mirror his own poems' ability to enter, with impassioned empathy, the intimate life of the other. It's as if he were entering the life of a host consciousness without sacrificing his own. His role as narrator helps: by keeping emotional distance he can close on the story itself, stories in which his parents, his wife, his daughters, his Akhmatova become characters, real *and* imagined. Of all his many collections of poems, certainly one of the most interesting is *Shaving*, a hundred-page sequence of some of the most remarkable prose-poems ever published. *Shaving* appeared in 1998, like a culmination of the voice in Berg's formally broken lyrics beginning with *Grief* (1975) and *In It* (1981) and stunningly realized in *Oblivion* (1995). Berg's prose-poems are massive, indeed are about mass, volume, displacement, a cityscape viewed from a clinical but caring distance. They make quotation daunting, thus all the more necessary.

*In a New Leaf*

Three weeks before he died, my father acted as an extra in *A New Leaf*, a movie about an alcoholic, her lover, and a stranger who showed up and

301

would, as it happened, try to save her. Cassavetes and May were making the film in Philly on 13th Street, using a defunct hotel, renamed The Royal, for the battles between the fucked-up couple. Night after night the crew would take their places—at the camera, yelling directions, searching for extras in the crowds lined up six deep around the roped-off set to watch Peter Falk (the stranger) do a scene in which he's passing The Royal on his way somewhere and a whisky bottle flies out a window and hits the ground at his feet and he looks up, sees someone (the woman, I think) in the window and dashes (there's a scream) into the dark building. It seems the woman and her lover (Cassavetes) are holed-up there, planning a robbery. Falk is tanned, dressed in a custom-cut Navy-blue silk suit and delicate black shoes, Italian style, the kind tap dancers use because they're so flexible, nearly weightless. In and out, in and out he goes, repeating the scene, bottle after bottle arcing from the window, the pieces swept away each time by one of the crew, while none of the fans and gawkers really knows what the story is. It was like watching real life, it doesn't matter whose life, with one big difference: that scene lost all meaning because it was shot so many times. It was beginning to get hot the way it does in Philly in early June—thick greasy humid air, hanging on for days so every little thing feels difficult, everything looks like it has sweat and dirt on it. My father had had a massive, fifth heart attack and when we picked him up at his house he was wearing a raincoat, single-breasted with a full button-in camel's-hair liner, and under it a suit, tie and scarf. A gray felt hat and gray doeskin gloves lent the finishing touches. His face was the color of those gloves, it had a dull shine like solder, like those Philly skies before a rain when blossoming puffs of air cool your face but it stays hot, the sun has disappeared, everything is drained of strong color. Well, he walked, shuffling one foot at a time very very slowly, stopping between each step, as if on a tightrope, almost floating, with great caution and weakness and fear, to the car. Settled in the front seat, he barely spoke. We heard the movie was being made, thought it would be fun to watch the production, a rare distraction from all he had gone through. We drove the few blocks to the place, parked, walked over to the people at the ropes circling The Royal, and faded into the crowd. My Dad, for some reason of his own, drifted to another side of the crowd and stood at the back of it. Everything on the street was blue-white under the lights; the mist of humidity in the glare put a fine pearly veil between you and whatever you saw. Once in a while I'd glance around to see how he was. Inch by inch he had slipped from the back of the mob until now he was standing up front pressing against the waist-high rope—all gray: raincoat, glove, hat, face. Except for his Watch-plaid cashmere scarf. He looked like a Mafia Don: implacable mask of a face, a man with secrets and power who refused the world any hint of emotion that might reveal who he was. Was his mind silent as he stood there or did he hear one of those primitive, sourceless, pure, self-defining voices that haunt us, left over from the gods, telling him not to smile, not to speak, not to show anything to the enemy world, telling him to be no one as the line between death and the future evaporated and he edged closer to the playground of the gods by obeying them, by adopting the hero's impassive mask? The fact is he looked like Edward G. Robinson, not Oedipus or Lear immortalized in the revelatory aftermath of cosmic self-discovery. Reticent, masochistic, mildly depressed all his life, he stood there, to me awesome because of his ordeal near death. "He'll never walk out of the hospital," the doctor had said, and here, five months later, he was, as fate would have it, a passerby about to act in a bad movie, about to play one of the gods as they are today. By now Elaine May was pacing the edge of the crowd inside the roped-off area, looking for extras, picking people by their faces to walk past under an arcade twenty or so feet behind Falk during the bottle-throwing scene. She saw my father, nodded a questioning "Yes?" He ducked under the rope, which May lifted for him, and joined a group of eight people, then moved to the outside of the crowd. By now I was standing beside him, listening. All were being told to begin walking, briskly, scattered apart, just before Falk reaches the front of the hotel when the bottle hits. Over and over he did it, briskly, until we thought he would drop dead. Over and over I watched his speechless face, betraying nothing, glistening under his hat in the lights, while behind me, off to my right—where the camera was, pointed away from the hotel at Falk and the extras walking by—Falk ran past into the hotel, yelling something, after the bottle crashed, and a woman yelled back at him from the window. Over and over. Finally they got it right and we went home. For months, I waited for the newspaper ads announcing the film so we could all see it. When it finally played, and we went, the scene wasn't even in it. The film was so mediocre it ran less than a week. I tried buying a copy of the scene but they wouldn't sell the footage. Several years since your walk-on part, and it happens anytime: the muggy summer night, the family, gauzy air, you doing what you're told by the director—I'll be teaching, washing dishes, reading, writing, talking with Millie and the kids, a middle-aged man, your son, watching his sick father, but not on the screen in a theater. It's still the street, the live, unknown people, you doing it over and over, over and over the scene being shot, the bottle, the scream, the lights, "Okay—try it again!" coming from behind lights and faceless faces, from the black steel bodies and silent blank lenses of the weapon-like cameras pointed at us.

This is poem as monolith, enormous in its vertical/horizontal tension. Its power is assertive, accumulative, exhaustive, yet it's also Chekhovian in its attention to and figurations of detail, detail so achieved it projects an almost pointillist totality. The *mise en scène*, the father's clothes, "the muggy summer night . . . the gauzy air," the hold on the setting of the street (the real versus the movie-making action), the gradual, subtle emergence of the speaker-narrator, the growth of the narrative itself all add up to parts equal to their sum. The fact that Berg's version of the movie story, involving John Cassavetes (the lover) and Peter Falk (the stranger), has nothing to do with the final edited released version of a comedy entitled *A New Leaf*, starring Elaine May and Walter Matthau, is beside the point. The poem is an elegy, a kind of family elegy, in which illusion and rehearsal, appearance and intention, imagination and text are little more than "walk-ons." Mortality is the story, and diminished at that.

Berg's talent for mixing self-witness with hard-eyed observation, vulnerability with objectivity, is impressive. More impressive is the mixture of lyric moment with narrative flow, the way the perpetual present tense of the movie-making is given grounding in the memory tense of the actual, and the way in which they move in and out of their separate realities, joining at the instant the father becomes an extra. "Extra" is exactly what he is, with his fifth heart attack, his eccentric dress (raincoat, suit, tie, and "Watch-plaid cashmere scarf"), his "implacable mask of a face," looking somewhere between a "Mafia Don" and Edward G. Robinson, as if he had come from another movie set instead of home or the hospital. Nothing in the making of a movie or life ever works out as planned. A film that starts as "a movie about an alcoholic, her lover, and a stranger" ends up as a nutty comedy about the con of a wealthy, glasses-wearing nerd botanist by a flush playboy. It will be a film the writer, director, and star herself, Elaine May, will disavow, as she too becomes extra to the final cut. And the speaker's father, "Reticent, masochistic, mildly depressed all his life," now an extra, now the color of his doeskin gloves, now "about to play one of the gods as they are today" will also not make the final cut.

What the full prose-poem form offers Berg is a seamless opportunity to orchestrate a postscript, a resolution and something of a reconciliation. No, first it has offered him all of it: exposition, complication, climax, and, yes, rest. In the klieg lights of film-making he has seen his father as he is, a man diminished but worthy, "to me awesome because of his ordeal near death." He has seen Philly, where he lives, as no less diminished—"thick greasy humid air, hanging on for days so every little thing feels difficult, everything looks like it has sweat and dirt on it." And he has seen his own life as a middle-aged man with a "walk-on part." At the lovely, lyric ending of this poem, the speaker speaks directly to the dead, remembering the scene, the long summer night of filming, he has just shown us, and sees it all, in summary, again, as trial and error, "over and over the scene being shot . . . 'Okay—try it again!' coming from behind lights and faceless faces, from behind the black steel bodies and silent blank lenses of the weapon-like cameras pointed at us." The nakedness of the emotion here is as much stated as understated, exposed as much as revealed. Verse would have clothed it in the qualifications of prosody. The figure-making function and the metric-making argument of verse present the virtues of indirection, even misdirection; when they are resisted through a more direct emotional, narrative contract, the result can be the muscular naturalism of a Dave Smith or C. K. Williams. When the imagination and music are romanced, the result can be the rich symbolist rhetoric of a Charles Wright; or, when they are muted but no less seductive, the result can be the silences of a Michael Palmer. When they are unmediated, except in the telling, the result is the open heart of Stephen Berg. Thus, the prose-poem can be yet another alternative to lyricism, sustaining a sentence rhythm, duration, and emotional texture less likely in lineation. The longer lyric—or compressed extended sequence—is yet another option.

# 10

As the 1995 sonnet-sequence *Kyrie* shows, Ellen Bryant Voigt is not shy of the book-length poem as a way of putting narrative in its place within the discipline of the lyric. The raw material—the influenza pandemic of 1918–1919—would be overwhelming without the fictional lens of a family for whom world catastrophe becomes individual and personal. The method is precisely how a novelist or a film-maker would have to deal with the size of the subject. Her most recent collection, *Shadow of Heaven* (2002), is more to the point: the impact of narrative value and lyric imperative is cotermi-nous, notably in carry-over poems such as "The Garden, Spring, The Hawk"—fifteen sonnet-sized linked poems—and "The Art of Distance"—a memory meditation of seven sections of varying length. Voigt's handling of the needs for story and the equal demands of form are at her personal best in these poems, as they are in the powerful coda of a generation, "What I Remember of Larry's Dream of Yeats," an elegiac paean not only to Larry Levis but to poetry itself. The verbal texture of the poem is close to essay-like, which is to say, it's a poem that explains, that tells as it shows; its tone, then, is one of expository memory. But because the speaker-narrator is will-ing to present herself as a less than perfect witness—although clearly a reliable source—the explaining itself becomes part of the flow of things. *Flow* here, however, means a meander, a turning and returning through al-luvial, allusive soil. Flow also means form, as the sentences find continuing resistance to their continuing on, in units measured out from their line-count—nine lines in each of nine stanzas. Voigt furthers her lyric logic by measuring the lines themselves.

A roomful of writers, three on the couch a cat
had pissed on, others clustered like animated trees,
Shahid benched at the melodiophobic piano
Reg had played while Deb and Karen sang;
and centered, under the fixture overhead, Larry,
pleated around a straight-backed chair, not drinking
then, not doing dope, his face above the mustache open
for company—although I heard him tell the dream
in North Carolina, after he moved to Virginia,

he'd dreamed it long before in Salt Lake City.
"Things not going very well," he summarized,
hurrying to what would make us laugh: him alone
and broke and barely hanging on, Strand advising
"'Buy silk sheets.'" I've forgotten whether or not
he did, whether or not the stained mattress
had been sheathed in silk, because he so expertly
buried for us that bed in papers, notebooks, volumes
underlined, low mound of the written word

as erudite, disheveled as Larry was,
taking a turn in the light of our attention, T-shirt
even though it was winter, distressed gray hair.
"In the midst of this" (here he lit another smoke),
"I'd been preparing for my class on Yeats," days, nights
on guided tours of the Variorum and *A Vision*;
also in the layers, the *L.A. Times*, manuscripts of poems
(his students' and his own), clean and dirty laundry,
letters, bills, an opened bag of chips.

Both white feet splayed flat on the splintered floor,
forearms on his knees, he leaned forward, maybe
to give this part some shoring-up, since labor
ran counter to his irony, his off-the-cuff,
his disaffected style—but didn't he know we knew
an intelligence as restless and large as his
needs feeding from time to time? (What did Dobyns say:
a billion who ought to die before Larry did?) Besides,
he looked so much like a caught thief coming clean,

none of us doubted he had read it all,
everything on Yeats, and fell asleep, and Yeats
stopped by, wearing a white suit. He'd come to retrieve
a last still-undiscovered poem, which he happened to keep
in Utah, in a locked drawer in Larry's room—just then
the kitchen howled and hooted, as if Larry
had also been in *there*, doing Justice, teacher
he loved, as an ice-cream man. Here's when Dr. Orlen
entered the room, stirring a short Scotch-rocks,

and Larry double-stitched: "Yeats in white,
pointing at my notes: 'Why do you bother with that?'"
Pause. Larry stared at Tony, next at me, the three of us
sharing the one ashtray, his eyebrows up, accents
*acute et grave*, like facing, aggressive bears:
"'Passion,' Yeats said, 'is all that matters in poetry.'"
Trawling the line to see if we would bite,
he leaned back in the chair, chair on its hind legs,
his legs straight out, his mouth a puckered seam.

In the dream Yeats turned away, as we ourselves
were starting to turn away now from the dream, to reach
for another fistful of chips or Oreos, another humiliation
from the Poetry Wars, another sensual or shapely thing
to throw at loneliness or grief, like what I'll hear
from Mary Flinn, how, when Richmond's ROBINSON'S REMOVAL
came for the body, days still undiscovered on the floor,
to wrestle it like a sodden log out to the hearse,
they swaddled it first in a scarlet velvet tarp,

then aimed for the stairs, headlong, the tapered end
under the arm of a ravaged small thin old black man
(that's Robinson), his doughy-bosomed lieutenant at the helm,
and Mary, foot of the stairs and looking up, expecting
Larry to break loose any minute, tumble forward—
the kind of punchline we were avid for
that evening in Swannanoa with good friends
(was Heather there? was Lux fanning the fire?) when Larry
pulled himself upright and dropped his voice

as Yeats paused at the door in a white silk suit:
ancient, graveled, this was the voice of the caged sibyl,
shriveled the size of a flea, when he read, from his long poem,
her song, "I want to die"; and saying now, as Yeats, "Passion
is also all that matters in life."
                    So weren't the dream,
and the telling of the dream, more lanky shrewd inclusive

Levis poems, like those in his books, those he left
in the drawer? If he comes back to get them, let him come
in his usual disguise: bare feet, black clothes.

Voigt deals with the difficult scene-narrative of this gathering of poets, this party for poetry, well: people appear and disappear as if on stage. Levis and the invoked Yeats are the center attractions, one barefoot, dressed in black, the other in his boots, dressed in white; one in the mourning cloth of death, the other in the immortal rags of dream-eternity. What could have been mawkish is controlled by irreverence, juxtaposition, affection, the very idiom of truth, and the vivid, poignant, beautifully rendered presence of Levis himself, in all his self-destructive, luminous fire. The closing scene involving Robinson's Removal is the perfect comic/tragic understatement in answer to the statement of the life, the Levis poems, the rare, summoning passion. But what stands out, for this reader, is the "lyricism," the self-reflection of the form, the rescue and return that achieved, even announced, form is. Roland Barthes speculates that since Rimbaud, poets have given "to their speech the status of a closed Nature, which covers both the function and structure of language. Poetry then is no longer a Prose either ornamental or shorn of liberties. It is a quality *sui generis* and without antecedents. It is no longer an attribute but a substance. . . ." Barthes is speaking here through assumptions of symbolist ideology. As a practical matter, though, narrative, with the usual mud on its shoes, is hard to keep out of the room. Its impurity, its quotidian values, its prose good sense are the antidote to preciousness, to the claustrophobia language in and of itself can be. No more than we want our poems to be poetic do we want our prose to be prosaic. Lyric form, to be alive, must *move*; that movement is its inherent narrative, sourced in an emotion discovered in time. That's the prose in the poetry, whose antecedent is, ultimately, the poet.

The temptation of the autobiographist—whether the autobiography starts in the emotion or the imagination—is to write as if one value outweighs another, one imperative transcends. The potential for self-indulgence, laxity, or free-verse narrative is obvious in Voigt's Levis elegy. Its easy but assured lyric form, its *count*, saves it from the miasmal mists of content. Its implicit narrative, on the other hand, saves it from the sentimentality of form, which too often seeks to solve experience, correct it, instruct it, improve it. It may well be that our living experience has no other meaning than its reconstruction, reconfiguration, representation. But it's axiomatic that what that experience is is inseparable, in good poetry, from how that experience is rendered, the way Ginsberg's "Howl" is opera, Plath's "Daddy" a nursery rhyme. The narrative is the emotion, the lyric form the imagination of a poem. At the end of the new poems section of Robert Pinsky's exceptional *The Figured Wheel* (*New and Collected Poems, 1966–1996*), there's a long meditation (165 lines) in free verse terza rima entitled "Impossible to Tell," an incredible poem I think. It moves by aggregate through a completely fluid, open, and concentric poetic form, appropriate to its title, which is intransitive and transitive at once, implying a linking-up as well as a reaching-out. It is what might be called a collaborative poem, or *renga*, an identity well explained in the poem

There is, in fact, no more adroit explainer in our poetry than Pinsky, who lifts the analytic lyric to sometimes sublime heights. "Impossible to Tell" is dedicated, for instance, to Pinsky's long-time friend Robert Hass, who is now a continent away, in California, and to the memory of Elliot Gilbert, who has died through medical blunder. The dedications, though, are not affectionate attachments; they are at the heart of the poem. They "explain" the emotion. The device of joke-telling is also at the center of the story: Gilbert, apparently, had an awesome memory for jokes, or what might be termed circular narratives, which the structure of the poem itself certainly emulates, in the spirit of Basho, "Banana Tree," and like Gilbert a top banana at "Threading a long night through the rules and channels" of jokes, linking-poems, collaborations.

> Elliot had in his memory so many jokes
> They seemed to breed like microbes in a culture
>
> Inside his brain, one so much making another
> It was impossible to tell them all:
> In the court-culture of jokes, a top banana.

Joke-telling becomes not only a way of organizing and unifying the poem but a version of whistling in the dark, a calling-across separations, a way for a child, as court jester, to entertain his mother out of suicide—he "cuts capers, he sings, he does imitations/Of different people in the building, he jokes. . . ." What links friends—the one absent, the other mourned— is the linking of little narratives "threading," "coursing," and "circling" throughout the poem, narratives that are, finally, death jokes, elegies of wit.

> In the first months when I had moved back East
> From California and had to leave a message
>
> On Bob's machine, I used to make a habit
> Of telling the tape a joke; and part-way through,
> I would pretend that I forgot the punchline,
>
> Or make believe that I was interrupted—
> As though he'd be so eager to hear the end
> He'd have to call me back. The joke was Elliot's,
>
> More often than not.

Everything is masterfully mixed in this poem: the terrible, accidental death of Gilbert at the hands of doctors; the memory of friendship dependent on "messages"; the distracting jokes themselves, tapering "Down through the swirling funnel of tongues and gestures/Toward their preposterous Ithaca"; the complex referencing of ethnicities, mythologies, and cultures; plus the rhetorical drive of the sentences, which insist on continuing, linking, enjambing, especially across stanzas. The poem's brilliance, however, has as much to do with Pinsky's ease with his authority as with his ability to move in and out of his "stories" in order to create and elevate the elegy he's intending. (Gilbert was Hass's friend too.) If jokes, regardless of origin, are "Universal," as he says, their fated punchlines are no less so—"Oh swirling petals, falling leaves." The humor, the sweetness of the renga form, the invocations of and imprecations to the "Powers and princes of earth" (Jehovah, Raa, Bol-Morah, Pluto . . . Provincial stinkers), the hyperbole played against understatement, the art and use of poetry itself—what good are they in the face of an "Allegiance to a state impossible to tell"?

But as the *renga* describes
Religious meaning by moving in drifting petals

And brittle leaves that touch and die and suffer
The changing winds that riffle the gutter swirl,
So in the joke, just under the raucous music

Of Fleming, Jew, Walloon, a courtly allegiance
Moves to the dulcimer, gavotte and bow,
Over the banana tree the moon in autumn . . .

We think of narrative as a linear experience, as if it were, in some imagined realm, a straight line. It is, in fact, a corner turned, a pattern traced, a
circumference circumscribed. The circular size of "Impossible to Tell," as
it winds around and continues, as it extends without attenuating its intensity, as it acquires its various detail within a slow-circling vortex, the size
of the poem works because, in spite of its linear length, it turns and returns
around the common center of "a one-man *renga*," whose linked stories are
impossible to tell straight—straight-faced, straight-on. As the form suspends
closure so Pinsky finds it impossible to talk *his* story—the poem overall—
to a punchline. The three-line stanzas formalize the verse structure in
order to facilitate its paralleling continuity, its circulating on-goingness, its
blending of tones. Hass is a silent partner, Gilbert the lost partner, Pinsky
the protagonist. The power of the poem lies in the degree to which the poet
surrenders himself to the material, its memory and the time it takes to re-
iterate how impossible it is to approximate, let alone articulate, pain. A joke
is, after all, a non sequitur leading to a misdirection and ending in the middle
of things, a perfect narrative lyric arc.

# 11

I need, I believe, to say something about Robert Hass, a poet whose work
so many of us love. American poetry has come a long way since mid-century
last when social codes kept the art objective to its subject. Now think of
the personal name-dropping in Voigt's Levis poem, of Pinsky's presump-

tion that his friends are our friends. You could argue, perhaps, that personalizing poetry started with the Confessionals, though the people in Lowell, Plath, Sexton, and so forth seem now more like dramatis personae than people on a first-name basis. You could argue that as far back as Keats, and before him Herrick, right on back to Horace, names are used. Yet names and relatives are one thing, intimacy is another. Hass, above all poets in my memory, has elevated naming to a level of intimacy and generosity new in our poetry. He does it across the board—in his critical prose, his unique prose-poems, and in his searching meditations. Naming, indeed, is his narrative, no less circular, interrupted, distracted, no less impossible to tell. For a lot of readers, Hass makes poetry valuable and compelling at once. Clearly his artless art is compelling, but the valuing of experience, the unforced intimacy of his narrative, the reconciling tone of his voice, suggest a quality extra-textual.

"*Of course, here*, gesturing out the window, pines, ragged green/winter lawn, the bay, *you can express what you like, enumerate the vegetation. And you! you have to, I'm afraid, since you don't excel at metaphor.*" This is an excerpt from a remembered conversation Hass is having with an Eastern European survivor of the pogroms of World War II. It's from the last poem, "Interrupted Meditation," in his last book, *Sun Under Wood* (1996), a meditation layered in time and significantly interrupted by enumerations of the vegetation and by an apparently unconnected marital conversation. Whether he excels at metaphor or not, Hass is good at rendering the natural world—at sketching it, then leaving it alone. He's good at conversation, too, which is an extension of his naming skills, his social skills in a poem, his charm. His relationship with his reader is a conversation as well, intimate, singular. The Eastern European, a friend of Polish poet Czeslaw Milosz (also a friend of Hass's), is raising moral questions regarding the importance of poetry compared to life-and-death politics.

Little green involute fronds of fern at creekside.
And the sinewy clear water rushing over creekstone
of the palest amber, veined with a darker gold,
thinnest lines of gold rivering through the amber
like—ah, now we come to it. *We were not put on earth*,
the old man said, he was hacking into the crust

of a sourdough half loaf in his vehement, impatient way
with an old horn-handled knife, *to express ourselves.*
I knew he had seen whole cities leveled: also
that there had been a time of shame for him, outskirts
of a ruined town, half Baroque, half Greek Revival,
pediments of Flora and Hygeia from a brief eighteenth-century
health spa boom lying on the streets in broken chunks
and dogs scavenging among them. His one act of courage
then had been to drop pieces of bread or chocolate,
as others did, where a fugitive family of Jews
was rumored to be hiding. *I never raised my voice,*
*of course, none of us did.* He sliced wedges of cheese
after the bread, spooned out dollops of sour jam
from some Hungarian plum, purple and faintly gingered.

The conversation, quasi-argument, goes back and forth, focusing, finally, on one of Hass's favorite themes, the relationship between the self, being, and language. It's important to know that this philosophizing encounter is taking place in memory in the speaker's mind, on a mountainside, where butterflies "hover lightly/over lupine blooms, whirr of insects in the three o'clock sun." Hass has set it up that pastoral beauty must be interrogated by political and ontological truth, that poetry, the language itself, must be somehow brought into the house justified.

> *You write well, clearly.*
*You are an intelligent man. But*—finger in the air—
*silence is waiting. Milosz believes there is a Word*
*at the end that explains. There is silence at the end,*
*and it doesn't explain, it doesn't even ask.* He spread chutney
on his bread, meticulously, out to the corners. Something
angry always in his unexpected fits of thoroughness
I liked. Then cheese. Then a lunging, wolfish bite.
*Put it this way, I give you, here, now, a magic key.*
*What does it open? This key I give you, what exactly*
*does it open? Anything, anything! But what?* I found
that what I thought about was the failure of my marriage,
the three or four lost years just at the end and after.

*For me there is no key, not even the sum total of our acts.*
*But you are a poet. You pretend to make poems. And?*

I'm once again reminded of two moments in Keats: one, in a letter, when he opines, "Let the fish philosophize away the ice in winter"; the other, in the confrontation with Moneta in *The Fall of Hyperion*, when she asks, "Art thou not of the dreamer tribe?" Hass's answer to his dreaming, his philosophizing, his valuing of language as "*responsible/to all of it, the texture of bread, the hairstyles/of the girls you knew in high school, shoelaces, sunsets/the smell of tea*"— Hass's answer is to think of "the failure of my marriage,/the three or four lost years just at the end and after." So life takes over; life inspires, but life takes over. And art takes over after that.

> She sat on the couch sobbing, her rib cage shaking
> from its accumulated abysses of grief and thick sorrow.
> I don't love you, she said. The terrible thing is
> that I don't think I ever loved you. He thought to himself
> fast, to numb it, that she didn't mean it, thought
> what he had done to provoke it. It was May.
> Also pines, lawn, the bay, a blossoming apricot.
> Everyone their own devastation. Each on its own scale.
> I don't know what the key opens. I know we die,
> and don't know what is at the end. We don't behave well.
> And there are monsters out there, and millions of others
> to carry out their orders. We live half our lives
> in fantasy, and words. This morning I am pretending
> to be walking down the mountain in the heat.
> A vault of blue sky, traildust, the sweet medicinal
> scent of mountain grasses, and at trailside—
> I'm a little ashamed that I want to end this poem
> singing, but I want to end this poem singing—the wooly
> closed-down buds of the sunflower to which, in English,
> someone gave the name, sometime, of pearly everlasting.

The segue to this closing moment is only a stanza break, befitting an interruption, and for the speaker of the poem an exhaustion of options in a high-minded yet heartfelt remembered argument. As in his "Meditation

at Lagunitas," the speaker's working-out of things occurs among a contrib-
uting nature, a transcending nature, a correlative nature. The fact that it
takes a hundred lines for Hass to come to his reconciling insights ("We live
half our lives/in fantasy, and words.") is what the stuff of narrative is—the
bent light, the broken path, the interruption. The connections we make of
our experiences, he suggests, are as much about separation as they are about
joining. Hass is also one of our great lyric talkers—his prose proves that,
and often, blessedly, the differences between the poems, the prose-poems,
and the prose is one of emphasis. He's a lyricist at heart, with a genius for
narrative, the narrative of scene, passage, disassembly. As lyricism heals so
narrative works its wounding. How well Hass understands that . . .

   That marriageable moment in Michael Palmer, at the Hotel de l'Odéon,
when Palmer misses meeting the poet Anne-Marie Albiach, leaves a copy
of one of his books, and decides, on reflection, that "this had been a most
excellent first meeting with the poet Anne-Marie Albiach . . . Our conversation, in short, had never deviated from the highest plane. And, as is the
case with absence generally, a trace of the erotic had lingered in the atmosphere, at least from my point of view." And that "incident" in Roland
Barthes's journal (*Incidents*, 1992, trans. Richard Howard): "I gave him some
money, he promised to be at the rendezvous an hour later, and of course
never showed. I asked myself if I was really so mistaken (the received wisdom about giving money to a hustler *in advance*!), and concluded that since
I really didn't want him all that much (nor even to make love), the result
was the same: sex or no sex, at eight o'clock I would find myself back at the
same point in my life."

   Missed meetings, lost opportunities, interrupted meditations. Narrative
dotes on such missed, lost, interrupted possibilities. For Palmer the possibility is positive, at least he says so; for Barthes, it is more neutral, perhaps
sad. In either case, the non-meeting and rhetorical response are more interesting. Anticipation, deceleration, articulation—somewhere in there
narrative constructs to verse, to form, to language, to the event in the words
turning into the event of the words. Time must pass, however. "I gradually
began to comprehend," says Palmer, "that this had been a most excellent
first meeting," this "in-place-of-an-encounter" encounter. The "result was
the same," says Barthes, "at eight o'clock I would find myself back at the
same point in my life." The emptiness, the nonness of the missed meet-

ing, the lost opportunity, the interrupted moment: that's where the energy is, the emotion, the heart of possibility, and only out of that will something real and true be made. But as a poem takes time it is of time. If verse is the creative distance, narrative is the creative source, the narrative of not meeting. Hass says at the end of "Interrupted Meditation" that he is "pretending/ to be walking down the mountain in the heat." Does this mean he did not walk down the mountain or that he is remembering walking down the mountain and saying so as if he were, right now, walking down the mountain?

Poetry, as verse, as we know, is pretense. But did I or did I not walk down the mountain? Of course I did, because I am, at this moment, walking down the mountain in the heat—because I say I am. Language, inherently, is narrative; verse makes something memorable of it. Language, inherently, is memory, the way "a word is elegy to what it signifies." The non-meeting, as it is remembered and reported, is elegiac experience in language, which is why Palmer wrote his "Five Easy Poems" in response to his non-encounter with Anne-Marie Albiach. Metaphor, whatever else it is, is an admission of a non-meeting. Hence, Hass ends his meditation singing, which, in lyric free verse, invariably comes out as seeing—seeing "the wooly/closed-down buds of the sunflower to which, in English,/ someone gave the name, sometime, of pearly everlasting." Poetry, then, as image, is also pretense, because behind the language, behind the idea and the emblem, the music and the metaphor, is the non-meeting, the non-encounter we call narrative experience, the experience of having walked down the mountain in the heat, piecing together, in the mind, the broken parts of what you thought were meetings.

2003

# AUTHOR INDEX

Agee, James, 209
Alberti, Rafael, 227
Albiach, Anne-Marie, 274, 275, 276
Alvarez, A., 129
Ammons, A. R., 279
Appollinaire, Guillaume, 123, 224–
    225
Arnold, Matthew, 5, 171
Ashbery, John, 104, 105, 187, 227,
    236, 270, 297
Audubon, John James, 63
Austen, Jane, 67

Barthes, Roland, 309, 316, 317
Baudelaire, Charles, 221, 300
Beaumont, George, 70
Beckett, Samuel, 259
Bell, Marvin, 195–200, 208
Benedikt, Michael, 225
Benn, Gottfried, 222, 259
Berg, Stephen, 301–305
Bernstein, Charles, 272
Berryman, John, 172, 270
Birkerts, Sven, 270
Bishop, Elizabeth, 271

Bly, Robert, 104, 181, 226, 239, 297
Bonnefoy, Yves, 227, 241
Borges, Jorge Luis, 227
Breton, André, 224, 276
Bronte, Anne, 4
Bronte, Charlotte, 4
Bronte, Emily, 5, 7, 8, 18
Brown, Charles, 7, 8, 9, 32, 33, 34,
    63, 65, 78
Browne, Thomas, 29
Browning, Robert, 123
Burton, Robert, 77
Byron, George Gordon, 123

Calvino, Italo, 227, 260
Carson, Anne, 279
Cezanne, Paul, 288
Char, René, 227
Chekhov, Anton, 24, 217
Christie, Agatha, 3
Clampitt, Amy, 279
Claude (Lorrain), 84
Coleridge, Samuel Taylor, 27, 30,
    31, 35, 37, 38, 82, 175, 210,
    233, 259, 278

Courbet, Gustave, 55
Crane, Hart, 139, 222–223, 269,
    271, 288
Cummings, E. E., 166

Dadd, Richard, 47
de Andrade, Carlos Drummond, 227
de Man, Paul, 269
DeQuincey, Thomas, 271
Dickens, Charles, 53
Dickinson, Emily, 24, 27, 49, 70,
    86, 88, 89, 98, 99, 100, 104,
    139, 149, 196, 231, 244, 245,
    269, 279, 284
Dilke, Charles Wentworth, 7, 63,
    78
Dryden, John, 98
Dubie, Norman, 251–255

Eliot, George, 3
Eliot, T. S., 56, 99, 119, 123, 144,
    148, 153, 172, 173, 175, 187,
    218, 221, 239, 269, 270, 273,
    286
Eluard, Paul, 272
Emerson, Ralph Waldo, 98, 99,
    101, 174

Flaubert, Gustave, 284
Forster, E. M., 105
Fowles, John, 46, 47
Frost, Robert, 27, 28, 88, 98, 174,
    211

Gainsborough, Thomas, 71, 84
Gallagher, Tess, 176–179, 211

Gautier, Théophile, 220
George, Stephan, 222
Ginsberg, Allen, 103–104, 175,
    269, 310
Glück, Louise, 282–285, 288
Graham, Jorie, 277–281, 282
Guillen, Jorge, 222

Hacker, Marilyn, 166–167, 169–
    171, 172, 173, 183, 185
Hall, Donald, 181
Halpern, Daniel, 228–230, 234,
    235–238
Hardy, Thomas, 3, 31, 211
Hass, Robert, 190–194, 220, 310,
    311, 312, 313–317
Haydon, Benjamin Robert, 7
Hazlitt, William, 7
Henley, W. E., 171
Heyen, William, 195, 200–205, 208
Hiroshige, Ando, 55
Homer, 191
Hopkins, Gerard Manley, 279
Housman, A. E., 211
Howard, Richard, 172
Hughes, Ted, 127, 171
Hunt, Leigh, 7, 8

Iyengar, B. K. S., 146

Jacob, Max, 123, 124
James, Henry, 24, 186, 284
Jensen, Laura, 230–238
Joyce, James, 194, 219, 220, 221,
    261, 269
Jung, Carl, 155

Keats, John, 7–11, 18, 30, 31–35, 37–40, 46, 49, 63–70, 75–84, 89, 90–94, 131, 149, 160–161, 187, 217, 278, 281, 284, 285, 286, 291, 313, 315
Kennedy, John, 103
Kenner, Hugh, 129
Kinnell, Galway, 171, 187
Klee, Paul, 255
Komunyakka, Yusef, 297–300, 301

Lauterbach, Ann, 292–295, 316, 317
Lensing, George, 181
Levis, Larry, 214–219, 250, 290, 306
Lincoln, Abraham, 28, 31, 100
Lorca, Federico Garcia, 221
Lowell, Amy, 68
Lowell, Robert, 25, 103, 104, 113, 127, 129, 166, 187, 269, 275, 313
Loy, Mina, 276
Lucrece, 29
Lucretius, 31

Mallarmé, Stephen, 138, 219, 220, 221, 224, 239, 272
Mandelstam, Osip, 255
Matthews, William, 211–214, 216, 218, 227, 246–249, 250
McCaffery, Steve, 277
McMichael, James, 290
McPherson, Sandra, 241–246, 250
Merwin, W. S., 106, 171, 181, 184, 186, 223, 241

Michaux, Henri, 227
Milosz, Czeslaw, 313
Milton, John, 29, 98, 269
Monet, Claude, 58
Montale, Eugenio, 221, 259, 288
Moore, Marianne, 23, 269
Moran, Ronald, 181

Neruda, Pablo, 221

Olds, Sharon, 265–268, 271
Oliver, Mary, 290
Olson, Charles, 102, 103, 269, 286
Ovid, 31

Palmer, Michael, 272–276, 277, 305, 316, 317
Paz, Octavio, 227
Pinsky, Robert, 263–265, 267, 271, 310–312
Plath, Sylvia, 11–15, 18, 19, 127–139, 269, 270, 310, 313
Poe, Edgar Allan, 27, 99, 300
Ponge, Francis, 227, 241
Popa, Vasko, 227, 241
Pope, Alexander, 98, 269
Pound, Ezra, 99, 102, 175, 181, 183, 185, 221, 239, 250, 269, 286
Poussin, Nicholas, 84

Rembrandt (van Rijn), 55
Reynolds, John Hamilton, 63, 64, 65, 66, 67
Rich, Adrienne, 171
Ricoeur, Paul, 282

Rilke, Rainer Maria, 134, 221, 224
Rimbaud, Arthur, 309
Ritsos, Yannis, 241
Roethke, Theodore, 11, 13, 15, 16, 19, 27, 99, 131, 279
Rousseau, Jean Jacques, 117
Ruskin, John, 55, 58

Salinger, J. D., 118
Severn, Joseph, 7, 9, 36, 38, 90–94
Sexton, Anne, 313
Shakespeare, William, 27, 29, 31, 70
Shelley, Percy Bysshe, 7, 27, 82
Sidney, Philip, 29, 30, 31, 32
Simic, Charles, 251, 255–259, 295–297, 298
Simpson, Louis, 173, 188, 224
Smith, Dave, 167–171, 172, 183, 185, 211
Snyder, Gary, 274
Spenser, Edmund, 98
Stevens, Wallace, 25, 48, 49, 89, 97, 99, 113, 117, 131, 144, 153, 154, 221, 234
St. John, David, 180–184
Strand, Mark, 188, 227, 241

Tate, James, 296–297, 298
Thomson, James, 70, 85
Turner, Joseph Mallord William, 55

Valéry, Paul, 59, 134, 137, 219, 222, 224, 227, 239, 272
Voigt, Ellen Bryant, 306–309, 312

Walton, Izaak, 29
Warren, Robert Penn, 122, 188
Wells, H. G., 24
Wenthe, William, 300
Whistler, James Abbott McNeill, 53–60
Whitman, Walt, 15, 16, 17, 18, 28, 31, 89, 98, 99, 100, 101, 103, 104, 171, 175, 269, 288
Wilbur, Richard, 98
Williams, C. K., 195, 205–209, 211, 223, 288, 289, 305
Williams, W. C., 99, 101, 102, 103, 104, 175, 198, 223, 227, 269, 286, 288
Woodhouse, Richard, 7
Woolf, Virginia, 255
Wordsworth, William, 24, 25, 30, 37, 49, 70, 117–118, 119, 173, 174, 175, 209, 210, 269, 286, 287
Wright, Charles, 251, 259–262, 288, 305
Wright, James, 104, 105, 119–124, 171, 181, 186

Yeats, W. B., 25, 26, 60, 87, 172, 221, 291
Yogananda, Paramahansa, 149